MENTORING PHYSICAL EDUCATION TEACHERS THE SECONDARY SCHOOL

Mentoring Physical Education Teachers in the Secondary School helps mentors of trainee and newly qualified physical education teachers in both developing their own mentoring skills and providing the essential guidance their beginning teachers need as they navigate the roller-coaster of the first years of teaching. Offering tried and tested strategies based on the best research and evidence, it covers the knowledge, skills and understanding every mentor needs and offers practical tools such as lesson plans and feedback guides, observation sheets, and examples of dialogue with beginning physical education teachers.

Together with analytical tools for self-evaluation, this book is a vital source of support and inspiration for mentors involved in developing the next generation of outstanding physical education teachers. Key topics explained include:

- Roles and responsibilities of mentors
- Developing a mentor–mentee relationship
- Guiding beginning physical education teachers through the lesson planning process
- Observations and pre- and post-lesson discussions

Filled with the key tools needed for the mentor's individual development, *Mentoring Physical Education Teachers in the Secondary School* offers an accessible guide to mentoring physical education teachers with ready-to-use strategies that support and inspire both mentors and beginning teachers alike.

Susan Capel, Emeritus Professor of Physical Education, Brunel University, UK.

Julia Lawrence, Head of Subject Group – Teacher Education, University of Hull, UK, and Senior Fellow of the Higher Education Academy.

MENTORING TRAINEE AND NEWLY QUALIFIED TEACHERS

Series edited by: Susan Capel, Trevor Wright and Julia Lawrence

The **Mentoring Trainee and Newly Qualified Teachers** Series offers subject-specific, practical books designed to reinforce and develop mentors' understanding of different aspects of their role, as well as exploring issues that beginning teachers encounter in the course of learning to teach. The books have two main foci: First, challenging mentors to reflect critically on theory, research and evidence, on their own knowledge, their approaches to mentoring and how they work with beginning teachers in order to move their practice forward. Second, supporting mentors to effectively facilitate the development of beginning teachers. Although the basic structure of all the subject books is similar, each book is different to reflect the needs of mentors in relation to the unique nature of each subject. Elements of appropriate theory introduce each topic or issue with emphasis placed on the practical application of material. The chapter authors in the subject books have been engaged with mentoring over a long period of time and share research, evidence and their experience. We, as series editors, are pleased to extend the work in initial teacher education to the work of mentors of beginning teachers.

We hope that this series of books supports you in developing into an effective, reflective mentor as you support the development of the next generation of subject teachers.

For more information about this series, please visit: www.routledge.com/Mentoring-Trainee-and-Newly-Qualified-Teachers/book-series/MTNQT

Titles in the series

Mentoring Physical Education Teachers in the Secondary School
Edited by Susan Capel and Julia Lawrence

Mentoring English Teachers in the Secondary School
Edited by Debbie Hickman

Mentoring Design and Technology Teachers in the Secondary School
Edited by Suzanne Lawson and Susan Wood-Griffith

MENTORING PHYSICAL EDUCATION TEACHERS IN THE SECONDARY SCHOOL

A Practical Guide

Edited by Susan Capel and Julia Lawrence

Routledge
Taylor & Francis Group

LONDON AND NEW YORK

First published 2019
by Routledge
2 Park Square, Milton Park, Abingdon, Oxon OX14 4RN

and by Routledge
711 Third Avenue, New York, NY 10017

Routledge is an imprint of the Taylor & Francis Group, an informa business

© 2019 selection and editorial matter, Susan Capel and Julia Lawrence; individual chapters, the contributors

British Library Cataloguing in Publication Data
A catalogue record for this book is available from the British Library

Library of Congress Cataloging in Publication Data
Names: Capel, Susan Anne, 1953- editor. | Lawrence, Julia Clare, editor.
Title: Mentoring physical education teachers in the secondary school :
a practical guide / Edited by Susan Capel and Julia Lawrence.
Description: Abingdon, Oxon ; New York, NY : Routledge, 2019. |
Includes bibliographical references.
Identifiers: LCCN 2018019590 (print) | LCCN 2018021955 (ebook) |
ISBN 9781315163444 (E-book) | ISBN 9781138059641 (hbk) |
ISBN 9781138059658 (pbk) | ISBN 9781315163444 (ebk)
Subjects: LCSH: Physical education teachers-Training of-Handbooks, manuals, etc. |
Mentoring in education-Handbooks, manuals, etc. |
Physical education teachers-Education (Secondary)-Handbooks, manuals, etc. |
Physical education and training-Study and teaching
(Secondary)-Handbooks, manuals, etc.
Classification: LCC GV363 (ebook) | LCC GV363 .M39 2019 (print) |
DDC 372.86-dc23 LC record available at https://lccn.loc.gov/2018019590

ISBN: 978-1-138-05964-1 (hbk)
ISBN: 978-1-138-05965-8 (pbk)
ISBN: 978-1-315-16344-4 (ebk)

Typeset in Interstate
by Out of House Publishing

Visit the eResources: www.routledge.com/9781138059658

CONTENTS

LIST OF ILLUSTRATIONS

Figures

Tables

TASKS

CASE STUDIES

CONTRIBUTORS

Jackie Arthur is a senior lecturer in physical and coach education at the University of St Mark and St John, Plymouth. For details, please visit www.marjon.ac.uk/about-marjon/staff-list-and-profiles/arthur-jackie.html

Deb Barrett is a senior lecturer in physical education at Brighton University. For details, please visit http://about.brighton.ac.uk/staff/details.php?uid=db49

Sophy Bassett is a senior lecturer in physical education at the University of Bedfordshire. For details, please visit www.beds.ac.uk/howtoapply/departments/teacher-education/about-us/staff/sophy-bassett

Jon Binney is a principal lecturer in physical education at Brighton University. For details, please visit http://about.brighton.ac.uk/staff/details.php?uid=jmb34

Mark Bowler is a senior lecturer and course coordinator for the BA (Hons) Physical Education (Secondary) (with QTS) degree in the School of Teacher Education at the University of Bedfordshire. For details, please visit www.beds.ac.uk/howtoapply/departments/teacher-education/about-us/staff/mark-bowler

Susan Capel is Emeritus Professor of Physical Education at Brunel University London. For details, please visit www.brunel.ac.uk/people/susan-capel

Suzie Everley is a reader in the sociology of physical education and activity at the University of Chichester, West Sussex. She has previously been subject leader for PGCE Secondary Physical Education and has been involved in initial teacher education in higher education for 15 years. For details, please visit www.chi.ac.uk/staff/dr-suzanne-everley

Gill Golder is director of teacher education, department head for education and programme leader for secondary education at the University of St Mark and St John, Plymouth. For details, please visit www.marjon.ac.uk/about-marjon/staff-list-and-profiles/golder-gillian.html

Simon Green is a senior lecturer in physical education at Brighton University. For details, please visit http://about.brighton.ac.uk/staff/details.php?uid=sg111

Will Katene is a senior lecturer in education, subject lead for both the Secondary PGCE Physical Education and Primary PGCE Physical Education 'Foundation Subject' Course and deputy director of the MA (Ed) Programme in the Graduate School of Education at the University of Exeter. For details, please visit http://socialsciences.exeter.ac.uk/education/staff/index.php?web_id=will_katene

Alison Keyworth is a senior lecturer in postgraduate and professional development at the University of St Mark and St John, Plymouth. For details, please visit www.marjon.ac.uk/about-marjon/staff-list-and-profiles/keyworth-alison.html

Julia Lawrence is subject group head for teacher education at the University of Hull. For details, please visit www.hull.ac.uk/Faculties/contact-list/Julia-Lawrence.aspx

Karen Low is a senior academy officer at the Physical Education and Sports Teacher Academy, Singapore, providing professional development for in-service physical education and sports teachers with the aim to deliver quality PE lessons and sports coaching in schools.

Paul McFlynn is a lecturer in education and course director for PGCE Physical Education at Ulster University, Coleraine campus. For details, please visit www.ulster.ac.uk/staff/p-mcflynn

Peter Mellor is the course director and manager of partnerships for the PGCE Secondary 11–16 Course at Leeds Beckett University. For details, please visit www.leedsbeckett.ac.uk/staff/peter-mellor/

Jon Mills is a senior lecturer at the University of Chichester, West Sussex. He is currently the subject leader for the PGCE Physical Education Secondary course and has been involved in ITT in both schools and higher education for 25 years. For details, please visit www.chi.ac.uk/staff/jon-mills

Julie Money is a principal lecturer at Liverpool John Moores University and has spent a number of years in the role of partnership mentor and link tutor with schools and colleges in the north-west region of England. For details, please visit www.ljmu.ac.uk/about-us/staff-profiles/faculty-of-education-health-and-community/sport-studies-leisure-and-nutrition/julie-money

Angela Newton is a principal lecturer in physical education at the University of Bedfordshire. For details, please visit www.beds.ac.uk/howtoapply/departments/teacher-education/about-us/staff/angela-newton

Joanna Phan is a senior academy officer at the Physical Education and Sports Teacher Academy, Singapore, providing professional development for in-service Physical Education and sports teachers with the aim to deliver quality PE lessons and sports coaching in schools.

Lucy Pocknell is a senior lecturer in physical education at Brighton University. For details, please visit http://about.brighton.ac.uk/staff/details.php?uid=lpp10

Clare Shaw is a senior lecturer in primary initial teacher education at the University of St Mark and St John, Plymouth. For details, please visit www.marjon.ac.uk/about-marjon/staff-list-and-profiles/shaw-clare.html

Warren Smart is a senior lecturer in physical education at Brighton University. For details, please visit http://about.brighton.ac.uk/staff/details.php?uid=ws101

Julie Stevens is a senior lecturer in physical and coach education and programme leader for the BEd (Hons) Physical Education – Secondary Education (with QTS) at the University of St Mark and St John, Plymouth. For details, please visit www.marjon.ac.uk/about-marjon/staff-list-and-profiles/stevens-julie.html

Barbara Walsh is director of school at Liverpool John Moores University. She is a national teaching fellow and a principal fellow of the Higher Education Academy. Barbara has a wealth of experience in mentoring both beginning and experienced physical education teachers and sport coaches. For details, please visit www.ljmu.ac.uk/about-us/staff-profiles/faculty-of-education-health-and-community/sport-studies-leisure-and-nutrition/barbara-walsh

Kerry Whitehouse is a principal lecturer of learning and teaching in higher education and physical education at the University of Worcester. She is a Senior Fellow of the HEA. For details, please visit www.worcester.ac.uk/discover/sport-kerry-whitehouse.html

Jane Woolliscroft is a lecturer in teacher education at the University of Hull. For details, please visit www2.hull.ac.uk/Faculties/staff-profiles/Jane-Woolliscroft.aspx

AN INTRODUCTION TO THE SERIES: MENTORING TRAINEE AND NEWLY QUALIFIED TEACHERS

Mentoring is a very important and exciting role. What could be better than supporting the development of the next generation of subject teachers? A mentor may have asked, or been asked, to do the role because they are an effective teacher. Being an effective teacher does not necessarily mean a person is going to make a good mentor, despite similarities in the two roles. This series of practical workbooks books covers most subjects in the secondary curriculum. They are designed specifically to reinforce mentors' understanding of different aspects of their role, for mentors to learn about and reflect on their role, to provide support for mentors in aspects of their development and enable them to analyse their success in supporting the development of beginning subject teachers (defined as trainee, newly qualified and early career teachers). This book has two main foci: first, the focus is on challenging mentors to reflect critically on theory/research/evidence, on their own knowledge, how they work with beginning teachers, how they work with more experienced teachers and on their approaches to mentoring in order to move their practice forward. Second, the focus is on supporting mentors to effectively facilitate the development of beginning teachers. Thus, some of the practical activities in the books are designed to encourage reflection, whilst others ask mentors to undertake activities with a beginning teacher.

This book can be used alongside generic and subject books designed for student and newly qualified teachers. These books include *Learning to Teach in the Secondary School: A Companion to School Experience*, 8th edition (Capel, Leask and Younie, 2019) which deals with aspects of teaching and learning applicable to all subjects. This generic book also has a companion Reader: *Readings for Learning to Teach in the Secondary School* (Capel, Leask and Turner, 2010) containing articles and research papers in education suitable for 'M' level study. Further, the generic book is complemented by two subject series: *Learning to Teach (subject) in the Secondary School: A Companion to School Experience*; and *A Practical Guide to Teaching (subject) in the Secondary School*. These books are designed for student teachers on different types of initial teacher education programmes (and indeed a beginning teacher you are working with may have used/currently be using them). However, these books are proving equally useful to tutors and mentors in their work with student teachers, both in relation to the knowledge, skills and understanding the student teacher is developing and some tasks which mentors might find it useful to support a beginning teacher to do.

It is also supported by a book designed for newly qualified teachers, the soon to be published *Surviving and Thriving in the Secondary School: The NQT's Essential Companion*

(Capel, Leask, Younie and Lawrence, 2019), as well as *Starting to Teach in the Secondary School: A Companion for the Newly Qualified Teacher* (Capel, Heilbronn, Leask and Turner, 2004). These titles cover material not generally needed by student teachers on an initial teacher education course, but which is needed by newly qualified teachers in their school work and early career.

The information in this book should link with the information in the generic text and relevant subject book in the two series in a number of ways. For example, mentors might want to refer a beginning teacher to read about specific knowledge, understanding and skills they are focusing on developing, or to undertake tasks in the book, either alone or with their support, then discus the tasks. It is recommended that you have copies of these books available so that you can cross-reference when needed.

In turn, the books complement a range of resources on which mentors can draw (including other mentors of beginning teachers in the same or other subjects, other teachers and a range of other resources including books, research articles and websites).

The positive feedback on *Learning to Teach* and the related books above, particularly the way they have supported the learning of student teachers in their development into effective, reflective teachers, encouraged us to retain the main features of that book in this series. Like teaching, mentoring should be research and evidence-informed. Thus, this series of books introduce theoretical, research and professional evidence-based advice and guidance to support mentors as they develop their mentoring to support beginning teachers' development. The main focus is the practical application of material. Elements of appropriate theory introduce each topic or issue, and recent research into mentoring and/or teaching and learning is integral to the presentation. Tasks are provided to help mentors identify key features of the topic or issue and reflect on and/or apply them to their own practice of mentoring beginning teachers. Although the basic structure of all the subject books is similar, each book is different to reflect the needs of mentors in relation to the unique nature of each subject.

The chapter authors in the subject books have been engaged with mentoring over a long period of time and are aiming to share research/evidence and their experience. We, as series editors, are pleased to extend the work in initial teacher education to the work of mentors of beginning teachers. We hope that this series of books supports you in developing into an effective, reflective mentor as you support the development of the next generation of subject teachers.

Susan Capel, Julia Lawrence and Trevor Wright
July 2018

Introduction
A Practical Guide to Mentoring in Physical Education

The importance of mentoring

The profile of mentors in supporting the development of beginning teachers is rising. Concerns regarding, for example, recruitment, retention, workload and work-life balance are all contributing towards a need to support those joining the profession not only during their beginning years, but also longer term. The importance of mentors supporting beginning teachers in England is reflected in the publication in 2016 of mentoring standards (Teaching Schools Council, 2016), which provide guidance and support for those engaging in mentoring.

The purpose of this workbook

Being a mentor is exciting, but it is also challenging. You work with different beginning physical education teachers and with one beginning physical education teacher with different needs at different times in their development. They have expectations of you as a mentor; likewise, you have expectations of them in being mentored.

Much of what you do as a mentor you will have experienced as a mentee, or you will have used similar skills in a teaching situation; for example, as a teacher you will have been observed on many occasions. Thus, you have your own experiences to guide you through what you think works well and what you might wish to develop further. However, you cannot rely on your own experience. What worked for you might not work for a beginning teacher you are mentoring. Likewise, you might identify a better way to do things through, for example, research and literature about mentoring, attending workshops and courses, and working and discussing with other mentors (e.g. physical education mentors in other schools, other subject mentors in your own school).

This practical workbook is designed to support you in your professional learning and development as a mentor to enable you effectively to be able to support beginning physical education teachers to learn and develop towards becoming outstanding teachers. It is designed to support you in reflecting on your own practice, identifying areas for your own learning and development as a mentor, developing your knowledge, understanding and skills, and considering different approaches you may use to meet the needs of a beginning teacher at a specific time.

In preparing this book, we have tried to draw on a broad range of expertise. The author(s) of each chapter have been identified for their experiences as mentors and/or tutors of beginning physical education teachers and/or their work in supporting the development of effective mentors. In turn, they have drawn on the expertise of others in their chapters, for example through research, evidence and case studies.

This workbook covers the practical application of a range of topics particularly relevant to mentoring beginning physical education teachers. As in teaching, there is basic knowledge, understanding and skills for mentoring. However, effective mentoring also requires the development of professional judgement in order to be able to adapt skills to meet the demands of a specific situation, to be able to use the right skill in the right way at the right time, to take account of the needs and abilities of each beginning physical education teacher. As a mentor, you have your own personality and characteristics. You will, therefore, refine and adapt basic mentoring skills and combine them in different ways to create your own unique mentoring style. Further, there is no one right way to mentor. Different approaches are appropriate in different situations.

There is a lot to learn to develop into an effective mentor. We cannot prepare you for a specific mentoring situation, but we can help you to understand the complexities of mentoring. We aim to help you to develop:

- knowledge and understanding about effective mentoring;
- competence in basic mentoring skills, to enable you to cope in most mentoring situations;
- the ability to apply these basic mentoring skills to meet the needs of specific situations;
- your professional judgement;
- your ability to reflect critically on what you are doing and on your values and beliefs about mentoring.

In so doing, you should be able to develop, adapt and refine your mentoring skills to meet the needs of any specific situation. You should also be able to look more critically and reflectively at aspects of mentoring and to begin to articulate your own values and beliefs about mentoring in physical education.

About this book

This book contains 18 chapters in four sub-sections, which cover the following topics:

Section 1 What is mentoring? This section includes two chapters, which cover mentoring theories and models; and why mentoring?

Section 2 About you as a mentor. This section includes four chapters, which cover understanding yourself, including your values and beliefs; understanding mentoring from a beginning physical education teacher's perspective; roles and responsibilities of mentors; and knowledge, understanding and skills mentors need.

Section 3 What a mentor does. This section includes two chapters, which cover the mentor-mentee relationship and a range of collaborative approaches to mentoring.

Section 4 Supporting the development of specific aspects of beginning physical education teachers' knowledge, understanding and skills. This is the largest section, and includes nine chapters, which cover: what knowledge, understanding and skills do beginning physical education teachers need?; supporting beginning physical education teachers to become reflective practitioners; supporting beginning physical education teachers to plan good lessons; supporting beginning physical education teachers to deliver and evaluate their lessons; observing beginning physical education teachers' lessons; supporting beginning physical education teachers to observe movement to support pupils' learning; holding pre- and post-lesson observation discussions with beginning physical education teachers; holding weekly debriefs; and moving beginning physical education teachers on when they have mastered the basics.

Although the material is divided into sections and chapters, some similar content is covered in a number of chapters. In such cases, the content is generally considered from different perspectives, and hence, the material reinforces that in other chapters. Where similar content is covered in a number of chapters, there is cross-referencing to relevant content in another chapter.

Each chapter is laid out as follows:

- **introduction** to the content of the chapter;
- **objectives**, presented as what a mentor should know, understand or be able to do having read and carried out the tasks in the chapter;
- **main content** of the chapter. Research and evidence underpin the practical focus of the content of each chapter. Links between theory and practice are emphasised by including examples from relevant practical situations throughout each chapter and interweaving theory with **tasks** designed to challenge you to reflect critically on practice or your knowledge and understanding, or to support you in supporting the development of beginning physical education teachers. Thus, some of the practical activities in the book are designed to encourage reflection, whilst others ask you to undertake activities with a beginning teacher;
- **summary and key points** of the main points of the chapter;
- **further resources**, selected to enable a reader to find out more about the content of each chapter.

Although this book has been written with the mentor as the main reader, you may find it useful to use parts of the text with a beginning teacher so that they start to understand how they are involved in the process.

Website

The main text is supported by a companion website (www.routledge.com/9781138059658). This contains all the tables, figures and tasks that require you to insert information. They can be downloaded and completed or printed off. The website also includes some further resources designed to support your development as a mentor, including additional material associated with particular chapters and links to some websites which may be of use.

Other resources

Whilst the book as a whole, and each chapter, is written to stand alone, this book will not suffice alone. We have attempted to provide you with guidance to further resources by two methods: first, by references to print and web-based material in the text, the details of which appear in the references; second, by further resources at the end of each chapter. These provide you with the opportunity to explore specific aspects of the content of the chapter in greater depth. We have tried to ensure that a range of sources are included; for example, text books, research papers and websites.

In addition, this book can be used alongside subject and generic books designed for student and newly qualified teachers, to which we refer in a number of chapters, including:

- Capel, S. and Whitehead, M. (2015) *Learning to Teach Physical Education in the Secondary School: A Companion to School Experience*, 4th edn, Abingdon: Routledge.
- Capel, S. and Breckon, P. (2014) *A Practical Guide to Teaching Physical Education in the Secondary School*, 2nd edn, Abingdon: Routledge.
- Capel, S., Leask, M. and Younie, S. (eds) (2019) *Learning to Teach in the Secondary School: A Companion to School Experience*, 8th edn, Abingdon: Routledge.
- Capel, S., Leask, M., Younie, S. and Lawrence, J. (eds) (2019) *Surviving and Thriving in the Secondary School: The NQT's Essential Companion*, Abingdon: Routledge.
- Capel, S., Heilbronn, R., Leask, M. and Turner, T. (2006) *Starting to Teach in the Secondary School: A Companion to the Newly Qualified Teacher*, 2nd edn, London: Routledge.

These books are designed for student teachers on different types of initial teacher education courses or for newly qualified teachers (and, indeed, a beginning teacher you are working with may currently be using/have used them). However, they are proving equally useful to mentors in their work with beginning teachers. Likewise, you may find it useful to use these books to enable you to support the development of a beginning teacher's knowledge, understanding and skill. You can do this by directing a beginning teacher either to some reading on a particular topic or to some of the tasks for them to undertake, either alone or with your support.

About you

We recognise that you, as mentors, have different amounts of experience. As you do not let a beginning physical education teacher plateau when they are competent in the classroom, it is important that you do not plateau as a mentor. Rather, mentoring is a process that both promotes and enables professional development to be viewed as continual reflection and lifelong learning. If you already have considerable experience, you need to reflect on how you can develop and enhance your practice further.

Likewise, you are working with different beginning physical education teachers (student, newly qualified or early career teachers) and in different contexts. Some of you will be supporting student physical education teachers who are on an initial teacher education course run in partnership with a university, whilst others will be supporting student physical education teachers on school-based courses or qualified physical education teachers starting out on their careers. As a mentor, you may get support from a university partnership, the school or another context. On the other hand, you may have limited support.

Further, we recognise that your role as a mentor is being undertaken alongside several other roles you have within school; hence, you are busy.

We therefore do not feel that there is one best way for you to use this book. The book is designed so that you can dip in and out, to enable you to focus on a specific aspect of mentoring to support a beginning physical education teacher's development, rather than read it from cover to cover (although you may want to use it in both ways, of course). However, we encourage you to use the book in ways appropriate to you.

We consider reflection essential to your development as a mentor and encourage you to engage in the reflective process in a number of ways throughout this book. First, you are encouraged to reflect on your current approaches to mentoring, to consider what you currently do and how this might change/develop as a result of reading and engaging with the materials contained in this book. In addition, the practical nature of this text encourages you to undertake a number of tasks within each chapter. Some tasks are designed explicitly to encourage you to reflect, whilst others ask you to apply aspects of knowledge, understanding and skill in your mentoring activities. We encourage you to discuss tasks whenever possible in order to enhance your reflection, learning and development. In this way, you can reflect on your own responses and identify other potential responses and others' views. Further, it is important that a teacher records professional development activities undertaken, their outcomes, and actions planned as a result. This enables them to evidence their learning and development. Can you evidence your learning and development as a mentor? If you do not already do so, it is recommended that you record your responses to tasks in an evidence folder or personal diary/journal, as this will allow you to chart your learning and development as a mentor.

Terminology used in this book

Different terminology is adopted in differing mentoring contexts. The terminology used in this book might not be the same as that used in the context in which you are mentoring. In such cases, use the terminology used in your context.

One example of different terminology in use is the term 'subject knowledge', which is highly problematic. It is used widely, but generally loosely. In physical education, it relates to what the subject is about and puts the child at the centre of the learning (Kay, 2004). However, mentors in schools often use the term to mean content knowledge. Hence, there is a 'dichotomy in perceptions as to what constitutes subject knowledge and content knowledge in physical education' (Kay, 2004, p. 19). In this book, we use the term 'subject knowledge' where we are referring to subject content, pedagogical content and subject curriculum knowledge, but '(subject) content knowledge', 'pedagogical content knowledge' and 'curriculum knowledge' when we are referring to one or another of these.

We have used the plural in relation to **gender** in order to avoid clumsy he/she terminology.

We call school children **pupils** to avoid confusion with students; the latter referring to people in further and higher education. We use **beginning teachers** for people whom you are working with. This term includes student physical education teachers, newly qualified physical education teachers and early career physical education teachers. Where reference is being made to one specific group, normally student physical education teachers, we use the specific term.

Although mentoring is generally referred to generically, where we do refer to specific requirements, we make reference to requirements in England. If you are not mentoring beginning physical education teachers in England, you should refer to the specific requirements of mentoring in your own situation at this point. We also suggest that you take the opportunity to reflect on the differences between mentoring in your situation and in England.

Different practices are adopted in different contexts, including different formats for lesson plans. Lesson planning proformas might require different ways of presenting the same information, but might also require slightly different information. For example, in some plans, lesson learning outcomes are written for the whole class, and achievement of pupils against the learning outcomes forms part of the formative and summative assessment. However, on other plans, it is the learning outcomes themselves that are differentiated to cater for the range of pupils in the class. For example, learning outcomes can be divided into three bands – those that can be achieved by most of the pupils in the class, with different learning outcomes for pupils who cannot achieve these and additional outcomes for those pupils who need to be extended further. The examples used in this book, and on the companion website for this book (www.routledge.com/9781138059658), may be different from the formats you use in the context in which you are working. We suggest you use these as examples of different ways in which similar information may be presented, and then use the format required in your context or select the format most appropriate for the needs of the beginning physical education teacher you are working with.

So,

We hope you find this practical workbook useful in your role as a mentor to support the development of beginning physical education teachers. If so, tell others; if not, tell us.

We wish you well in an exciting role, supporting the development of the next generation of physical education teachers.

Susan Capel
Julia Lawrence
March 2018

SECTION 1

What is mentoring?

1 Models of mentoring

Gill Golder, Alison Keyworth and Clare Shaw

Introduction

Your job as a mentor is to develop a positive working relationship with a beginning teacher to enable them to grow and develop both professionally and personally. How you go about this will be influenced by a number of factors, such as your own experience of being mentored in the past and your common-sense opinions of the role. These are important starting points, but you are likely to grow as an effective mentor when you also base your approaches on evidence. This chapter (and this book) is designed to support you in considering the evidence to underpin your practice.

The chapter starts by looking at different definitions of mentoring. It then looks at the importance of the context in which you are working as a mentor, highlighting a number of documents from England and other countries, which impact on your mentoring practice. The chapter then considers three mentoring models which a mentor could adopt to inform their practice. These models underpin various roles you undertake and hence the other chapters in this book.

Objectives

At the end of this chapter, you should be able to:

- Have a greater understanding of what is meant by the term 'mentoring' for a beginning teacher;
- Have an appreciation of the key context in which you work, which may influence the manner in which you act as a mentor in school;
- Have an awareness of the plethora of mentoring models that exist;
- Compare and contrast three developmental mentoring models and how these could be used to support your role as a mentor.

Before reading further, undertake Task 1.1.

Task 1.1   Mentor reflection: Reflecting on your understanding of mentoring

Reflect on what you understand by mentoring by considering the following questions:

How would you define mentoring?

How does your definition inform your practice as a mentor?

How do the various policy and guidance documents relevant to your context influence your mentoring practice?

Do you base your mentoring practice on personal experience or on a model(s) of mentoring? If a model, which one(s)? Why?

Definitions of mentoring

Mentoring is widely used in many contexts for the purpose of helping people to learn and develop, both professionally and personally. There are numerous and frequently contradictory definitions of mentoring, with accompanying models of how mentoring is best approached (Haggard et al., 2011). Whilst different models might utilise different terminology and vary in emphasis regarding the role of a mentor, what remains consistent is the view that mentoring is a supportive, learning relationship. The mentor, with his or her more extensive experience, is there to support the learner's development. The quality of the relationship between mentor and mentee is extremely important.

The terms 'mentoring' and 'coaching' are at times used interchangeably. Both aim to develop the professional or professional competencies of the client or colleague. Although mentoring and coaching have much in common, an important difference between the two is the focus of developmental activities. In mentoring, the focus is on development at significant career transitions, whereas in coaching, the focus is on the development of a specific aspect of a professional learner's practice (CUREE, 2005a).

Montgomery (2017) suggested that definitions of mentoring often involve the concept that advice and guidance is given to a novice, or person with limited experience, by an experienced person. In this way, mentoring can be seen to be hierarchical; a top-down approach largely based on a one-way flow of information.

> Mentoring involves the use of the same models and skills of questioning, listening, clarifying and reframing associated with coaching. Traditionally, however, mentoring in the workplace has tended to describe a relationship in which a more experienced colleague uses his or her greater knowledge and understanding of the work or workplace to support the development of a more junior or inexperienced member of staff.
>
> (Chartered Institute of Personnel and Development (CIPD), 2012, p.1)

In contrast, other definitions of mentoring follow a less hierarchical structure. These include peer mentoring (Driscoll et al., 2009) and group mentoring (Kroll, 2016). In these approaches to mentoring, the flow of information is more bidirectional. Montgomery (2017) suggested that they are more personalised, as mentoring is adapted to an individual mentee's goals and needs more effectively. Higgins and Thomas (2001) suggested that top-down mentoring had greater impact on short-term career outcomes, and individually driven mentoring supported long-term career development more effectively. Whether the focus is on short- or long-term tailored development of a mentee, there are common aspects to all forms of mentoring. CIPD (2012, p.1) identified four characteristics of mentoring:

- It is essentially a supportive form of development.
- It focuses on helping a person manage their career and improve skills.
- Personal issues can be discussed productively.
- Mentoring activities have both organisational and individual goals.

In education, school-based mentors play a vital role in the development of student teachers and induction of newly qualified teachers. They also support other staff at points of career development. As with mentoring in other contexts, there is a focus on learning, development, and the provision of appropriate support and encouragement. The definition of a mentor outlined in the *National Standards for School-based Initial Teacher Training (ITT) Mentors* in England (Department for Education (DfE), 2016b, p.11) is someone who 'is a suitably experienced teacher who has formal responsibility to work collaboratively within the ITT partnership to help ensure the trainee receives the highest quality training'. However, in initial teacher education in many countries, including England, assessment of the beginning teacher is integral to the mentor's role. This is supported by Pollard (2014), who suggested that the role of the mentor in ITT has developed because of three aspects: the complexity of the capabilities teachers need to meet, the focus on high professional standards in school, and the transfer of knowledge from one generation to another. Before reading any further, undertake Task 1.2.

Task 1.2   Mentor reflection: Understanding the term 'mentoring'

1. Research the terms 'mentoring' and 'coaching'.
2. List a variety of terms that you associate with coaching and mentoring.
3. Make a list of common and unique characteristics for both.

The context in which you are working, which underpins your mentoring practice

Mentoring is increasingly important in a range of fields, both in the UK and internationally, as a tool to support recruitment into a profession, retention in that profession, professional learning, networking and career development. In teaching, it is widely recognised that there is a strong relationship between professional learning, teaching knowledge and practices, educational leadership and pupil results (Cordingley et al., 2015). As such, there has been an increase in the development of policy and guidance documents as well as frameworks, toolkits and factsheets produced over the past few years to support educators and others in fulfilling their roles as mentors.

As a mentor, it is important to recognise and embed current policy and statutory guidance into your mentoring practice. There are a number of key documents that underpin the mentoring process in initial teacher education and beyond in England and elsewhere. These constitute the key external drivers in shaping mentoring practice in school. Being aware of these is important, but knowing how to use them to support your work with a beginning teacher can add purpose and validity to what you do (there are examples of how to do this in other chapters in this book). They also enable you to recognise the value of being a mentor in school, as 'effective professional development for teachers is a core part of securing effective teaching' (DfE 2016c, p. 3).

Table 1.1 highlights policy and guidance documents that influence the work you do in school with a beginning teacher in England and also signposts you to examples of international equivalence documents to enable you to make comparisons internationally.

Now complete Task 1.3.

Task 1.3   The context in which you carry out your mentoring duties

Reflect on the context in which you carry out your mentoring duties. Ensure you are familiar with the relevant documents listed earlier (or, if you are working outside England, documents specific to your context). What aspects of these documents do you identify as being of most use to your work and why?

Effective mentoring models

As alluded to earlier, there are a number of mentoring models which a mentor could adopt in order to support the growth and development of a beginning teacher. Attempts have been made to categorise different approaches to mentoring; for example, Maynard and Furlong (1995) suggested that there are three categories of mentoring: the apprentice model, the competence model and the reflective model. The apprenticeship model argues that the skills of being a teacher are best learned by supervised practice, with guidance from imitation of experienced practitioners. The competence model suggests that learning to teach requires learning a predefined list of competences (the current Teachers Standards in England (DfE, 2011a) could be described as a competence model). In this model, the mentor becomes a systematic trainer supporting a beginning teacher to meet the competences. In the reflective model, the promotion of reflective practice through mentoring is key. This requires a beginning teacher to have some mastery of the skills of teaching to be able to reflect upon their own practice and for the mentor to be a co-enquirer and facilitator rather than an instructor. Task 1.4 asks you to look at three different mentoring models.

Table 1.1 Key external drivers influencing mentoring work

	Policy/guidance document	Author and date introduced	Key purpose
Teacher Standards Documents	Teachers' Standards (England)	DfE (2011)	Used to assess all student teachers working towards qualified teacher status (QTS) as well as newly qualified teachers completing their statutory induction period. 'Providers of ITT should assess trainees against the standards in a way that is consistent with what could reasonably be expected of a trainee teacher prior to the award of QTS' (DfE, 2011a, p.6).
	The Australian Professional Standards for Teachers (Australia)	Australian Institute for Teaching and School Leadership (AITSL) (2011)	The Standards are designed so that teachers know what they should be aiming to achieve at every stage of their career; to enable them to improve their practice inside and outside of the classroom. 'The Standards do this by providing a framework which makes clear the knowledge, practice and professional engagement required across teachers' careers' (AITSL, 2011, p.2).
Core Content requirements for Initial Teacher Education	Framework of core content for Initial Teacher Training (England)	DfE (2016a)	The aim of this framework is to improve the consistency and quality of ITT courses by supporting those involved in training teachers and student teachers themselves to have a better understanding of the key elements of good ITT content.
	Differentiated Primary and Lower Secondary Teacher Education Programmes for Years 1-7 and Years 5-10 (Norway)	Ministry of Education and Research (2010)	These regulations apply to universities and university colleges that provide primary and lower secondary teacher education. They aim to ensure that teacher education institutions provide integrated, professionally orientated and research-based primary and lower secondary teacher education programmes of high academic quality.
National or Regional Standards for Educators acting as mentors	National Standards for school-based initial teacher training (ITT) mentors (England)	DfE (2016b)	The standards were developed to bring greater coherence and consistency to school-based mentoring arrangements for student teachers. They set out the minimum level of practice expected of mentors. They are used to foster consistency in the practice of mentors, raise the profile of mentoring and build a culture of mentoring in schools.
	The New York State Mentoring standards Albany (USA)	The State Education Department/ The University of The State of New York (2011)	A set of standards that guide the design and implementation of teacher mentoring programmes in New York State through teacher induction.

(continued)

Table 1.1 (Cont.)

	Policy/guidance document	Author and date introduced	Key purpose
National or Regional guidelines for general coaching and mentoring practice	National framework for mentoring and coaching (England)	Centre for the Use of Resource and Evidence in Education (CUREE) (2005a)	The framework was developed in order to help schools implement mentoring and coaching to assist with continuing professional development and other activities. It sets out ten principles based on evidence from research and consultation which are recommended to inform mentoring and coaching programmes in schools. The framework provides a tool for reflection on existing practice and further development and assists a mentor in self-regulation and monitoring of their own practice.
	NTC Continuum of Mentoring Practice (USA)	New Teacher Center (NTC) (2011)	Designed to assist programme leaders as they seek to implement mentoring to support induction programmes that are capable of accelerating the development of beginning teacher effectiveness, improving teacher retention, strengthening teacher leadership and increasing pupil learning. 'It presents a holistic view of mentoring, based on six professional standards … The continuum of mentoring practice describes three levels of development, labelled Exploring/Emerging, Applying, Integrating/Innovating' (NTC, 2011, p. 2).
Professional Development expectations for teachers	Standards for teachers' professional development (England)	DfE (2016c)	This is intended for 'all those working in and with, schools in order to raise expectations for professional development, to focus on achieving the best improvement in pupil outcomes and also to develop teachers as respected members of the profession' (DfE, 2016c, p. 4). There is an emphasis on using the standards to support regular reflection on existing practice and discussion between all members of the teaching community. There are five parts to the standard, which, when acted upon together, ensure effective professional development.
	Ohio Standards for Professional Development (USA)	Ohio Department for Education (2015)	These define the essential elements of a strong professional learning system, which is one way that school systems can support all educators and encourage improved teaching and learning.

Task 1.4   Three different mentoring models

- What are the features of practice for each of these models: apprentice, competence and reflective?
- Which features of these models do you use/want to use in your mentoring?
- When do/would you use each model of mentoring?

Maynard and Furlong (1995, p.18) acknowledged that these three models exist but suggested that they should be taken together, in order to contribute to 'a view of mentoring that responds to the changing needs of trainees'. It is this recognition that mentoring practices and approaches evolve as a beginning teacher develops and the need for an examination of different stages of development that lead us to exploring three models of mentoring in more detail. We explore three well-known models (Daloz, 2012; Katz, 1995; and Clutterbuck, 2004), all of which focus on the need for the mentor to be flexible in their style and approach to best fit the needs of a beginning teacher at any given stage of their development, in initial teacher education and/or their teaching career.

Daloz's (2012) developmental model identifies two key aspects that need to be present in order for optimal learning to take place: **challenge** and **support**. The challenge aspect refers to your ability as a mentor to question a beginning teacher to enable them to reflect critically on their own beliefs, behaviours and attitudes. The support aspect relies on you being able to offer an empathetic ear, actively listen and encourage a beginning teacher to find solutions in order to continue to develop and progress.

Daloz (2012) argues that a combination of high challenge and high support needs to be offered by you as the mentor for a beginning teacher to learn effectively and to '**grow**' (High challenge + high support = **growth**). At the opposite end of this spectrum is what Daloz refers to as '**stasis**'. A beginning teacher's learning in this zone is very limited indeed as a result of their mentor offering low levels of challenge and support (Low challenge + low support = **stasis**). Where challenge is high but support is low, a beginning teacher is likely to '**retreat**' from development (High challenge + low support = **retreat**). However, where challenge is low but support is high, a beginning teacher is unlikely to move beyond their present situation despite their potential for growth being on the increase. Daloz refers to this as '**confirmation**' (Low challenge + high support = **confirmation**). You therefore need to be aware of both the level of challenge you offer and the level of support needed by the beginning teacher.

The second model is Katz's stages of development model (1995), which describes a model for professional growth in four stages:

1. Survival stage
2. Consolidation stage
3. Renewal stage
4. Maturity stage

During the first stage, '**Survival**', a beginning teacher is likely to show signs of being very self-focused and just 'getting by' or coping from day to day. They are likely to experience their practice from a position of doubt and be asking questions like 'can I get to the end of the week?' or 'can I really do this day after day?' During this initial stage, a beginning teacher may show a reluctance to take responsibility for things and, instead, look to blame others; for example, the pupils, colleagues, the school. As a mentor, observing a beginning teacher during the survival stage, you are likely to see elements of confusion and a lack of any clear rules and routines in their lessons. The beginning teacher may also demonstrate little, if any, consistency in their approach to managing behaviour. Their teaching style is often very teacher-centric and they show a reluctance to deviate from their 'script' in any way.

By the second stage, '**Consolidation**', it is likely that a beginning teacher will have begun to implement clearer rules and routines into their classrooms. There is evidence of them starting to question their own practice and being more open to alternative ways of doing things. Whilst observing a beginning teacher at this stage, you are likely to notice that their classes are generally well managed and that the needs of the average pupil are predominantly well catered for. In addition, the beginning teacher is likely to demonstrate a greater awareness of individual pupils and their learning needs. However, they are unlikely to have gained a true grasp of how to support and cater for the needs of pupils within specific subgroups; for example, special educational needs and disability (SEND), English as an Additional Language (EAL) and Gifted and Talented (GandT).

The '**renewal**' stage is the point at which a beginning teacher is becoming much more self-aware and self-critical. They have generally mastered the basics and are now striving for ways in which they can improve their practice. They are looking for strategies and ideas of how to introduce more creative and innovative activities into their lessons. As a general rule of thumb, at the 'renewal' stage, beginning teachers are often at their most self-motivated and are eager to contribute to departmental discussions, offer suggestions, design additional resources and/or become involved in the running of lunch-time and after-school clubs.

The final stage of Katz's model, '**maturity**', is where a beginning teacher is demonstrating signs of developing their own beliefs, teaching style and strategies. They are regularly asking themselves a number of questions which support deeper levels of reflection, both in and on practice (Schön, 1983). They are still looking to improve their practice and are still interested in new ideas and resources. However, their focus has shifted from an inward perspective to a much broader one. They are now very interested in the impact of their teaching on their pupils' learning and progress. Task 1.5 focuses on the responsibilities of the mentor and beginning teacher at each stage of Katz's stages of development model (1995).

Task 1.5   Responsibilities of the mentor and beginning teacher at each stage of Katz's stages of development model (1995)

In each of Katz's stages, there are responsibilities for both the mentor and the beginning teacher. Identify what you would do to support a beginning teacher at each stage.

And finally, Clutterbuck's (2004) model of developmental mentoring suggests that an effective mentor wants to draw on all four of the 'helping to learn' styles (guiding, coaching, counselling and networking) (see Figure 1.1). Figure 1.1 shows that in any given mentoring

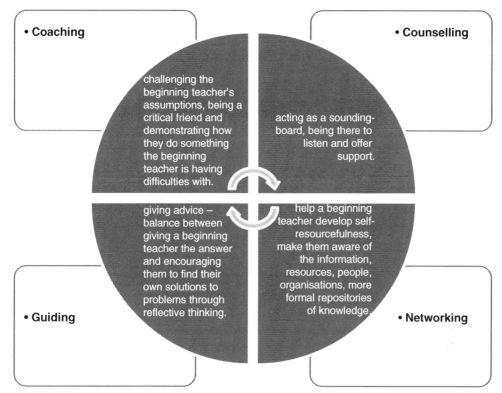

Figure 1.1 Helping to learn styles
(Source: adapted from Clutterbuck's model of developmental mentoring (2004, p. 9))

relationship, a mentor may need to adopt a different style and/or approach to challenge and support a beginning teacher at various stages of their development. In developmental mentoring, the beginning teacher sets the agenda based on their own development needs, and the mentor provides insight and guidance to support the beginning teacher to achieve the desired goals. A more expert mentor will be able to select the right 'helping to learn' style for a beginning teacher's needs.

Now complete Task 1.6, which looks at Clutterbuck's model.

Task 1.6 Helping a beginning teacher to learn using Clutterbuck's (2004) model

- Consider which of the four 'helping to learn' styles you feel most comfortable with and why.
- Which do you use the least often and/or feel the least comfortable with and why?
- What could you do to overcome this?

Your ability to assess and identify the developmental stage in which a beginning teacher is operating at any given point is a significant aspect of your role in becoming an effective mentor and ensuring growth takes place. Of equal importance, however, is your skill in adapting your own approach to fit the developmental needs of a beginning teacher. It is worth remembering that none of the three models (Daloz (2012), Katz (1995) or Clutterbuck (2004)) is linear in structure, and, therefore, it is likely that a beginning teacher will move 'to and fro' between stages/zones, for example if teaching different aspects of the curriculum in which they have greater or lesser knowledge and/or confidence or starting at a new school. With each of the models considered, it is possible to see elements of all three approaches to mentoring described by Maynard and Furlong (1995). Regardless of the mentoring model on which you prefer to base your practice, the attributes of the mentor play a crucial role in making decisions about the approach to mentoring.

There have been a number of attempts to characterise attributes of mentors. For example, Child and Merrill (2005) sought to generate an understanding of the attributes of a mentor in initial teacher education. Cho et al. (2011) described personal qualities that lie at the core of the mentor's identity and professional traits that relate to success in work-related activities. The DfE (2016b) described four separate, but related, areas in the *National Standards for School-based Initial Teacher Training (ITT) Mentors*: personal qualities, teaching, professionalism and self-development, and working in partnership. Ragins (2016) described the attributes of a mentor as an antecedent to high-quality mentoring; as something that needs to be in place before a mentor–mentee relationship begins. Task 1.7 asks you to consider the attributes of an effective mentor (see also Chapter 2).

Task 1.7   Attributes of an effective mentor

1. Considering the context and models of mentoring outlined in this chapter, reflect upon what you think the attributes of an effective mentor are. Attach a level of significance to each attribute, using three categories of significance: *essential, desirable* and *highly desirable*.
2. Having identified the attributes and the levels of significance, place five of the attributes in a prioritised list that best captures the ideal profile of a mentor of a beginning teacher.
3. Reflect on your own practice as a mentor; how might you develop the attributes that you have prioritised?

Finally, Task 1.8 asks you to reflect again on your mentoring practice after having read this chapter.

Task 1.8   Mentor reflection: Reflecting on your mentoring practice

After having read this chapter, reflect on how your understanding of definitions of mentoring, relevant policy and guidance documents, and models of mentoring have impacted/will impact on your practice.

Summary and key points

Effective mentoring is a complex and demanding task, but, as with any role that enables you to have a positive impact on the development of others, it is hugely rewarding. In this chapter, we have considered the importance of:

- being aware of different definitions of mentoring
- understanding the context in which you are carrying out your role and what moral, political or theoretical drivers might influence the education system that you work in and/or your work as a mentor
- having a broad understanding of different models of, or approaches to, mentoring in order to make decisions about how to carry out your role as a mentor

Further reading

Chambers, F. (2015) *Mentoring in Physical Education and Sports Coaching*, Abingdon: Routledge.
Section 1 explores different models of mentoring, how these models can be used to support professional development, and practical ideas for putting the models into practice. It sets a specific context of mentoring for physical education.

Maynard, T. and Furlong, J. (1995) 'Learning to teach and models of mentoring', in T. Kerry and A. Shelton-Mayes (eds.) *Issues in Mentoring*, London: Routledge, pp. 10-14.
This chapter should help to deepen your knowledge of the three categories of mentoring: the apprentice model, the competence model and the reflective models.

Cordingley, P., Higgins, S., Greany, T., Buckler, N., Coles-Jordan, D., Crisp, B., Saunders, L. and Coe, R. (2015) *Developing Great Teaching: Lessons from the International Reviews into Effective Professional Development*, London: Teacher Development Trust.
This should help you to gain an understanding of how mentoring fits into current ideas of effective continued professional development and learning.

See also the companion website for this book (www.routledge.com/9781138059658).

You may also find it useful to refer to/use the text books written for student and newly qualified physical education teachers with a beginning teacher you are mentoring (see list on Page 4).

2 Why mentoring?

Suzie Everley

Introduction

Mentoring is an ever-evolving role that is responsive to the changing demands of education contexts and our understanding of what works most effectively.

This chapter explores the nature of mentoring and the value it has in supporting beginning physical education teacher development. As a mentor, you have a crucial role to play in the development of a beginning teacher and their continued engagement in the teaching profession (Hudson and Hudson, 2016; Lord, Atkinson and Mitchell 2008). Ensuring your own understanding of the reflective capacities required as a mentor will facilitate the support you are able to give a beginning teacher in their journey to become a truly reflective, autonomous practitioner.

The chapter begins with an exploration of what is meant by mentoring. It continues by considering school mentoring contexts for physical education specialists. The chapter then focuses on your readiness to mentor and how you might approach this responsibility, as well as what the benefits of becoming a mentor are, not only to yourself and to the beginning teacher, but also to pupils learning, the school and the wider teaching profession. The chapter concludes by looking at qualities of a good mentor.

Objectives

At the end of this chapter, you should be able to:

- Understand what mentoring is and the different approaches you might adopt;
- Understand school mentoring contexts for physical education specialists;
- Demonstrate an understanding of your readiness to mentor;
- Identify the benefits of mentoring for yourself, the beginning teacher, pupils learning, the school and the wider teaching profession;
- Consider qualities of a good mentor and your own strengths and areas for development.

What is mentoring?

Before you embark on reading this chapter, complete Task 2.1, which encourages you to consider what your own interpretation of mentoring as a concept is and how this is likely to affect your engagement with the role.

Task 2.1 Mentor reflection: What is mentoring?

- What do you understand by the term 'mentoring'?
- Why have you taken on the role/would you become a mentor?
- What do you see as the advantages/disadvantages of becoming a mentor?
- What are the implications of this for you as you take on the role of/consider whether to become a mentor at this stage of your career?
- How does being/becoming a mentor support your career aspirations?
- As you read this chapter, reflect on your answers to these questions.

It is not unusual for mentoring to be described on a basic level as a form of apprenticeship in which a beginning teacher simply receives advice and guidance from more experienced colleagues (see models of mentoring in Chapter 1 and one model in Chapter 4). In the apprenticeship model, the mentor is the central figure in the process, providing advice and guidance and acting as a role model (Chartered Institute of Personnel and Development (CIPD), 2017; Kell and Forsberg, 2016, 2014; Wright, 2010). Whilst this is a key part of the role, arguably the reality presents a far more complex set of challenges and a deeper sense of commitment than this would convey.

Too often there is an implied hierarchy in mentoring, whereby a beginning teacher feels they must change their behaviours to reflect the expectations of their mentor (or those making judgements on them) rather than developing their own individual teaching approaches. However, the process is generally more effective if there is a sense of collaborative practice (see Chapters 8 and 9) in what you are doing.

However, the etymology of the term, deriving from 'mentos', suggests a passionate, purposeful commitment to development (*Online Etymology Dictionary*, 2017). It is this purposeful commitment to development that forms the basis of the work you engage in as an effective mentor. As well as supporting a beginning teacher in developing the knowledge, skills and understanding needed to teach (see Chapter 9), you are supporting a change from one self-perception to another.

One key aspect of mentoring a beginning teacher is concerned with professional career development and transition (National College of School Leadership (NCSL), 2017), the nature of which varies greatly. For example, this may be a transition to learning to teach from having been an undergraduate student, or being employed in, for example, a sports-related coaching role or other professional post within education, such as a learning support assistant; or it may be the transition from student teacher to newly qualified teacher and then early career teacher. The complexities of mentoring within any of these contexts requires you to consider carefully how you approach and manage the mentor relationship and how you identify and prioritise areas for support and development with a beginning teacher (see Table 4.1 for one example of different approaches at different stages of a beginning teacher's development).

Case study 2.1 illustrates how different approaches to mentoring affect the progress a beginning teacher might make in the short term.

Case study 2.1 Different approaches to mentoring

Tom (a student teacher)

Of the two school experience placements I had, I made most progress with my second mentor; not because I'd already been in school but because she sat down and we genuinely went through everything together. I had a mentor meeting every week which was a requirement of the university on both placements. On the first one, Mark (mentor) was really helpful but just kind of told me what I should be doing; he was a good teacher and I respected him so it worked but I just hadn't realised how much further you could get if you were 'made' to think for yourself. With Lucy, I had to come with suggestions as to how to improve before we could begin our conversation; we really worked together to find new ways for me to do things. The emphasis was on working out what would be most effective for me; not just to copy her, so I ended up finding my own way of teaching that suited me. Also, I would've been reluctant to admit it at the time but, she used the academic work that we were doing in our institute and it all made sense; the reflective practice assignment and the tasks ... it really enforced their purpose.

Tom's example highlights a number of issues to consider as a mentor. First, it shows that beginning teachers themselves have expectations of their mentors (we explore this in more detail in Chapter 4); that mentors adopt different approaches to support a beginning teacher (see Chapter 1 for further information); and that effective mentors should encourage a beginning teacher not only to reflect on their practice, but also to make links between theory and practice.

However, it is also important to consider the context in which mentoring is taking place with respect to physical environments and relationships with other staff regarding the nature and status of our subject within the wider school.

School mentoring contexts for physical education specialists

Chapter 1 focused on the broad context of mentoring in beginning teacher development. However, it is also important to consider the specifics of a physical education context within school settings in relation to your role as a mentor. These include subject status, geographical location within the school and additional responsibilities outside teaching. Mentoring is not just supporting the development of subject content and pedagogical knowledge. It provides an opportunity to help a beginning teacher, and others, to understand the complexities of the place of their subject within the wider curriculum.

Whilst a beginning physical education teacher is likely to have a clear awareness of the far-reaching benefits of their chosen specialism to pupils' learning in school, they may be less aware of the professional marginalisation of the subject (Kell and Forsberg, 2014). For example, although many physical education teachers are not seen as having high marking loads, in practice there is a growing requirement to teach theory courses and to set homework, which means that this is not actually the case. In addition, they spend a lot of their time supporting extra-curricular activities, which is not always highlighted. Further, the sports hall is frequently requisitioned for exams, a situation that does not occur for other subjects. Maintaining a positive orientation to the value of our subject will be an integral thread to the wider context of your mentoring.

The location of physical education facilities and the siting of the department staff work-space means it is not unusual for physical educationalists to be geographically isolated from other subject areas. This can sometimes create a sense of being removed from the school not only physically but also in terms of the informal relationships that might otherwise develop with staff from different subjects or senior management (Kell and Forsberg, 2016); for example, through staffroom conversations. As a mentor, you should consider how the impact of this can be minimised. For example, are there opportunities for a beginning phys-ical education teacher to observe in other subject areas, or could specific efforts be made to ensure that at least some breaks are taken in a common staff room?

Finally, contributing to the department's extra-curricular programme, whilst highly rewarding, involves what are likely to be new challenges for a beginning physical education teacher (Banville, 2015); for example, in the organisation of 'peripheral' considerations such as transport, risk assessments and obtaining parental consent. Importantly, as a mentor, it is important that you take account of the level of commitment expected in order that a beginning teacher does not become overburdened, resulting in a negative impact on their teaching. You also need to be cognisant of other demands that are possibly being placed on the beginning teacher. If you are working with a beginning teacher in their initial teacher edu-cation (ITE) phase, candidates are required to complete reflective academic work (Everley and Flemons, 2014) and keep records to track their progress. Whilst this is always designed to support their development, in some instances, this can be seen by a student teacher as conflicting with the demands of school. As a mentor, you need to help a beginning teacher to manage conflicting demands and not to overburden themselves through a high commitment to supporting extra-curricular activities.

It is important to note that such contexts as these constitute the framework within which effective approaches to support a beginning teacher might be developed. Task 2.2 asks you to reflect on the context of physical education and how it might impact on your work as a mentor.

Task 2.2   Identifying your mentoring context

Reflect on the points raised in this section: how does your own situation relate to the contexts identified?

To identify your mentoring context, consider:

- the status of physical education in relation to others
- where the department features in the presentation of the school to pupils and the wider public
- how often you see senior management in your teaching environment
- to what extent your success in both curricular and extra-curricular activities is celebrated

- any other aspects of the subject context that you feel are relevant and you need to consider

Now reflect on how:

- the answers to these questions might affect a beginning teacher's perception of their own professional development
- this working context can affect your practice as a mentor with the particular beginning teacher you are working with
- you can most effectively utilise the context to support the development of the beginning teacher

Having acknowledged the need to incorporate consideration of the specific professional context in which you are working, a pertinent question is your readiness to mentor and, if you are deciding whether to take on the role, why you wish to mentor and whether this is the right choice for you.

Readiness to be a mentor

The mentor is a critical figure in the development of a beginning teacher. Since not all mentoring is necessarily good, it is important to be sure that this is a role you wish to take on and for which you are ready (Kell and Forsberg, 2014, Keel, 2009). Mentoring can be a highly rewarding role and one that is very attractive once you are established as an effective teacher. However, it is also challenging; the skills, knowledge, personalities, and socialisation of beginning teachers vary greatly, and you are unlikely to employ a single approach to mentoring – either with one beginning teacher over time (see Table 4.1) or with different beginning teachers. The ability to be both proactive and responsive is a necessary attribute of an effective mentor. Case study 2.2 takes us through the journey of Claire, a physical education mentor in a university-led ITE programme who, through engaging in the role, clearly changed her opinion as to what being a mentor actually means.

Case study 2.2 Claire's (mentor) journey

In all honesty, when I first went into mentoring I had thought it was a good way of getting myself noticed for promotion later in my career; it always looks good to the head teacher to have done these things, you know, adds something to the cv. I also thought there'd be the added bonus of having lessons planned for me and delivered by someone else. Added to this, an extra pair of hands in extra-curricular activities never goes amiss.

Claire initially undertook the role for career advancement. Her perceptions were that it would potentially reduce aspects of her own workload and support the school's extra-curricular activities. As a mentor (or before taking on the role), it is very important to be clear about why you are a mentor and what your role as a mentor is. However, Claire soon changed her perception of the role, as shown in the second part of case study 2.2.

> Once I'd started, I realised that really, mentoring wasn't as straightforward as I'd thought. We had a student teacher who had some experience working in school before starting their ITE but it really didn't show. She wasn't proactive at all and seemed to want to get off as soon as the bell went. Her relationships with the pupils were pretty poor and there were some groups that just really didn't respect her as she came across as really not bothered.

Rather than taking work away from Claire, it was clear that becoming a mentor was going to give her more work. Claire needed to consider why the beginning teacher clearly lacked engagement in even being in the school environment. Questioning herself (and the beginning teacher) on why this may be happening is important (Zachary, 2012). As a mentor, you need to support a beginning teacher in transitioning between their current position and the one they need to be in, and identify the *processes* through which they might get there. Often, simply articulating a reflection can facilitate recognition that progress is not as expected and that, as in Claire's case, student teacher behaviour is not consistent with teacher behaviour (the transition you are supporting). In developing an appreciation of the mentoring role, Claire was beginning to have opportunities to develop her own competencies and understanding of the role of the teacher, highlighting one of the benefits of mentoring (professional development), as identified in Figure 2.1.

Back to Claire in the third part of case study 2.2.

> In a weird way, I learnt a lot from that first student teacher. It forced me to reflect on what I was doing and my reasons for having wanted to be a mentor in the first place. Quite frankly it made me do what I should have done before taking on the role and made me understand the sort of processes that I would need to take student teachers through in order to qualify as teachers themselves.

It is clear that Claire was already engaging in the process of reflective practice, supporting the suggestion by Zwozdiak-Myers (2015a) that reflective practice may well already form part of your practice as a critical practitioner. As a mentor, it is necessary for you to think carefully about your own role and what you are doing and to develop a reflective and reflexive approach to your role (Zachary, 2012). Mentoring is not a case of imposing your ideas and approaches on a beginning teacher, but of awakening in them new capacities and finding their own way of working. This is evidenced in Claire's final thoughts in part 4 of case study 2.2.

> [M]ore than that, I realised that we were actually in the process together. We'd tried quite a lot of things out where she tried to do what I do. Some of it worked but some didn't I think. It was a bit of a roller-coaster; we both realised we needed to take a collaborative approach in looking at what was going on and developing the most effective way she (beginning teacher) could develop her teaching and whole role in school. In short, I then felt ready to mentor!

Supporting a beginning teacher in becoming a continually evolving practitioner (as they will need to continue throughout their career) involves facilitating progress towards them becoming a reflective and reflexive professional, that is, one who can identify the relationship between events, their intentions, and outcomes (Everley and Flemons, 2015). Within the scenario depicted, the beginning teacher Claire was mentoring started by adopting similar strategies to teaching as her mentor. However, Claire worked with the beginning teacher to identify how her own beliefs about physical education and her knowledge could be integrated effectively in her own practice (Everley and Flemons, 2015).

Claire clearly developed her understanding of why someone might become a mentor and their role. It was not about reducing her workload by giving up some teaching. Rather, it was about working alongside someone to support their development as well as developing herself. It required her to rethink not only aspects of her own teaching, but also the way she worked.

Clearly, there is no one type of person who makes a good mentor, but it is important to scrutinise your reasons for wanting to be one. In particular, as Claire found out, it is important to remain mindful that mentoring is a role that requires a great deal of support, demanding time and personal commitment (Kell and Forsberg, 2014). It is also important to remember that for some mentors it can be

> honestly one of the most rewarding things in the job
>
> (James, mentor for three years)

Indeed, having considered the need to reflect on your readiness to mentor, it is important to acknowledge the benefits of mentoring. These are considered in the next section of the chapter.

Benefits of mentoring

Benefits of mentoring accrue to both the mentor and the beginning teacher. However, there are also benefits to the pupils being taught, your own school and the wider profession. Before looking at these in any detail, undertake Task 2.3, which is designed to help you identify what you feel are the benefits.

Task 2.3   Identifying the benefits of mentoring

Reflect on your own teacher education process and, in light of the preceding discussion,

- Identify key incidents that affected your journey towards becoming a teacher.
- Detail these incidents by considering the contexts within which they occurred, how they were managed and the consequences of this.
- Identify how you benefited from being mentored.
- Consider the implications of these for your own mentoring practice.

Benefits to you as mentor

When taking on a mentoring role, it is important to understand the value of what you will be doing that makes your work purposeful and meaningful. For example, it allows you to reflect upon your own teaching as well as potentially to see how others teach. In terms of your own personal development, being engaged in mentoring has been shown to significantly enhance a sense of self-discovery and growth (Kennett and Lomas, 2015). One of the drivers for a person to become involved in mentoring has been identified as the sense of worth mentors gain from supporting the development of a colleague (Kell and Forsberg, 2016). Indeed, the very fact that you were asked to mentor may have had this effect (Kennett and Lomas, 2015).

As mentoring takes a great deal of commitment and rarely attracts additional remuneration, it is important to identify the intangible personal, professional and career development value of becoming involved (see Figure 2.1). These elements involve deriving a sense of meaning, developing your professional skills and enhancing career progression. This builds on the work of Kennett and Lomas (2015), who identified that mentors benefited from the fact that their role met three basic psychological needs: competency, autonomy and relatedness. In essence, your role as a mentor adds meaning and purpose to your professional identity. Taken as a whole, effective mentors also see their work as part of a wider contribution to social responsibility and the development of the teaching profession. Engagement in work and commitment to a profession have been identified as important for experiencing meaning in a role (Kennett and Lomas, 2015). Using your own experience as a teacher and the expertise that you offer to support others gives purpose to your work, and seeing others develop as a result of this is a highly motivational factor; as a result, you are likely to feel more valued, committed and driven to improve yourself.

Further, it also provides you with an additional aspect of your role that makes a meaningful contribution to your professional practice (Kennett and Lomas, 2015). It supports your professional development. By being involved in the mentoring process, you are likely to develop your own reflective capacities, aspirations and ability to contribute to the professional culture of your institution (Lord et al., 2008). You are likely to become a more reflective and reflexive practitioner and therefore enhance the quality of your own teaching and career development.

On a more pragmatic level, being engaged in the mentoring of a beginning teacher is likely to support your career development (Kennett and Lomas, 2015) in the sense that it

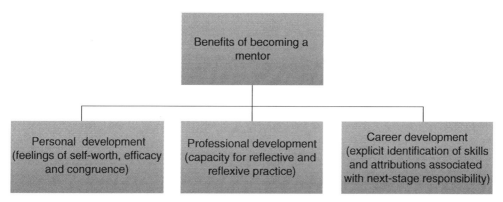

Figure 2.1 The benefits to mentors in fulfilling their role

enhances your curriculum vitae. However, as already discussed, because of the level of commitment and contingent nature of the role of mentor, this is not a simple road to recognition. Generally, mentoring requires much more commitment than a description of the role the mentor is presented with ordinarily suggests.

Benefits to a beginning teacher

In the scenario in case study 2.2, it is clear that Claire and the beginning teacher both benefited from the experience. Of key interest here is the value derived from collaboratively engaging in the process. Kennett and Lomas (2015) have suggested that the benefits of mentoring for a beginning teacher are axiomatic. Research has demonstrated that the benefits of mentoring significantly exceed those of experience alone (Kell and Forsberg, 2014; Wright, 2010; Zachary, 2012). Being engaged in the mentoring process supports a beginning teacher to develop more quickly, therefore becoming a better teacher earlier, which is obviously to the benefit of learners.

Mentoring supports beginning teachers in developing skills of teaching and also key capacities that are essential to their development. In particular, as a result of the mentoring process, beginning teachers demonstrate a greater capacity for self-management/learning and working with others, and a more positive orientation towards the profession (Lord et al., 2008).

Benefits to pupils, the school and the profession

In terms of benefit to your school, being engaged in the mentoring process has been identified as creating a sense of meaningfulness in professional roles, which, in turn, positively affects work-based motivation (Kennett and Lomas, 2015). Therefore, it would appear self-evident that a potential rise in commitment by staff as a result of engaging in the mentoring process is of great benefit to the school. Indeed, it creates an 'upward spiral' of positive orientations to work (Kennett and Lomas, 2015).

Teacher attrition in some areas of Europe, the Americas and Australia has been a key cause for concern within the teaching profession (Banville, 2015), and large numbers of teachers leave before they have completed five years' service (Hudson and Hudson, 2016). This not only has cost implications (Hudson and Hudson, 2016; Kell and Forsberg, 2014) but also has an impact on the profession as a whole and the culture of valuing teachers (Lord et al., 2008). Effective mentoring has been suggested as a means through which retention can be addressed, as it provides emotional and practical support in dealing with the challenges of teaching (Kell and Forsberg, 2014), which is highly significant.

Effective mentoring that enhances the quality of teachers and the retention of staff has immense value for pupils' education. Improving the quality of teaching and engagement with assessment and planning processes enhances learning opportunities and, therefore, progress. Beginning teachers can arrive with fresh ideas and approaches, which, when they are mentored into realistic, focused learning opportunities, can energise the teaching environment and the response of learners. When such beginning teachers remain in the profession, pupils' progress is likely to be enhanced through the establishment of stable learning contexts.

A weaker beginning teacher carries potential risk to learner progress and can clearly negatively impact development. Whilst a beginning teacher needs to learn and develop, it is important that pupils are not negatively affected through being taught by a beginning teacher. Rather, they should continue to achieve their potential and benefit from their school supporting the development of beginning teachers. The centrality of mentoring in ensuring a high calibre of delivery is therefore essential to the ultimate goal of the profession, which is to ensure high-quality learning.

Task 2.4 is designed to enable you to explore the benefits of mentoring.

Task 2.4   Reflecting on the benefits of mentoring

Having read this section, and using your responses from Task 2.3, reflect on what you now see as the benefits of engaging as a mentor. Have these changed? Can you add any benefits to your original thoughts?

Using Figure 2.1, write down three targets (one for each area) which you aim to achieve as a mentor. For example: Personal Development: to use observations to reflect on my own approaches to lesson delivery.

Clearly there are benefits to being a mentor; however, equally important are the qualities you require to undertake the role effectively.

Qualities of an effective mentor

A good mentor is respected by colleagues at all levels in the school. Her/his contribution as a member of staff is appreciated, but what qualities enable a mentor to be effective? What is the difference between a good mentor (one whom a beginning teacher speaks positively about and says, for example, I learned a lot, I am grateful to x for, etc.) and a less effective mentor (one whom a beginning teacher is less likely to speak positively about; for example, they were not supportive, I could not wait to finish my placement, etc.)? Task 2.5 asks you to identify qualities of a good mentor, and task 2.6 asks you to identify experiences, skills and characteristics you are bringing to the mentoring role that enable you to be effective as a mentor (this will be particularly useful if you are thinking about becoming a mentor and/or are presenting a case to your head of department as to why you would be effective in this role or are reflecting on your qualities as a mentor).

Task 2.5   Qualities of a good mentor

Before reading the next part of the chapter, write down a list of what you perceive to be qualities of a good mentor.

Table 2.1 The experience, skills and qualities you bring to your role as a mentor

Question	Your personal response	Evidence?
What experience do you have in teaching that gives you the expertise to mentor?		
What interpersonal skills do you have that enable you to develop as an effective mentor?		
What characteristics do you have that mean you can effectively provide and assess development opportunities supportively?		
How are you reflective and reflexive in your own practice?		

Task 2.6   Experience, skills and characteristics you are bringing to the mentoring role

Complete Table 2.1. In column 2 you are asked to respond to the questions, then provide evidence (implicit or explicit) in column 3 to support your response in each case.

Qualities of an effective mentor as identified from a range of sources are identified in Table 2.2.

These qualities of mentoring are highlighted throughout the remainder of the book.

Task 2.7 asks you to identify your own qualities as a good mentor.

Task 2.7   Personal qualities as a mentor

Identify your strengths and areas for development on each of these qualities. To enable you to do this, use Table 2.2 on the companion website for this book (www.routledge.com/9781138059658), to which two additional columns have been added for you to record how you perceive you fare on that quality and to record evidence for the grade you have given yourself.

Identify mechanisms to help you further develop your strengths as well as areas identified for development.

Task 2.8 asks you to reflect on experiences that enable you to have empathy for, and accept, a beginning teacher as a developing professional.

Task 2.8   Revisit your own beginning teacher experiences

Revisit and reflect on your own early years as a teacher in light of theoretical and research-based perspectives. Identify how this helps you to have empathy for, and accept, a beginning teacher as a developing professional, regardless of their age or previous life experiences.

In addition, or if you prefer, complete this task for a selected quality of your choice.

Table 2.2 Qualities of an effective mentor

Self-awareness	This enables the mentor to recognise: their beliefs and values; what drives them; their strengths and aptitudes as well as their weaknesses; what enables them to succeed and what prevents them from succeeding; what they would like to be better at and what they lack confidence in. This should enable them to better support a beginning teacher. This requires skills of reflection.
Is committed to the role of mentoring and to helping beginning teachers recognise and achieve their potential and satisfaction in teaching	The mentor understands that they need to be there for a beginning teacher when they need support or help. They also understand that mentoring is challenging, needs commitment and persistence and takes significant time and energy. However, they believe that, as a mentor, they are capable of having a significant, positive impact on a beginning teacher.
Recognises that each mentoring relationship is unique	The mentor recognises that each beginning teacher comes with different backgrounds, experiences and expectations. They adjust their mentoring to the needs of each beginning teacher.
Is able to draw on a range of theoretical models	The mentor is knowledgeable about a range of mentoring models (including their own self-generated models developed from personal experience) and can draw on these, as appropriate, as a framework to support a beginning teacher's development.
Takes a personal interest in the mentoring relationship	The mentor invests in the success of a beginning teacher as they are committed to helping a beginning teacher to develop their own strengths, beliefs and personal attributes to find success and satisfaction as a teacher. Responsibilities as a mentor are not taken lightly.
Is organised	A common characteristic identified by beginning teachers is the need for their mentor to be organised. Many seek clarity as to what is expected of them from the start of the relationship. A mentor is likely to be a very busy person. However, it is important to be organised in order to be able to give time to supporting a beginning teacher. Successful mentors give time to a beginning teacher, building a trusting relationship and supporting progress. A beginning teacher should feel confident in their mentor's commitment to them. Where practical and appropriate the mentor should prioritise them.
Is able to develop a constructive, trusting relationship with a beginning teacher	It is important to build rapport with a beginning teacher. This involves focusing on a beginning teacher, building trust, having empathy, acknowledging their goals and empowering them. Beginning teachers value what their mentor thinks, so it is important that a beginning teacher trusts the mentor and feels it is all right to make a mistake and tell the mentor about it. Honesty and truth is the foundation of any relationship. Constructive criticism is important for learning. Thus, it is important that the mentor thinks about how they will respond (a mentor forgets what they said a lot sooner than a beginning teacher). A beginning teacher should know the mentor will stand up for them; both in front of them and to others when a beginning teacher is not there.
Is respected by a beginning teacher	Respect needs to be earned. To achieve this, the mentor needs to reach out to a beginning teacher to make sure they are involved, their opinion is valued, they are being taken seriously. For example, the mentor sits with a beginning teacher at break or takes her/him to a meeting. The mentor should treat interactions with confidentiality where needed.

(continued)

Table 2.2 (Cont.)

Has clear expectations of a beginning teacher	Mentors expect certain things of beginning teachers (just as beginning teachers expect certain things of the mentor). A mentor might need to spell out what you expect of a beginning teacher. Likewise, you might need to help a beginning teacher think about what being a good beginning teacher is (this includes listening to suggestions and acting on advice/recommendations, showing commitment to developing as a teacher and taking responsibilities (and career) seriously).
Has good communication skills	Good communication is two-way. It includes being able to adopt appropriate tone, volume, pace, language of verbal communication as well as non-verbal signals to communicate with the beginning teacher. It also involves listening, reflecting on and analysing what the beginning teacher is saying and making an appropriate response in a timely manner. This helps the mentor to know whether a beginning teacher is having a good day or is stressed to enable them to react accordingly (e.g. sharing and celebrating their successes, giving advice, helping her/him to de-stress). Each of us has our own personal communication style. A mentor must understand their own communication style as well as the preference of a beginning teacher and be adaptable in order to adjust their communication to meet the needs of each individual beginning teacher and the situation.
Motivates others by setting a good example, demonstrating a positive attitude, acting as a positive role model and displaying the personal attributes it takes to be successful as a teacher and showing enthusiasm	By showing a beginning teacher what it takes to be productive and successful, the mentor demonstrates the specific behaviours and actions required to develop into a good teacher. They believe (and communicate that belief – both privately and publicly) that a beginning teacher is able to overcome current challenges. They communicate hope and optimism and build a beginning teacher's confidence in what they can become. They share their own struggles and frustrations and how they overcame them in a genuine and caring way that fosters trust. Being enthusiastic conveys to a beginning teacher that the job has meaning. It also supports learning. It is useful if this is supported by a sense of proportion and good humour. Laughter, used appropriately, is invaluable in developing rapport and bringing enjoyment to beginning teacher–mentor meetings.
Has empathy for, and is accepting of, a beginning teacher as a developing professional	The mentor remembers what it was like for them starting out as a teacher; that not everything goes smoothly. They share their own stories of their development as a teacher. They appreciate the ongoing effort of a beginning teacher and empower them through positive feedback and reinforcement. They are non-judgemental. They view problems, areas for development or characteristics of a beginning teacher (such as being poorly prepared, overconfident or defensive) as challenges to be overcome in delivering meaningful support. They listen to, and are a sounding board for, a beginning teacher to bounce ideas off, give advice, smile or say a kind word. They approach mentoring from the perspective of we are all in it together. They work well in a team environment.
Is skilful at providing support for beginning teachers	Whatever knowledge, skills and understanding the beginning teacher brings to the teaching situation the mentor is able to identify a beginning teacher's current strengths and areas for development and can provide support in order to enhance both teaching performance and pupil learning. This requires a number of skills, including working cooperatively, e.g. co-planning, team teaching, observing beginning teachers teach and discussing/giving constructive feedback and guidance on these observations.

Table 2.2 (Cont.)

Is willing to share professional knowledge, skills and expertise	The mentor accepts a beginning teacher at their current stage in their professional development, is available to answer any questions relevant to the job and is willing continually to share information and provide ongoing support.
Challenges a beginning teacher to foster professional development and a feeling of achievement	The mentor pushes a beginning teacher's thinking and helps them grow in new ways. They question a beginning teacher to develop and improve by discovering and learning for themselves, for example, new teaching methods or how to handle various situations throughout the year.
Values ongoing/ continuous learning and development and sets and meets ongoing personal and professional goals	The mentor has clear goals and personal development plans which show a beginning teacher that teacher development is ongoing, even after many years in the profession. They continually set a good example by showing how their personal habits are reflected by personal and professional goals and overall personal success. They are open about not always having the right answers; rather, they value the opinions and initiatives of others; therefore actively seek feedback from others, take part in new experiences and experiment with new ideas as they look for better ways to do things. They take every opportunity to learn with a beginning teacher. The can refine their own ideas, learn new ideas, challenge their own thinking etc. by working collaboratively with a beginning teacher. They are also able to support a beginning teacher in establishing what they want to achieve and why.
Celebrates and shares successes of a beginning teacher	It is important that the mentor celebrates and shares successes of a beginning teacher, however small. It might be that these successes are partly due to the support and guidance of the mentor.

Task 2.9 asks you to reflect on what mentoring is in light of your reading of this chapter.

Task 2.9   Mentor reflection: What is mentoring?

Having read the chapter, now return to Task 2.1 and reflect on whether your understanding of mentoring has changed. If so, how?

How does this influence your work as a mentor of a beginning physical education teacher?

Summary and key points

The key considerations that have been made in this chapter for you as a mentor concern conceptualising what mentoring is and the different approaches you might adopt, focusing on:

- Understanding school mentoring contexts for physical education specialists
- Demonstrating an understanding of your readiness to mentor

- Identifying the benefits of mentoring for yourself, the beginning teacher, pupils' learning, the school and the wider teaching profession
- Considering qualities of a good mentor and your own strengths and areas for development

It may be that you feel you have a rather dichotomous existence, as you are simultaneously seeking to protect and support a beginning teacher whilst guiding them on a path to take responsibility for themselves as an independently functioning professional. However, what you are ultimately doing is supporting a beginning teacher by provoking them to deal with challenging ideas - to truly be a 'mentee', that is, someone who learns by being caused to think (Lane and Clutterbuck, 2004).

Recommended resources

Wright, T. (2010) (ed.) *How to be a Brilliant Mentor:Developing Outstanding Teachers*, London: Routledge.
This is an accessible text that will assist you in the navigation of the ambiguities associated with being a mentor and help you develop as a mentor.

www.davidclutterbuckpartnership.com/
This website represents an organisation that focuses on generic issues in mentoring that can be applied in a variety of contexts. Articles and videos are included to explain key concepts and their application.

www.youtube.com/watch?v=6zbSArFHJsE
This short video summarises key feedback to mentors from mentees - a summary of the points covered in this chapter and evidence that you matter as a mentor!

See also the companion website for this book (www.routledge.com/9781138059658).

You may also find it useful to refer to/use the text books written for student and newly quali-fied physical education teachers with a beginning teacher you are mentoring (see list on Page 4).

SECTION 2

You as a mentor

3 About you as a mentor

Barbara Walsh and Julie Money

'Know thyself is the beginning of wisdom' Socrates

Introduction

The importance of mentoring in supporting beginning teachers, and also to ongoing profes-sional development, has taken on renewed attention with the publication of international league tables such as the Programme for International Student Assessment (PISA), which show the results of pupil attainment. League tables have reaffirmed the importance of effective teachers and high-quality mentoring (Furlong, 2015). The Carter Review (2015) in England, the Furlong Review (2015) in Wales, the Aspiring to Excellence review (2014) in Northern Ireland and the Donaldson Review (2014) in Scotland have all made it clear that mentoring should have greater status and recognition and that the qualities of effective mentors should be better understood. Mentoring can be challenging, requiring significant investment of time and energy.

Without awareness and understanding of ourselves, and a sense of being self-rooted in our own values, it is hard, if not impossible, to be aware of and respond to the needs and emotions of others. Self-awareness is all about knowing your emotions, your personal strengths and weaknesses and having a strong sense of your own worth (Stanulis and Ames, 2009). Being self-aware means understanding your emotions as they occur and as they evolve. It also means being able to differentiate whether they are appropriate or inappropriate to the situation and environment you are in. People who are self-aware and good at self-assessment generally, not only have a good understanding of their strengths and weaknesses; they also show a good sense of humour about themselves and their limitations. They are usually very reflective, learn from experience and are open to feedback. This chapter gives an overview of knowing yourself, your values and beliefs and the importance of these in your work with beginning physical educa-tion teachers. Within both of these areas is a range of elements linked to emotional intelligence.

Objectives

At the end of this chapter, you should be able to:

- Reflect on the importance of understanding yourself, including understanding your own emotional intelligence competencies as a mentor of physical education;

- Recognise your own values and beliefs about teaching and mentoring in physical education;
- Recognise your strengths as a good mentor and areas for development.

People who have influenced you

Most successful teachers can point to one or more people who have been particularly important to their growth and development. Task 3.1 asks you to consider one such person.

Task 3.1   People who have influenced you

Identify a person who positively influenced your development.

What was it that made them stand out to you? What is it you remember about them?

How did they influence you?

Did they encourage you to believe in yourself?

Did they support you in developing knowledge and skills?

Did they point you to the right resources or give you the right advice when you needed it?

Did they challenge and question your beliefs and values?

These people are mentors. Mentors can serve many purposes, from helping individuals with immediate needs to longer-term support and guidance. Mentoring is a giving and receiving relationship; it is about helping each other to expand and grow so that everyone wins.

Mentoring others is an excellent way to accelerate your own learning, develop talent and build collaborative relationships.

> I can't believe how good I felt at that moment. I had learned and he had learned, but there was no one to take credit. There was only the glimmer of a realisation that we were both participating in a wonderful process.
>
> (Gallwey, 2015, p.86, *The Inner Game of Tennis*)

It is likely that these people have influenced how you think about yourself as a teacher and mentor. However, it is important that you do not copy exactly what they did; rather, you need to understand yourself, your strengths and areas for development. The next section looks at understanding yourself.

Understanding yourself

Knowing yourself shows you are congruent; you see yourself as consistent with who you are (Johnson and Ridley, 2004). Knowing yourself is as crucial to good teaching as knowing your pupils and your subject. In fact, knowing your pupils and your subject depends heavily on self-knowledge. When you do not know yourself, you cannot know who your pupils are (Palmer, 1998).

Likewise, being a good mentor means knowing yourself. Good mentoring, like good teaching, cannot be reduced to technique; good mentoring comes from the identity, empathy and integrity of the individual. Good mentors are self-reflective; they take time to become reacquainted with their own needs, feelings, wishes and fears.

Self-reflection is a process by which you analyse your own practice, evaluate it and plan to improve it. It is the link between theory and practice. It cannot be assumed that increased knowledge leads to a change in behaviour. Newly acquired knowledge needs to be applied and then reflected upon in order to change it. With experience, this process becomes more effective. It is important to understand the need for regular reintroduction of the self.

One important personal quality is emotional intelligence. Emotional intelligence is the capacity to recognise, express and manage one's own and others' emotions and to handle interpersonal relationships empathetically and with good sense (Salovey and Mayer 1990). Daniel Goleman (1998), the author of the book *Emotional Intelligence*, identified self-awareness as the first of the five competences that make up emotional intelligence. The other competences are self-regulation, motivation, empathy and social skills.

Task 3.2 returns to people who have influenced you.

Task 3.2   The five competences that make up emotional intelligence of people who have influenced you

Using your answers from Task 3.1, as well as your own capabilities, write down the capabilities in the emotional intelligence competencies of the individuals who have influenced you.

Competencies	As a mentor	Awareness	Capabilities
Self-awareness	Recognise and understand your own emotions	Being aware of your own actions, moods and emotions and their effect on other people	Capable of recognising your own strengths and limitations, open to new information and experiences
Self-regulation	Able to regulate and manage your emotions appropriately	Being aware of waiting for the right time, place and pathway to express your emotions	Capable of being flexible and adapting well to change. Good at managing conflict and diffusing tense or difficult situations
Motivation	Recognise how you are intrinsically motivated	Being aware of seeking things that lead to internal rewards, of realising your own potential	Capable of being action-orientated, setting goals and always looking to do things better. Good at taking the initiative and committed to seeing things through

Empathy	Have the ability to understand how others are feeling	Being aware of how someone feels will influence your response by taking extra care or buoying their spirits	Capable of sensing who possesses power in different relationships, understanding how these forces influence feelings and behaviours, and accurately interpreting different situations that rely on such power dynamics
Social skills	Able to interact well with others	Being aware of how to build relationships and connections with others	Capable of being an active listener, have good verbal and non-verbal communication skills, are a good leader and are persuasive

Emotional intelligence can only really be measured by your ability to manage your own emotions and personal skills and how you as an individual develop meaningful relationships with others, your interpersonal skills and understanding (Goleman 1998). Emotional intelligence can be developed and improved by learning new skills.

In every story you will have heard about good mentors, they share one trait: a strong sense of personal identity infuses their work. Understanding your own and others' emotions also requires a good understanding of your personal strengths, weaknesses, inner resources and, perhaps most importantly, your limits (Hobson et al., 2009). It can be particularly hard to admit to weaknesses and limits, especially in a busy school environment, but it is crucial for emotional intelligence and for your own wellbeing. Either as a teacher or as a mentor, if you are faced with a problem you cannot solve, are you happy to say 'I don't know but I will try and find out', rather than inventing knowledge?

In understanding yourself, it is important to know your strengths and areas for development. Task 3.3 is designed to help you with this.

Task 3.3   Your strengths and areas for development as a mentor

Write down in each column of the table the important skills and personal qualities you believe are required to be a successful mentor. The list in Table 3.1 may help you, as might the interpersonal skills self-assessment at www.skillsyouneed.com/general/emotional-intelligence.html, which includes a section on emotional intelligence.

Skills	Strength/area for development	Personal qualities	Strength/area for development

Once you have completed the list of skills and qualities, reflect on, and record in the table, your strengths and any areas you think you might need further support to develop further as a mentor. Completing Task 3.4 will help you to undertake a reflection of your strengths and limitations/areas for development of self-awareness.

Table 3.1 Skills and personal qualities of mentors

A good listener	Caring
A good role model	Supportive
A good teacher	Encouraging
Problem-solver	Understanding
Someone to look up to	Honest
Professional	Consistent
Organised	Approachable
Use different strategies to control pupils	Enthusiastic
Good subject knowledge	Punctual
Good communicator	Available
Insightful	Reflective
Challenge thinking	Celebrates success

Table 3.2 Strengths and areas for development

Awareness	Strengths	Limitations/areas for development
Being aware of your own actions, moods and emotions and their effect on other people	I keep calm when things go wrong I learn from my mistakes I stay positive	I am happy to stay in my comfort zone I am not a risk taker
Being aware of waiting for the right time, place and pathway to express your emotions		
Being aware of seeking things that lead to internal rewards, of realising your own potential		
Being aware of how someone feels will influence your response by taking extra care or buoying their spirits		
Being aware of how to build relationships and connections with others		

Task 3.4   Mentor reflection: Strengths and limitations/areas for development of self-awareness

Reflecting on your current areas of strength and areas for development, fill in Table 3.2 to identify your awareness of your emotions. There is a worked example in the first box to give you an indication of what you need to reflect on to complete the task.

Being aware of your own values and beliefs is very important. Values affect our behaviours and character, whereas beliefs affect our morals and values. Values can emerge from a combination of background experiences and an evolving sense of self. Examples of values are loyalty, fairness and truthfulness. Beliefs are judgements about ourselves and the world that we generally accept to be true; they provide context for our experiences and connect our experiences to our values. They can be influenced by various factors such as religion, culture and society. Examples of beliefs are: lying is bad; cheating is immoral (Giddens et al., 2014).

Do your values and beliefs bias how you react to certain behaviours or in particular envir-onments? Task 3.5 is designed to help you with this.

Task 3.5   Mentor reflection: Biases

Having completed Tasks 3.3 and 3.4, do you have any biases that cloud your judgement? What are these? You might also want to reflect on your capabilities as a mentor in task 3.12 on the companion website for this book (www.routledge.com/9781138059658).

Values and beliefs about teaching physical education

Your own journey of becoming a teacher has gone through complex landscapes of practice. Your experiences as a pupil yourself (the type of school and their approaches to physical education), your experiences of sport, both inside and outside of school, the interactions you have had with physical education teachers, coaches and team members, and your own success in both physical education and sport will all have influenced your values and beliefs (Palmer, 1998). These socialising processes have helped to shape your knowledge, values and beliefs about the purpose of physical education, how it is taught and what it consists of. Perhaps the values and beliefs you have internalised because of your own experiences have led you to believe, naively, that teaching is teaching, regardless of the context. How do you challenge your own and others' beliefs and practices in teaching in order to make physical education more relevant to young people (Capel, 2015)?

Task 3.6 asks you to reflect on your values and beliefs about teaching physical education.

Task 3.6   Your values and beliefs about teaching physical education

How can physical education help to value fairness and cooperation?
How can physical education help you to accept diverse viewpoints?
How are these reflected in your teaching and in your approach to mentoring?

Values and beliefs about mentoring beginning physical education teachers

Being a good mentor entails knowing yourself psychologically and emotionally. You need to spend some time understanding your own feelings, needs, wishes and fears (Jones, 2009). As a mentor, you have to be accepting of a beginning physical education teacher as a developing person and professional. It is sometimes easy to forget that not all beginning teachers are created equal, nor are all mentors, and therefore, it is critical that as a mentor you understand yourself and your own values and beliefs to help you respond appropriately to the needs and emotions of a beginning teacher. A successful mentor will lead the process of self-reflection but will continually seek to empower the mentee.

As a mentor, you will want to develop knowledgeable, innovative teachers and not settle for those who have a busy, happy and good approach to teaching (Placek, 1983). You are bringing your own worldviews on a beginning teacher, which will end up shaping how you mentor (Langdon, 2011). Do you, for example, assume that, as a physical education teacher, you can transfer your knowledge about teaching without any formal professional development in mentoring?

Now read case study 3.1, which forms the basis for Task 3.7. As a mentor, you are vital in supporting the development of a beginning teacher. You do not just offer subject support and assessment of a beginning teacher's competence; you also provide guidance in the complexities of becoming a teacher, so a positive relationship with a mentor is fundamental to a beginning teacher. A good mentoring experience does not just happen, you make it happen.

Case study 3.1 Cath (student teacher)

Cath's first placement was in an inner city comprehensive school, where the mentor was set in her ways and did not allow her to introduce any new ideas. Cath felt very restricted in what she could do, as she had to structure and deliver the lessons as her mentor would do, as her mentor believed this was how she would 'pick up' subject content and pedagogic content knowledge.

I felt I had to teach in the style my mentor wanted me to and not necessarily how I would teach, so I would get good feedback.

As a beginning teacher, Cath felt conflicting levels of professional recognition due to the fact that being a student teacher and a teacher at the same time became a source of tension. She wanted to know

When could she be herself in the classroom?

Cath realised that, in order to please her mentor, she had to teach like her. This was just about performing the professional role of the teacher rather than being herself.

Cath felt she constantly needed to perform and prove herself to a range of different staff – including her mentor, who was judging whether or not she had met a required standard.

I felt you had to always put on an act.

Putting on an act influenced how Cath learned things and took on board feedback. It was not Cath's experiences of working with the children that caused her doubt about going into teaching, but the relationship with her mentor.

The presence of conflict between Cath and her mentor or other members of the department created a negative emotion. Critiques of lessons became a focus of this tension, as Cath could not differentiate between constructive feedback and criticism.

I felt I could never do anything right.

Task 3.7   Supporting the development of a beginning teacher

Each mentoring relationship occurs in a unique interpersonal context that is built on trust and caring.

What attributes are important from the list in Task 3.2 in mentoring Cath?

How important is it to identify where the teacher is on their journey?

Is there anything wrong with 'putting on an act'?

What are the values and beliefs of the mentor mentoring Cath?

Write down what you would do in this situation; what are your initial thoughts?

As a mentor, you are not only expected to provide support and guidance for a beginning teacher but, if you are mentoring a student teacher in England, you are also required to be their assessor and gatekeeper to the teaching profession. It is a common misassumption that the purpose of mentoring is to resolve a beginning teacher's problems or issues (Stanulis and Ames, 2009). The dangers with such an assumption are that it shifts responsibility subtly from the beginning teacher to you, and it then encourages you to do too much. In reality, the purpose of mentoring is to help a beginning teacher become more aware of their own strengths and weaknesses; to use reflection to help them ask questions of their practice. You may not be able to fix every problem that occurs in a relationship with a beginning teacher. This could be for a number of reasons, but it is important that you recognise the signs and act accordingly. It is important that you set as a priority the professional and developmental needs of the beginning teacher and not show your disappointment or get angry when things do not go according to plan. Understanding your own values and beliefs, reflecting, analysing and consulting on the situation will help you to resolve any issues. Now read case study 3.2 and answer the questions in Task 3.8.

Case study 3.2 Adrian (student teacher)

Adrian's first placement school had a traditional approach to physical education. It reinforced his beliefs about teaching games, as it was taught in a skills-based approach, with games being planned at the end of the lesson, if there was time. Adrian's mentor's beliefs about teaching physical education, and games in particular, were based upon the prerequisite of predetermined motor skills being taught and perfected first before introducing a game. He was told by his mentor:

Make sure they can perform the skill first before going into a game.

This resonated with his beliefs at the time, and, therefore, he felt happy to teach as his mentor wanted him to.

Adrian's second placement school was a sports college. He had an experienced mentor who wanted to provide a productive learning space for him. He asked Adrian if he would like to try any different ideas in his teaching. Although still not convinced about Teaching Games for Understanding (TGfU), Adrian had covered this as part of his university programme, and he was encouraged by his peers to *'give it a go'*. Knowing he had the support of his mentor, Adrian explained about the TGfU approach. Although his mentor had heard of it, he did not employ it in his school. However, his mentor was keen to see how it could be utilised and encouraged Adrian to plan for its use. Adrian was tasked with writing and teaching a series of six rugby lessons for a Year 8 games group using TGfU.

Adrian really enjoyed using the approach, and he received positive feedback from his mentor, who had also used it as a learning experience himself. His mentor asked Adrian to write further units of work for him to use before Adrian left the school. At the end of his PGCE year, Adrian concluded:

> Although I was sceptical at the start about TGfU, as it put me outside my comfort zone, I realise that it not only helped the children enjoy their games lessons more, but it also helped me to differentiate and facilitate my teaching rather than showing and telling all the time.

Adrian realised that the TGfU model helped him incorporate pedagogic content knowledge and aspects of subject content knowledge most applicable to the ability of the various groups he was teaching.

Task 3.8   Professional and development needs

Adrian was influenced in his first placement by the mentor's traditional approaches to teaching physical education.

Reflect on your own values and beliefs around approaches to teaching.

Reflect on your own values and beliefs about mentoring.

How might you encourage a beginning teacher to utilise a broad range of approaches?

When was the last time you pushed the boundaries of your own comfort zone?

In addition to theoretical and practical aspects of knowledge, mentors need to be aware of another dimension, the kind of cultural knowledge that provides 'the lens through which teachers' practical knowledge is viewed and interpreted' (Maynard, 2000, p. 8). This is a particularly pertinent aspect of mentoring, as the extent to which a beginning teacher establishes positive relationships with their colleagues and conform to their expectations of them influences, in part, how much knowledge is ultimately transferred to them (Jones and Straker, 2006). Therefore, being a professional does not simply include familiarity with a specific body of knowledge, but also what sort of person one is, how one appears and conducts oneself, and how far all these behaviours are deemed by others to be appropriate professional conduct.

Now read case study 3.3 and then complete Task 3.9.

Case study 3.3 Mark (student teacher)

> Mark is 23. He attended an all-boys grammar school in the north-west of England. After completing his sports studies undergraduate degree (where there was a small element of practical teaching), he spent a year in a local school as a curriculum support assistant in the physical education department. He had a positive view of the profession as a result of his own experiences and he made it clear he wanted to become a positive presence in the classroom.
>
> > I excelled in physical education, so I wanted to continue doing something I was good at.
>
> He had a good grasp of the content, as he had completed a number of level one coaching awards. At the start of his initial teacher education year, Mark was confident about his teaching when he first went into his placement school.
>
> > I felt I had a good understanding of the subject going into my first placement.
>
> However, when he started solo teaching, he soon realised that knowing the activity and being able to progress learning were far harder than anticipated:
>
> > I taught my first full week of lessons and I came home and, honestly, I cried and I was like 'that's not gonna work' and I completely re-jigged everything.
>
> In failing to identify the broader frameworks to which learning objectives relate, it could be argued that Mark, at this stage, was not genuinely participating in the discourse of the subject or structuring learning experiences so as to help pupils to participate. He was more concerned about keeping control of the class:
>
> > In terms of behaviour management first, you worry that the kids might prove you to be a weak teacher.
>
> Mark's biggest fear was the pedagogical content knowledge, as it was exploring what he knew about teaching, not just what he knew about physical education.

Task 3.9   The use of questioning as a mentor

What type of questions would you use to develop Mark's understanding and clarity? Why is the use of questioning important?

What type of questions could you use that would allow a beginning teacher to search inwardly for answers to their own questions?

You might want to refer to Task 3.11 on the website associated with this book, which focuses on the communication style of someone you speak with.

In case study 3.3, Mark demonstrated a good understanding of physical education; he was a keen sportsman and represented various school teams. He was also a football coach, so he was confident in his knowledge of games. However, on his first placement, he struggled to progress learning. This not only frustrated him, but also knocked his confidence. Mark appeared to have a grasp of the content, but not of how the content connected within the subject and the ways of knowing that are intrinsic to physical education. Consequently, the knowledge of physical education that some beginning teachers operate with (and seek to develop in pupils) is a narrow, restricted version at the start of their journey. It is important that a beginning teacher delivers their lessons with an understanding of the pedagogical principles of teaching and learning (Jones and Straker, 2006). Making the knowledge, which manifests itself in their day-to-day practice as a teacher, available to others is facilitated through the process of personal reflection (see Tasks 3.2, 3.3 and 3.4). Making explicit the pedagogical processes at work and integrating theoretical aspects with the practicalities of classroom action enables existing craft knowledge of teaching to be articulated. It is up to you as the mentor to widen their vison and explore new approaches.

As a mentor, you follow the same path of continuous professional development you promote to a beginning teacher. To be able to improve yourself as a mentor, you need to be able to reflect on your own mentoring experiences and your current practice.

Summary and key points

This chapter has highlighted

- the importance of awareness and understanding of ourselves, and being self-rooted in our own values. It has stressed that, without this, it is hard, if not impossible, to be aware of and respond to the needs and emotions of others.
- that good mentors are always aware of self and are congruent. How you see yourself is congruent with who you really are, and there is no void between the external front the beginning teacher sees and the internal self-experience.

In order to develop self-awareness, you need to

- spend quality time reflecting and learning from your experiences
- deliberately seek out views and perspectives that do not align with your own; this is important in your own development as a mentor
- try to release yourself from the constraints of your own areas of expertise in physical education, as these can reduce your openness to original ideas

In order to support the development of a beginning teacher:

- Do not withhold honest and constructive feedback, as this will help a beginning teacher to flourish.
- Be patient; it is easy to lose the emphasis of mentoring in the urgency to resolve short-term issues.
- When we measure the success of a mentoring relationship, it is most common to look at what changed for the beginning teacher in terms of their career or their job-related learning. In a really effective mentoring relationship, however, a critical outcome is 'How much wiser are you than before?'

- Safeguard your physical and emotional health in order to benefit a beginning teacher; mentoring is hard work.
- Be a good role model. A beginning teacher wants to see you 'walk the talk'. They want to know whether they can have a successful career and still have a satisfying personal life, and they will look to you for an answer.

As a mentor, you will be grateful for the opportunity this role provides you with to build your own wisdom by reflecting with another person on their experiences. Every session brings some insight that makes you reorient your own experience and modify your own understanding of yourself and your environment.

Further resources

www.skillsyouneed.com/ps/self-awareness.html
This resource gives you more information on emotional intelligence and offers you downloadable resources.

www.skillsyouneed.com/general/emotional-intelligence.html
This resource has an online interpersonal skills self-assessment tool, which helps you understand your personal and social competencies.

www.education.vic.gov.au/Documents/school/principals/profdev/learngteacherm.pdf
This learning guide is written for teacher mentors and has many useful tips and advice on becoming a mentor.

See also the companion website for this book (www.routledge.com/9781138059658). This includes three tasks specific to this chapter, which are designed to support you in reflecting on your strengths and areas for development in relation to qualities, capabilities and skills required by mentors.

You may also find it useful to refer to/use the text books written for student and newly qualified physical education teachers with a beginning teacher you are mentoring (see list on Page 4).

4 Beginning physical education teachers' expectations of their mentors

Suzie Everley and Jon Mills

Introduction

A large part of this book focuses on the knowledge, skills and understanding you need to be an effective mentor. However, understanding how your behaviours as a mentor impact on a beginning teacher is an essential component of effective mentoring. Some expectations of a mentor by a beginning teacher are covered within the other chapters: for example, expectations that you will return a lesson plan or other document at the time you said, and that you will hold a post-lesson observation discussion in a timely manner. This chapter looks at some key expectations beginning teachers have of their mentors that are not covered elsewhere in the book. These include providing an induction programme for a beginning teacher, supporting a beginning teacher to observe lessons taught by the mentor and other teachers, and developing independence through target setting and task design.

In initial teacher education (ITE) courses in England, the mentor undertakes what is probably a unique role: assessing a student teacher against the relevant professional standards. It is therefore important that you consider how externally set criteria might impact on a beginning teacher and their development within the profession. This role is also covered in this chapter.

Throughout your reading and your work with a beginning teacher, you should reflect upon your own practice as a mentor and consider how your behaviours as a mentor can impact on a beginning teacher. In doing so, you are encouraged to consider the characteristics of an effective mentor and how these might be reflected in the expectations a beginning teacher has of you.

Objectives

At the end of this chapter, you should be able to:

1. Understand expectations a beginning teacher may have of you and hence what makes a good mentor from a beginning teacher's perspective;
2. Design an appropriate induction programme for a beginning teacher;
3. Support a beginning teacher in critically observing you and other teachers in order to improve their own practice;
4. Evaluate a beginning teacher's progress;
5. Engage in critical reflection of your own practice as a mentor.

What makes a good mentor from the perspective of a beginning teacher?

As stressed throughout this book, it is important to reflect on your own professional practice in order to continually improve your practice (Everley and Flemons, 2015). Identifying key events and the impact they have had on you as a practitioner is a highly effective way of utilising experience (Everley, 2011; Everley and Flemons, 2015). Before continuing, Task 4.1 is designed to help you reflect again on your experiences of being a mentor and a mentee.

Task 4.1   Mentor reflection: Your experiences of being a mentor and a mentee

Having read Chapters 1–3 and based on your own experiences, consider the following:

1.   What do you feel makes a good mentor?
2.   What impact have any mentors you have worked with had on your own professional development?
3.   In your work with beginning teachers:

    a.   What challenges have you experienced?
    b.   How did you deal with these?
    c.   What feedback (if any) have you had from a beginning teacher?

4.   Based on these reflections, what would you say are the key expectations a beginning teacher would have of you as a mentor?

Reflecting on your own experiences allows you to consider what you feel are important components of the mentoring process. However, you need to consider that what works for you might not reflect the needs/expectations of those whom you mentor. You also need to remember that each beginning teacher is different, so it is important to find out what they each need (likewise, the same beginning teacher might need a different approach at different times in their development; see, for example, Table 5.2).

Chapter 2 covered the qualities of a good mentor. Task 4.2 asks you to consider these qualities in relation to what a beginning physical education teacher would expect of a mentor who has these qualities.

Task 4.2   Qualities of a good mentor from the perspective of a beginning physical education teacher

Using Table 2.2, add a column entitled 'What a beginning teacher would expect of the mentor who has this quality' (available on the companion website for this book (www.routledge.com/9781138059658) with the additional column added). With a beginning teacher, work through the list of qualities of a good mentor and complete this additional column.

Consider how effective you are on each quality.

Getting to know a beginning teacher

Being a good mentor requires you to have a good relationship with a beginning teacher (see Chapter 7).

For many beginning teachers, the expectation that the mentor will offer affective/emotional support as well as professional guidance is key to their success. As a mentor, you need to support a beginning teacher's transition into the classroom. Understanding their previous experiences and the level at which they are currently achieving is a key starting point. For those in ITE, some arrive straight from an undergraduate sport-related programme with little previous experience of a school environment. Others have already spent a year in a school setting working as a support assistant in a variety of curriculum areas or as a sport-specific graduate assistant. Likewise, a student teacher may have progressed particularly well in their first placement but may find a second placement more challenging, or a newly qualified teacher may find the new challenges expected of them to be challenging (e.g. being a form tutor or having to plan across a whole year). Therefore, understanding a beginning teacher forms an integral part of the review meetings you undertake with a beginning teacher (see Chapter 15 for details as to how these can be organised).

Even beyond differences in experience, beginning teachers are not all the same as individuals; they have different personalities and levels of self-confidence and resourcefulness. Therefore, perhaps the most important professional learning dimension is the interaction with other people and the daily challenges of the work itself (Eraut et al., 1998). Good mentors have a holistic approach to the role and should be sensitive to the needs of a beginning teacher in relation to each professional learning situation encountered. The mentor is there to share information and provide guidance in professional practice to the beginning teacher (Fletcher, 2000).

Thus, getting to know a beginning teacher is an important characteristic of an effective mentor. Task 4.3 encourages you to consider how you can start developing a mentor relationship through getting to know a beginning teacher.

Task 4.3   Getting to know a beginning teacher

Talk to a beginning teacher to find out more about them; you already have information about their academic qualifications and formal experience, but discuss the meaning of these experiences and the implications they have for their development:

1.   What situations make a beginning teacher feel confident?
2.   What kind of support will they value; are they an independent worker or do they value specific guidance in their practice at this stage?

3. How do they envisage using their experience in their work/to support their development?
4. What are their expectations of you as a mentor?

You may also find it helpful to find out more about a beginning teacher's home situation. The support (or otherwise) of family and friends, personal sporting commitments and possible additional work responsibilities may all impact on the way in which they work and their expectations of you as a mentor.

This knowledge should help you build a good relationship with a beginning teacher and enable you to support them in an appropriate way. Whilst no single model of mentoring is recommended, different countries have guidelines to provide a structured approach to supporting beginning teachers, particularly during ITE (e.g. Department for Education (DfE), 2016d). Such frameworks have developed over time, and many have historically focused on approaches to mentoring, in particular the apprenticeship, competence and reflective models. The apprenticeship model is based on a beginning teacher's emulation of an experienced professional; the competence model on meeting requirements of the capacity to execute certain tasks evaluated through regulated observation and feedback. The reflective model encourages in a beginning teacher the ability to 'switch focus' from their own practice to pupils' learning and identify how to make their own practice most effective (Maynard and Furlong, 1995) (see Chapter 1 and Table 5.2 in this volume for a range of mentoring models and approaches).

Models can be highly valuable tools for both you and a beginning teacher to provide a framework against which to develop your own mentoring approach. However, drawing on a range of approaches to meet the needs of the beginning teacher is crucial, as no one size fits all (Maynard and Furlong, 2013). The fact that you are reading this text is indicative of your own ability to see the importance of creating a theoretical basis for your work as a mentor. Mentors or beginning teachers who have studied mentoring literature generally are able to articulate the nature of their practice (Williams, 2010) and plan more effectively for their role.

The expectations that a beginning teacher may have of the balance of support and challenge they will receive is likely to be subject to their experience, confidence and previous mentoring. In essence, their expectations are linked to the values and beliefs they hold towards the process, in the same way as your mentoring approach is influenced by your own values and beliefs (see Chapter 3). However, it is important to remember that there can be discrepancies between a beginning teacher's experience, perceived abilities and practical competence. For example, we have sometimes had instances where a student teacher spent a period of time working in school in the capacity of being a teaching assistant or cover supervisor (wherein they either work with small groups or are simply responsible for overseeing the execution of tasks). They are familiar with school contexts and are able to establish good relationships with both pupils and staff; therefore, ostensibly, they are starting their development as teachers from a relatively strong foundation, and both they and the mentor may expect them to make better progress as compared with other beginning teachers. However, because the nature of their previous role has not necessarily required them to take responsibility for pupils' learning, when challenged to undertake this, they struggled. The need to take on a new identity as a 'teacher' was actually limited by their familiarity with working as a supervisor in that context.

Thus, we identified that all beginning teachers are different and that their progress will vary. Case study 4.1 illustrates the experience of Jenny as a student teacher as a result of her mentor's ability to get to know her on a personal level.

Case study 4.1 Jenny's experience

> I think what helped me most initially with my mentor was that we could talk informally about everyday things I was dealing with. This meant that I felt comfortable asking him questions about more specific issues concerning my training. It pretty much established a basis for me to communicate. Listening and talking from both sides; that worked well to know expectations.

As in case study 4.1, the sharing of information and provision of guidance is best initiated through first establishing relationships through informal conversations. Such interactions can establish rapport (Caddick, 2017) and provide a foundation for mutual understanding that, in turn, supports professional communication. There will be clear roles and expectations within the relationship (see ground rules in Chapter 7). Productive dialogue initially develops an understanding of goal setting and how to achieve these goals, and highlights the level of support that can and will be given to the beginning teacher.

The rest of the chapter considers four aspects of your work as a mentor which are not covered in greater depth in later chapters, highlighting the expectations a beginning teacher might have:

1. Providing a beginning teacher induction programme
2. Support and development; providing progressive responsibility
3. Observation by a beginning teacher of an experienced teacher's teaching
4. Evaluating a beginning teacher's progress

Beginning teacher induction programme

When you are working with a beginning teacher, their induction into the school environment through a beginning teacher induction programme is important. The aim of an induction programme is to develop a beginning teacher's functional acuity by making them aware of all the information and resources available and where and how to access them. When a beginning teacher arrives at a school, they expect to be given the practical information required to begin functioning in a new environment. Establishing an induction programme that enables a beginning teacher to understand the basic mechanics of the school is an essential foundation for their progress. The school may already have a programme, to which you contribute subject-specific parts. Otherwise, you need to create one for a beginning physical education teacher. If a school induction booklet is not available, it is worth creating one. This may include the following:

1. A message of welcome to the beginning teacher
2. General information about the school, including ethos/mission statements
3. Information about staff
4. Information about the student body
5. An overview of activities for the induction period, which should include reference to systems and procedures for the whole school and the physical education department:
   a. Safeguarding
   b. Professionalism and Expectations
   c. Health and Safety
   d. School Behaviour Policies – Sanctions/Rewards
   e. Inclusion – Special Educational Needs and Disability (including Gifted and Talented pupils and those with English as an Additional Language)
   f. Pupil Tracking
   g. Pastoral System

An induction programme should incorporate introductions to key members of staff, including the head, the professional tutor, the department, support staff and grounds staff. It might include a tour of school with a pupil, pupil shadowing, a learning walk with a senior member of staff, and a learning walk with the head of physical education, where a specific focus is visiting physical education teaching staff and gaining 'snapshots' of good practice. Additionally, shadowing a member of staff to gain an insight into individual practice and to see how they support different groups can be a highly valuable experience for a beginning teacher. Through these activities, you are encouraging a beginning teacher to develop their understanding of the operational workings of a department and its philosophy as applied in context.

Once a beginning teacher has been introduced to the school and department and is familiar with the nature of the school and department and the expectations they may have of their new teaching environment, it is important to frame the context through which a beginning teacher can take progressive steps towards developing their teaching, which, as a student teacher, will be taking increasing responsibility and gaining independence as an effective practitioner. The following section discusses this process.

Support and development: Providing progressive responsibility

Any one beginning teacher needs different types of support at different times. Likewise, different beginning teachers need different types of support. Although a beginning teacher may need a lot of advice initially, the aim is to support by advising where necessary but largely asking key questions, giving space for a beginning teacher to think for themselves and devise their own solutions in order to progress. This is significant, as mentors have been found to dominate conversations and therefore potentially limit a beginning teacher's development (Mena et al., 2017). Thus, a beginning teacher expects you to have strong skills of communication, facilitation and active listening to create an effective learning dialogue with them to improve their depth of thought and analysis (Caddick, 2017) (see qualities of a good mentor in Chapter 2).

Planning for a beginning teacher's development requires the ability to attend to a mix of task-orientated foci, challenge, supporting behaviour and nurturing (Lane and Clutterbuck,

2004). The balance between these is crucial. Setting too great a challenge can lead to a beginning teacher retreating due to a sense of being out of their depth. This can, in turn, damage the relationship of trust you have built. Conversely, an overemphasis on directing and supporting without any real challenge falsifies the teaching context, inhibits progress and makes independence unlikely. This is in line with Daloz's model (see Chapter 1).

If you are mentoring a student teacher, you could consider providing a structured observation programme that allows a beginning teacher to observe other teachers to identify how they plan, deliver and evaluate their lessons. This provides a beginning teacher with the opportunity to see practice modelled before delivering lessons themselves. This can be followed by a gradual introduction to classroom experience, so that the beginning teacher is ready to take on responsibility for teaching whole classes. Throughout, you need to consider the rate of progress and work with the beginning teacher to plan their next steps. Figure 4.1 illustrates the possible components of this progression with a student teacher during initial teacher education.

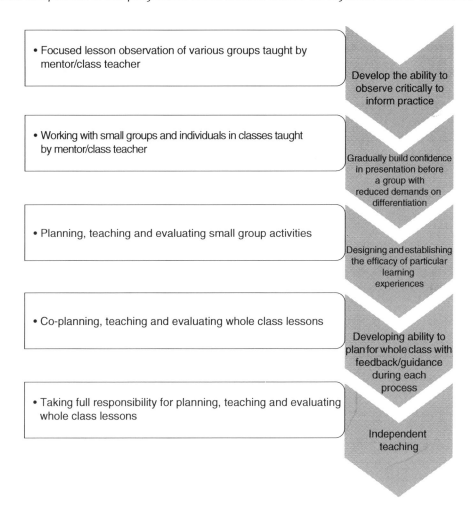

Figure 4.1 Progressive nature of student teachers' serial school experience (stages with purpose)

In order to address the first stage of this process, the following section discusses the nature of lesson observations by beginning teachers, how they might be utilised with beginning teachers and how to ensure their efficacy.

Beginning teachers' observation of experienced teachers' lessons

Learning from the practice of existing practitioners in the field can be a highly effective and efficient tool to support progress, particularly for beginning teachers (Hudson and Hudson, 2016). In our experience, this is highly variable in its efficacy, particularly as when they are asked to observe, many beginning teachers are not sure what they are looking for and view observing lessons as simply watching what is done, rather than purposefully engaging in observing the teaching and learning that is occurring. Thus, one expectation of a beginning teacher might be to be taught how to observe. To support a beginning teacher to purposefully observe lessons, as a mentor, you could look at how a beginning teacher engages in the observation process by asking them to record their observations whilst watching an experienced teacher without any prior direction from yourself, as in Task 4.5. Before you engage in providing any feedback on their observations, complete Task 4.4 to consider how you undertake observations.

Task 4.4   Mentor reflection: How you undertake observations

Consider the last lesson you observed.
What did you focus your observations on?
Why did you choose this focus?
How did you evidence your observations?

Task 4.5   Using unguided lesson observations with guided review

Ask a beginning teacher to observe and take notes on a lesson without first giving them guidance. Following the session, annotate the record and then collaboratively review the quality of the observation in light of its efficacy for improving a beginning teacher's practice.

Figure 4.2 provides an example of an observation completed by Hannah, a beginning teacher, when observing lessons with no guidance to help inform her practice.

How would you describe the observations Hannah made? What aspect of the lesson did Hannah focus on? What feedback would you give Hannah to develop her observational skills?

In this case, the mentor was surprised at the lack of detail and criticality in Hannah's observations. However, the process of completing an unguided observation was very effective in making Hannah's thought processes explicit. This enabled the mentor to discuss with Hannah how she could improve. The mentor subsequently annotated the record with

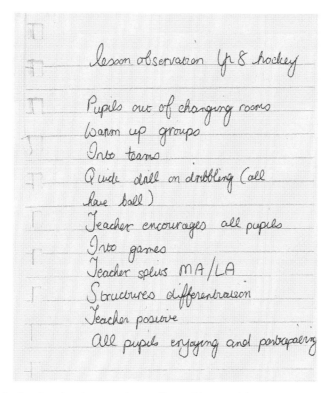

Figure 4.2 Beginning teacher lesson observation with no guidance

a number of questions for Hannah to consider before they next met (see Figure 4.3). This served to direct Hannah's thoughts but still required her to engage in the process of critically thinking about what she needed to focus on in her observations in order for them to be effective in influencing her own planning and teaching (Figure 4.3).

Following an initial exercise such as this one, you may wish to agree a focus for observation(s) a beginning teacher undertakes that relate to their weekly target for development. These evolve over time but may include key questions around, for example, planning and delivery (Table 4.1 identifies some key questions that may support this; further questions and some observation sheets can be found on the companion website for this book (www.routledge.com/9781138059658). The beginning teacher could ask the teacher they are about to observe questions *before* the lesson or ask for suggestions as to what they should focus on during the actual observations. Attending to just a few selected areas (to be agreed prior to the observation), ideally areas that relate to the beginning teacher's targets for development, is important. It is impossible to focus on too many, or too broad an area, at any one time. The comments recorded should be backed up by examples/evidence/comments from the observation. These can then inform the considerations the beginning teachers make in their own planning.

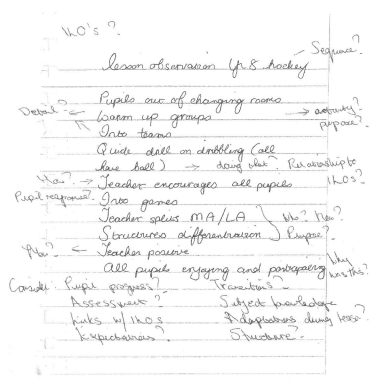

Figure 4.3 Annotated observation indicating points for reflection

Table 4.1 Questions for planning

Key questions for planning	Examples/evidence/comments
What are the learning objectives?	
What are the intended learning outcomes?	
What assessment is built into the planning?	
How is the teacher planning for differentiation?	
What Health and Safety considerations have been made?	
Key questions for observing teaching	
What progress are the pupils making? How do you know this?	
In what ways is the lesson content (including resources) appropriate for the needs of the pupils?	
What different teaching strategies are used?	
How are transitions managed?	
What types of questioning does the teacher use with pupils?	

Once an observation has taken place, the beginning teacher needs to reflect on its efficacy and identify what they have learned from it. For these purposes, it is useful for the beginning teacher to consider:

1. the strengths of the lesson and related impact on pupil progress
2. how the strengths might inform their own practice

3. any possible alterations or alternatives to approaches used in the lesson
4. areas for further discussion

The lesson observation and reflection can then be used to inform aspects of the discussions you have with a beginning teacher about their progress, influencing the extent of support or challenge you provide them with. In order to ensure continued improvement, it is important to secure a specific time each week when you meet with a beginning teacher to reflect and set targets for progress (weekly meetings are covered in Chapter 16).

Monitoring/evaluating progress

Part of your role as a mentor in England is to monitor the progress and achievements of a beginning teacher against specific criteria. This obviously occurs as an ongoing process of formal assessment and forms part of collaborative evaluation with a beginning teacher. This section considers how elements of progress tracking and summative evaluation work both independently and together.

There are a number of ways in which evaluation may be structured, but two key designs predominate: identifying first, the degree to which a beginning teacher is making progress and second, the level at which they are 'performing' against set criteria, as shown in Figure 4.4.

Although explicit assessment criteria against which you may assess a beginning teacher exist in many places, particularly in the initial teacher education phase, it may be that you choose to simply indicate the level of progress being made rather than the 'grade' being achieved. As a mentor, how you feed back to and support a student teacher is crucial in relation to maintaining their motivation as well as developing their understanding of how the evidence they are collecting supports the conversations you have around progress. Therefore, you must consider carefully whether you grade the progress a student teacher is making in relation to their own starting point, or specifically in relation to assessment criteria against which you finally report. In some respects, you need to consider whether final outcome is key, or whether it is the progress the student teacher makes over time (value added) that is important. Indeed, the process itself may involve a degree of stress for a student teacher, and therefore, finding the best way to assess in light of individual disposition is crucial here.

In our work with mentors and student teachers, we would suggest that a combination of these may be the most effective way of encouraging student teachers to become the best practitioners that they can. Student teachers like to know how they are progressing (and the

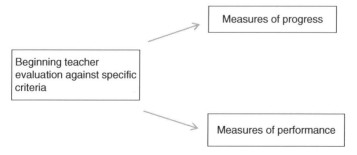

Figure 4.4 Two aspects of evaluating beginning teachers

Assessment summary progress phase

Progress (against personal targets)	The candidate has made significant progress	The candidate has made good progress	The candidate has made satisfactory progress	The candidate has not made progress
	X			
Achievement (against standards)	The candidate is achieving standards to a high level	The candidate is achieving standards at a good level	The candidate is achieving standards at a minimum level	The candidate has yet to achieve minimum standards expected
		X		

Figure 4.5 Overview of progress and achievement

final grade should not be a surprise). Therefore, particularly in any formal report made prior to assessment of qualified teacher status, giving both a progress and an achievement grade may be the most effective way of motivating a student teacher and ensuring that they understand how well they are functioning. Figure 4.5 provides an example of how a simple progress and performance template can be used to provide feedback to a student teacher.

Here, the student teacher had met some challenges; in particular, their ability to differentiate was below the level expected by the standard at that stage within their training. Weekly meetings had identified this as a target for development, and focused feedback was provided against this target when lessons were observed. Over a short period of time, the student teacher secured sufficient evidence to demonstrate that they were able to teach appropriately differentiated lessons employing a range of strategies effectively. Within the period of time given, the progress made was significant, whilst 'performance' against teaching standards was good. If this is a summative assessment, as a mentor, you need to consider the longer-term progress of a student teacher, and this requires you to include action planning for their continued practice in the profession.

Summary and key points

This chapter has focused on expectations a beginning teacher may have of you as their mentor. In summary, it is important that you establish a positive relationship with a beginning teacher and ensure they have the opportunity to maintain good professional relationships with other staff. Clear direction needs to be given, but it must be underpinned by a collaborative approach to evaluating progress and ensuring that a beginning teacher journeys towards independence. The chapter focused on four aspects:

1. Providing a beginning teacher induction programme
2. Support and development; providing progressive responsibility
3. Observation by a beginning teacher of an experienced teacher's teaching
4. Evaluating a beginning teacher's progress.

Finally, complete Task 4.6.

Task 4.6 Mentor reflection: What does a beginning teacher expect of a mentor?

Having read this chapter, consider:

1. how you know what a beginning teacher you are mentoring expects from a mentor
2. how much you consider what you are doing from a beginning teacher's perspective
3. how effectively you induct a beginning teacher into the school and/or department
4. how effectively you support a beginning teacher in critically observing you and other teachers in order to improve their own practice
5. how you consider a beginning teacher's perspective when you evaluate their progress
6. any changes you might make to develop your practice further.

Further resources

'Powerful Questions' with David Clutterbuck, available on: www.youtube.com/watch?v=QXU-tAkz_TY
This is a short presentation by David Clutterbuck focusing on how 'Powerful Questions' might be asked. These are those questions that have a clear impact on the thinking of the person we are asking the question of and how they rationalise their actions. It is very useful for thinking about how a beginning physical education teacher can be supported in reflecting on their practice, particularly, perhaps, at points where they feel they are struggling.

Building successful mentorships, available on:
www.mentorcloud.com/blog/2015/1/12/trust-and-time-building-successful-mentorships
This website gives an assessment of how a beginning teacher might expect you to give time and develop trust as an essential part of the mentoring relationship.

Wright, T (2017) *How to be a Brilliant Trainee Teacher*, 2nd edn, London: Routledge.
This text is a guide for beginning teachers to understand the relationship between teaching and learning and would be a helpful tool to be used within the mentoring process. It includes a section on reflection and evaluation that may be of particular value.

See also the companion website for this book (www.routledge.com/9781138059658).

You may also find it useful to refer to/use the text books written for student and newly qualified physical education teachers with a beginning teacher you are mentoring (see list on Page 4).

5 Roles and responsibilities of mentors

Julie Money and Barbara Walsh

Introduction

As a mentor working with a beginning physical education teacher, your major responsibility is supporting their professional development during the early stages of their career. As a mentor, you have a key role to play in supporting the growth and development of a beginning teacher, as behind every successful teacher it is essential that someone cares for them.

This requires you to fulfil a range of roles that constitute a formal arrangement for the mentoring process. Here, the focus is on completing specific requirements demanded by the relevant initial teacher education and/or development processes. However, you also play an informal role. Informally, the focus is on supporting a beginning teacher into the culture of the profession and encouraging them to become autonomous, reflective and reflexive practitioners (Everley and Flemons, 2015).

It is acknowledged that the roles and responsibilities of being a mentor to a beginning teacher are varied, extensive and demanding. It is vital that as a mentor you provide support for a beginning teacher for their professional development, as well as for retention of individuals to the profession (see Chapter 2).

Within the specific context in which you are working, you are likely to be given a list of specific roles and responsibilities as a mentor. However, this chapter outlines roles and responsibilities of mentors when working with a beginning teacher, which would be included on any such list. As a result, it illustrates the multi-dimensional aspects of your role and responsibilities as a mentor. Other chapters in this book consider your roles and responsibilities in greater detail.

Objectives

At the end of the chapter, you should be able to:

- Understand **key roles of a mentor**, including:
    - Being an 'excellent' role model to a beginning teacher;
    - Observing a beginning teacher and giving feedback in a variety of contexts;
    - Providing regular meetings with a beginning teacher and other associated personnel;
    - Co-planning and co-teaching with a beginning teacher to ensure a collaborative approach to personal and professional development;
    - Supporting a beginning teacher to develop their content and pedagogic knowledge, including behaviour for learning strategies and motivating pupils, and so on;

- Supporting a beginning teacher's understanding of safeguarding and child protection issues, as well as safety and risk assessment procedures.
- Understand the **main responsibilities of a mentor**, including:
  - Building positive relationships between the mentor and a beginning teacher, including effective communication channels;
  - Reflecting on practice, which includes your own practice as a teacher and mentor as well as reflecting on the practice of a beginning teacher;
  - Promoting the school's culture, ethos and values.

Before you start reading this chapter, complete Task 5.1 to reflect on your understanding of your roles and responsibilities as a mentor. In Task 5.2 you are asked to consider four different situations.

Task 5.1   Mentor reflection: Roles and responsibilities

What are your main roles and responsibilities as a mentor? If there is a list of roles and responsibilities specific to your current mentoring role, use this; if not, use those covered in this chapter and book.

Do you understand what these mean for you in practice?

How well prepared do you feel to take on these roles and responsibilities?

Task 5.2   Assisting a beginning teacher in different situations

Examples follow of four different situations in which you may find a beginning teacher, along with what you can do as a mentor to support them. List as many other situations as you can that have occurred or may occur and identify how you can support a beginning teacher in each.

A beginning teacher is:	Things you can do as the mentor:
Like a 'cat in the headlights' situation, very nervous, no confidence.	• *Let them establish their own way with your guidance.* • *Step in and support them during the lesson (without it being obvious to pupils that they are being 'rescued').* • *Discuss the issues, then beginning teacher watch mentor/other colleagues to focus on 'good practice'.*
Unconfident, still need help with classroom management, use of voice, pace of lesson.	• *Use suitable resources/text to address the issue of managing the learning environment.* • *Beginning teacher to observe more experienced colleagues with an agreed focus.* • *Video a beginning teacher's lesson (or section of a lesson); mentor and beginning teacher observe and discuss in relation to the agreed focus.*

Overconfident, too friendly with the pupils, doesn't listen to any advice.	*Some suggestions as to how can you change this and re-channel their energies:* • *Feedback from pupils, peers, mentor and colleagues.*
Disorganised, pupils in lessons suffering because of this.	*Some suggestions as to what action can you take:* • *Video the beginning teacher's teaching, with agreed criteria for observation; have a peer or mentor reflect and discuss.* • *With agreed criteria for observation, ask a beginning teacher to evaluate their teaching video.*

Stages of beginning teacher development and the mentor's role

Jones and Simmons (2010) used a sequence of stages in relation to a beginning coach (this can relate directly to a beginning teacher) and the role that their mentor has at

Table 5.1 Beginning teacher learning stage characteristics and a mentor's role

Beginning teacher's learning stage	Beginning teacher characteristics	Mentor's role
'Modelling'	A beginning teacher needs routines and set of skills and will attempt to copy behaviours.	*Role model, observer.* *The role of the mentor is to demonstrate 'good practice' through own teaching and share key content and pedagogical principles with a beginning teacher within observations of their and the mentor's own teaching.*
'Competence'	A beginning teacher aims to master a set of skills.	*Observer, provider of feedback.* *Observation of a beginning teacher by the mentor. This will have an agreed focus, and a beginning teacher will show a depth of understanding in terms of the feedback given by the mentor. Evidence of progression is essential.*
'Reflective/ Questioning'	A beginning teacher develops their own set of teaching beliefs and philosophy; they reflect on their own and others' practices.	*Challenger, facilitator.* *The mentor takes on a role that is less instructional. Rather, they encourage a beginning teacher to take ownership of their development and to become more innovative in their practice by challenging themselves and, where possible, 'take risks' in order to engage pupils in their learning (taking risks is covered in Chapter 17).*
'Autonomy'	A beginning teacher has a strong set of pedagogic beliefs and values. They are constantly seeking new opportunities, experiences and information to enhance their teaching pedagogy.	*Partner in critical enquiry.* *There is further collaboration between mentor and beginning teacher, whereby they work together in the exploration of different pedagogical approaches to enhance a beginning teacher's teaching and pupils' learning.*

(Source: adapted from Jones and Simmons (National Coaching Foundation (NCF), 2010, pages 8 and 11)

each of the identified stages. The stages are progressive, though it is acknowledged that each beginning teacher will go through the stages at different rates and may go back and forth between the stages. They are likely to have different needs, related to their previous experience, the progress they make, and their capacity and understanding to take on the feedback.

Table 5.1 provides a summary of this.

Key roles of a mentor

Being a role model to a beginning teacher

Being a role model is essential in your role as a mentor. Walsh (2008, p. 45) focused on mentoring being an opportunity to influence others by your own 'behaviour, beliefs and values'. In order for you to be the 'good role model' that a beginning teacher requires, you need to look at your own practice as a teacher; for example, are you well planned and organised for your teaching? Do you set a good example in terms of appearance and body language? A beginning teacher should be invited to observe you in a teaching and learning situation, with agreed key observation points. Observation of best practice is valuable throughout a teacher's career, but should have a focus related to their stage of professional development. Whilst you should not set out to 'clone' a beginning teacher, you may encourage them to take on board and model behaviours and beliefs based on your own philosophy of teaching, but as such, you should not make the experience constrained for them. Task 5.3 asks you to identify the pre-requisites of a good role model.

Task 5.3   Pre-requisites of a good role model

What do you consider are important pre-requisites of a 'good' role model to be in your school?

1.
2.
3.
4.
5.

Observation by, and of, a beginning teacher in a teaching context

There are two aspects to observation within the role of mentoring a beginning teacher: first, a beginning teacher observing the mentor and/or other members of the learning community (i.e. within the department and school) and second, a beginning teacher being observed by you, as the mentor, and other teachers. It is valuable for a beginning teacher to observe teachers from other departments as well as within PE, as this ensures that pedagogically they see a wide range of teaching skills, styles and approaches. There is an assumption that observation by a beginning teacher of experienced teachers takes place within the 'modelling phase' of their professional development (see Table 5.1); this is not the case. Throughout all stages of development, a beginning teacher benefits from observing others in their professional practice, in order that they can support their own development. By observing other teachers in the learning environment, a beginning teacher can take, for example, ideas, tips, and features of good lessons and content. However, the sophistication, depth and focus of an observation will be different, depending on a beginning teacher's stage of development. Observing a beginning teacher in a variety of situations and contexts is a key part of your role as a mentor, as is facilitating observations of other teachers within the school/department. Observation of other teachers by a beginning teacher is covered in Chapter 4, and observation of a beginning teacher is covered in Chapter 13.

Providing regular meetings with a beginning teacher and other associated personnel

Arranging meetings with a beginning teacher is one of your essential responsibilities. Meetings provide an opportunity for face-to-face communication, which is essential, particularly in a world dominated by electronic and virtual communication. It is your responsibility to ensure that time is allocated to both yourself and the beginning teacher so that time is provided to discuss both positive aspects of teaching and areas for development. The meetings can take a variety of formats; for example, a formal weekly meeting that has a pre-set agenda (see Chapter 16), pre- and post-lesson observation meetings (see Chapter 15), or an informal 'need to know' meeting that may not be planned but results from a 'situation' that has arisen. The membership of these meetings will normally be yourself and the beginning teacher, although it is your responsibility to invite key personnel as and when required.

Co-planning and co-teaching with a beginning teacher to ensure a collaborative approach to the beginning teacher's personal and professional development

Arshavskaya (2016) stated that where the mentor and the beginning teacher engage in activities of co-planning and co-teaching, they ultimately share the responsibility for enhancing pupil learning. There are a range of ways in which co-planning and co-teaching may be undertaken; for example, plan/teach together, beginning teacher plans/teaches a small part of a lesson and the mentor the rest, and so on.

You and the beginning teacher should then co-generate possible solutions to the various issues that may arise from the co-planning and co-teaching. Using the method of working with three parties (yourself as the mentor, the beginning teacher and the pupils), as you have a responsibility to both the pupils and the beginning teacher, this co-planning and co-teaching model can contribute to a more effective learning environment for everyone. Task 5.4 focuses on co-planning and co-teaching with a beginning teacher, and Task 5.5 focuses on mentor evaluation of the lesson with the beginning teacher.

Task 5.4   Co-planning and co-teaching with a beginning teacher

Co-plan a lesson with a beginning teacher and then co-teach that lesson (use any of the strategies described earlier or any other strategy which is appropriate).

   List the agreed learning objectives for the lesson below (maximum 3).

1.

2.

3.

Evaluation:

   How did the lesson progress in terms of the beginning teacher's teaching?

   How did the lesson progress in terms of pupils' learning?

Task 5.5   Mentor evaluation of the lesson with a beginning teacher

After the lesson taught in Task 5.4, ask the beginning teacher to reflect on the agreed learning objectives with you. Were they achieved or not, and why? What evidence do they have that supports this evaluation?

1.

2.

3.

Supporting a beginning teacher to develop content and pedagogic knowledge

As the mentor, you support a beginning teacher in developing their confidence within the teaching environment. This can be in relation to, for example, content and pedagogical knowledge. It is your responsibility to facilitate and provide opportunities for a beginning teacher to develop both content and pedagogical content knowledge. Much of the required continuing professional development (CPD) the mentor and beginning teacher identify to support the development of content and pedagogical content knowledge can be 'in house' or across a cluster of schools, where staff in the department or in another school can support a beginning teacher. This can be, for example, through sharing resources, inviting a beginning teacher to observe or co-teach, for example, curricular or extra-curricular activities. However, teaching pedagogy can also be developed through CPD with staff from other departments within the school.

Supporting a beginning teacher's understanding of Safeguarding and Child Protection issues and safety and risk assessment procedures

Safeguarding and Child Protection is important in all teaching and learning contexts, and it is your role to support a beginning teacher in ensuring they have the relevant knowledge and understanding of issues. Each school has its own Safeguarding and Child Protection Policy. It is important that a beginning teacher is familiar with the content of this and seeks help with anything they do not understand/do not know how to implement. There are a range of appropriate resources, many available online, to support Safeguarding and Child Protection; for example, in the UK, the National Society for the Prevention of Cruelty to Children (NSPCC) provides helpful resources. As a mentor, you can help a beginning teacher identify appropriate resources. Other staff are also a resource; for example, the school's Safeguarding and Child Protection Officer.

Safety and risk assessment is particularly important in physical education and hence an essential component of a beginning teacher's professional development. As with child protection, each school has its own safety and risk assessment policy. It is important that a beginning teacher is familiar with the content of this and seeks help with anything they do not understand/do not know how to implement. Within every physical education lesson that a beginning teacher plans and delivers, there should always be specific details on the health and safety of pupils within each aspect of the lesson (see Chapter 11 on lesson planning).

In both areas, school policy is developed in light of statutory requirements for the country in which a beginning teacher is working. It is, therefore, important that a beginning teacher is familiar with the appropriate legislation. Task 5.6 looks at supporting a beginning teacher with lesson planning.

Task 5.6   Supporting a beginning teacher with lesson planning

Ask a beginning teacher to identify a lesson plan they have developed in relation to, for example, gymnastics or athletics. For every aspect of the lesson, add a column at the end and identify how safety will be ensured in relation to the content as well as the organisation and management of the group. Discuss with the beginning teacher. Observe the lesson and, following the lesson, discuss how this worked in practice, giving any suggestions for improvement.

Responsibilities of a mentor

Your major responsibility as the mentor for a beginning teacher is to support professional development during the early stages of their career. A major responsibility is for you to build a working relationship with a beginning teacher (see Chapter 7). Your responsibilities are multi-faceted and varied, and key responsibilities are addressed in the following subsections.

Building positive relationships between the mentor and a beginning teacher, including effective communication channels

A major responsibility is that you build a working relationship with a beginning teacher, so this must involve you being 'open minded and willing to reflect' on your own teaching performance and beliefs (Jones and Simmons 2010). You and the beginning teacher have a responsibility to develop, foster and maintain a mutually positive and trusting professional relationship, as this is essential to a beginning teacher's professional development. This may not occur naturally and may require careful negotiation. This requires soft skills such as empathy towards others, self-empathy, good interpersonal skills, ability to manage your own emotions and the emotions of others, and an awareness of the feelings and needs of a beginning teacher, to whom a mentor needs to be tactful, compassionate and sensitive (Tschannen-Moran and Carter, 2016). Other skills include good communication skills; verbal, non-verbal and written (see also qualities of a good mentor in Chapter 2). As the mentor, you may need to support a beginning teacher to develop their communication skills. However, as the mentor, you have a responsibility to adopt a 'listen and ask approach, rather than a tell approach' (Jones and Simmons, 2010, p. 3). One of the fundamental requirements is that both mentor and beginning teacher are honest. You should not always 'tell' a beginning teacher, for example, how they should teach, or deal with certain issues, but instead allow honest reflection and sharing of ideas in order that professional development can be enhanced.

A major concern for many beginning teachers is to be accepted by you as the mentor. Beginning teachers do not want to be a burden and need to be accepted as a 'work in progress', though not the finished article (Walsh, 2008). Learning from each other through collegiate collaboration is the ideal situation for both parties in this professional relationship (Eliahoo, 2016; Arshavskaya, 2016). Mentoring should never be one-directional; rather, there should be a reciprocal relationship in which both you and the beginning teacher can contribute to each other's professional expertise and development.

Time is an essential requirement in a positive relationship between yourself and a beginning teacher. It is vital that you are provided with 'protected time' by the school's management team. This in itself reflects the value that is placed on the professional relationship. In order for mentoring to be successful, protected time made available for your role as a mentor must be used to good effect. This time may be used to observe a beginning teacher, hold a mentor meeting, or co-plan and/or co-teach a lesson; therefore, try to manage this time well and ensure you always use the time wisely. Get into the habit of keeping the time 'sacrosanct' so that, as such, mentoring activities become a timetabled event (like teaching your timetable).

Supporting a beginning teacher to reflect on their practice

Whilst it is acknowledged that there are a variety of ways that beginning teachers learn and develop their professional practice, reflection is considered to be a valuable learning tool (supporting a beginning teacher to reflect on their practice is covered in Chapter 10). One way of doing this is to identify critical incidents. Critical incidents do not necessarily have to be dramatic events, but can be actions, circumstances or situations considered to be worthy of reflection in order to develop and progress professionally. For example, a beginning teacher may consider how they use a more positive approach to motivate a pupil to learn rather than automatically reprimanding them. Such critical incidents may be triggered by issues or incidents that are usually personal to and instigated by a beginning teacher. However, a critical incident can also be identified by another person, such as you, the mentor, or another teacher observing a beginning teacher, but should always have a focus related to a beginning teacher's professional development. After identification of a critical incident, the beginning teacher should attempt to improve practice by reflecting on the situation and how they dealt with it. You need to monitor the critical incidents raised by a beginning teacher and use your own experiences to support them in addressing the incidents (Eliahoo, 2016). On occasions, there may be a situation where a beginning teacher cannot, or does not want to, identify a critical incident. As the mentor, you will then need to guide them using sensitivity to identify a critical incident that you have observed.

Task 5.7 looks at a critical incident.

Task 5.7   A critical incident

Meet with a beginning teacher to discuss a critical incident.

First, ask the beginning teacher to identify a critical incident from a lesson/situation in their school (they may have identified this before they come to the meeting).

Ask questions and discuss:

- How did they initially deal with the critical incident?
- Has the incident been fully addressed?
- What advice would you give to them after they initially dealt with the incident?
- What further action do they need to take?
- What development do they need to enable them to address the incident/avoid similar critical incidents in future?

The ability to give feedback is an essential skill for a mentor in supporting a beginning teacher to develop the ability to reflect. The Clean Feedback Model (Walsh et al., 2015) is an evidence-based model that can contribute to the improvement of a mentor's reflective practice. By giving 'clean feedback', you describe what you have seen or heard and keep this separate from what you've taken the behaviour to mean. You state what is actually happening rather trying to make sense of the events. There must be evidence to reflect the viewpoint of a beginning teacher; therefore, the 'feelings' related to the situation are taken out of the event, and as such, the 'personalisation' of the event is removed. An example of using clean feedback is shown in Figure 5.1.

Task 5.8 asks a beginning teacher to look at three critical incidents and give feedback using the 'clean feedback' model.

- **What worked well** *in the activity?*
The pupils responded well to the 3v1 game played.
- *What evidence have you seen/heard?*
All pupils were on task throughout this section, they could answer questions about how the attacking team found ways of outwitting an opponent.
- **What didn't work well** *in the activity?*
The transitions between activities didn't work as well.
- *What evidence have you seen/heard?*
Pupils appeared confused and were asking lots of questions as they embarked on the different activities.
- **What you will do next time** *when you teach this activity again?*
Next time, towards the end of the activity, have a group practice a demonstration of the next activity in order that the task is clear and the pupils are not waiting around for too long.

(Source: adapted from Walsh et al, 2015) (examples *in italics*)

Figure 5.1 The Clean Feedback model

Task 5.8   Using the Clean Feedback Model to reflect on critical incidents

Ask a beginning teacher to list three critical incidents that have happened in the last six weeks (or agreed period) (if they cannot identify any, you might need to help them).

Using the Clean Feedback model (Walsh et al., 2015), work through each of the critical incidents one at a time. The beginning teacher should consider clear evidence when they are making the key points (rather than putting their feelings onto the event).

Once the beginning teacher has completed the clean feedback cycle, that is, 'What will you do next time?', they can then put this into practice during the next lesson, activity or event, and then reflect on whether improvements have been made. Guidance and support from the mentor is useful in many situations to enhance progression.

Promoting the school's culture, ethos and values

In relation to the professional development of a beginning teacher, it is important that the culture, ethos and values of the school are promoted. In order that the culture, ethos and values of the school as a whole are understood and followed by a beginning teacher, the mentor should encourage and support a wider professional role for a beginning teacher. Many beginning teachers will consider their role to be solely within the physical education department; however, it is important that a beginning teacher understands that they have a much broader role in relation to the school in which they are working. A beginning teacher needs to understand how they fit into the department/faculty and school and within the field of education overall.

Thornton (2014) argued that, through working with a beginning teacher, a mentor may see the profession from a different perspective and, as a result, may challenge the culture in the school and be a catalyst for change within the school. In turn, this may have an overall positive effect on the whole school, including learning and teaching in the wider school community. Task 5.9 looks at the culture, ethos and values in your school.

> ### Task 5.9   Culture, ethos and values of your school
>
> Outline what the culture, ethos and values of your school are and share this with a beginning teacher. Discuss these with the beginning teacher and clarify whether they share the same culture, ethos and values of the school that the staff have and that are described in the key policy documents.

Summary and key points

In summary, there are a number of key points in relation to your roles and responsibilities when mentoring a beginning teacher:

- Roles and responsibilities are wide and varied, and if you take these on with a serious responsibility you can have a major impact on a beginning teacher.
- As a mentor, you will need to
    - Be an 'excellent' role model to a beginning teacher;
    - Observe a beginning teacher and give feedback in a variety of contexts;
    - Provide regular meetings with a beginning teacher and other associated personnel;
    - Co-plan and co-teach with a beginning teacher to ensure a collaborative approach to personal and professional development;
    - Support a beginning teacher to develop their content and pedagogic knowledge, including behaviour for learning strategies and motivating pupils, and so on;
    - Support a beginning teacher's understanding of safeguarding.
- As a mentor, you and the beginning teacher have a shared responsibility to ensure the professional relationship is successful; this includes supporting the development of a beginning teacher's ability to reflect on practice and in understanding the culture, ethos and values of the school.
- Face-to-face communication between you and a beginning teacher, both formally and informally, is essential. Whilst electronic communication has its value, the mentor and beginning teacher must consider the appropriate medium of communication.

Further resources

Capel, S., Leask, M., and Turner, M. (eds) (2016) *Learning to Teach in the Secondary School: A Companion to School Experience*, 7th edn, Abingdon: Routledge.
The following chapters from this book will be useful for both yourself and a beginning teacher to read and then discuss.
Unit 2.1 Reading classrooms: How to maximise learning from classroom observation. Ana Redondo
Unit 3.3 Managing classroom behaviour. Adopting a positive approach. Philip Garner
Unit 5.4 Improving your teaching: An introduction to practitioner research, reflective practice and evidence-informed practice. Marilyn Leask and Tony Liversidge
Unit 5.7 Developing critical thinking. Hazel Bryan
Unit 8.2 Developing further as a teacher. Jeanne Keay

Unit 8.3 Accountability, contractual and statutory duties. Dawn Leslie and Sue Collins

Jones, E. and Simmons, G. (2010) T*he National Coaching Foundation. Recruit into Coaching: Mentoring Guide*, Leeds: Sports Coach UK/Coachwise.
Whilst this is based on recruitment into coaching, there are many useful similarities in terms of building relationships and support in terms of professional development.

Walsh, B., Nixon, S., Walker, C. and Doyle, N. (2015) 'Using a clean feedback model to facilitate the learning process', *Creative Education* 6, 953–960.
This article discusses the use of the Clean Feedback Model, which is an alternative method of encouraging reflection whilst synthesising people's feelings.

Walsh, B. (2008) 'Being a mentor is like what?' *Innovations in Practice*, 1(1), 44–50.
Simple and easy to follow, this journal article summarises the roles and responsibilities of a mentor. It is realistic, and you will be able to identify with many different aspects.

See also the companion website for this book (www.routledge.com/9781138059658).

You may also find it useful to refer to/use the text books written for student and newly quali-fied physical education teachers with a beginning teacher you are mentoring (see list on Page 4).

6 What knowledge, understanding and skills does a mentor of beginning physical education teachers need?

Julia Lawrence and Jane Woolliscroft

Introduction

As a mentor, you require a range of knowledge, understanding and skills, many of which you possess as a teacher. However, according to van Ginkel et al. (2016, p. 214), mentoring 'requires the development of "second-order competences", concerning knowledge about how teachers learn and become competent teachers'. By this, they suggested that effective mentors are able to identify the differing needs of beginning teachers and are able to adapt their approaches to mentoring to reflect those needs. In essence, as a mentor, you utilise existing knowledge, understanding and skills and apply them to different contexts, including working with adult learners as individuals or in small numbers, each with different needs. Thus, in undertaking the role of a mentor, you need to consider what knowledge, understanding and skills you already possess as a teacher and how these might be used to support both you as a mentor and those beginning teachers with whom you work. However, it is also important to consider that you may also need to develop new knowledge, understanding and skills. As you do with a beginning teacher, identifying your strengths and areas for development is a key component of your professional development as a mentor.

Kleinknecht (2016) observed that beginning teachers may require substantial support, direction and guidance. This chapter aims to support you to identify and develop some aspects of knowledge, understanding and skills in order to provide a beginning teacher with the support, direction and guidance they need. It looks specifically at reflective practice and at working with a beginning teacher as a learner. In developing reflective practice, you are asked to reflect on both your teaching and your mentoring in order to develop your own ability to reflect and to be able to support a beginning teacher to reflect. Throughout the chapter, you are encouraged to reflect on the knowledge, understanding and skills you currently have and look for opportunities to develop these further.

Objectives

At the end of the chapter, you should be able to:

- Know what knowledge, understanding and skills are needed by an effective mentor;

- Understand, reflect on and know how to develop your own strengths and the knowledge, understanding and skills you need to develop as a mentor;
- Develop your reflective practice as a mentor.

Before reading further, complete Task 6.1.

Task 6.1 Mentor reflection: What knowledge, understanding and skills do I need to be an effective mentor?

Consider the following questions:

1. Based on your existing experiences, what do you feel are the key knowledge, understanding and skills required to be an effective mentor?
2. What knowledge, understanding and skills do you consider to be your strengths as a mentor?
3. What knowledge, understanding and skills do you consider you need to develop?
4. What activities could you undertake to support your development as a mentor in these particular areas?

This activity has been used a number of times with mentors, and the key skills that emerge commonly relate to reflection, openness, empathy, patience, collaboration and expertise.

The next section looks at skills of reflection for mentoring. The range of qualities of effective mentors are covered in Chapter 2 and highlighted in other chapters as appropriate.

Developing your reflective practice as a mentor

In your day-to-day teaching, you adopt a reflective approach. Dewey (1933, p. 118) defined reflection as 'active, persistent and careful consideration of any belief or supposed form of knowledge in the light of the grounds that support it and the further conclusions to which it tends'. In the context of teaching, Saric and Steh (2017, p. 71) presented an argument for reflection to be 'considered as a basis for professional learning because it enables the learning process in and from the everyday classroom experience of teachers'. This premise builds on the work of Belvis et al. (2013), who argued that effective reflection underpins a teacher's ability to improve their professional practice.

Working as a mentor is no different. It is important that you reflect on your own practice as a mentor. Indeed, you may have identified this as an area for development when completing Task 6.1. Taking time to think about how you are working with a beginning teacher and the impact this has is as important as thinking about how you teach and the impact this has on pupils' learning. However, in this chapter we ask you to do both; that is, to reflect not only on your mentoring, but also on your teaching. This will help you develop your own ability to reflect as well as understand how a beginning teacher reflects on their teaching, to enable you to support them in developing their ability to reflect.

Being able to identify what is or is not working well, to explore alternative approaches to mentoring and evaluate the effectiveness of your approach and the impact it is having on a beginning teacher, not only enhances your own practice but is beneficial and supportive for a beginning teacher. Reflecting on different approaches to mentoring and identifying your preferred approach(es), at the end of this chapter, is part of that reflection. Reading Chapter 10, which looks at how you, as a mentor, can support a beginning teacher in developing their capacity to reflect on their own teaching and on pupils' learning, may also be helpful in developing your own reflective practice as a mentor. Tasks 6.2 and 6.3 ask you to consider how you currently engage in self-reflection in teaching and mentoring.

Task 6.2   How do you engage in self-reflection of your own teaching?

This task encourages you to think about how you currently reflect on your own teaching. We ask you to do this to enable you to consider how you might support a beginning teacher to develop their ability to reflect.

Identify a specific incident that has occurred recently in a lesson you have taught.

1.   What was your understanding of the situation?

    a.   What specifically happened?
    b.   How did you feel about it?

2.   Could you explain why the incident occurred?

    a.   What led up to the incident occurring?
    b.   What other factors might have had an influence?

3.   What impact did you see on pupils' progress?
4.   Did you make any links to anything you have read, learned or engaged in previously?
5.   If the situation arose again, what would you do differently?

Task 6.3   How do you engage in self-reflection of your mentoring?

Identify a recent mentoring experience you had with a beginning teacher.

1.   How would you describe the experience?
2.   Think about how the mentoring experience developed and whether there were any key incidents during the relationship that made you stop and think (or reflect).
3.   What was it about these incidents that prompted you to reflect?
4.   How did you react to the incidents?
5.   Did you change any aspects of your mentoring in response to the incidents?

In completing Tasks 6.2 and 6.3, you have engaged in a formal reflective process. The questions posed are based on the model of reflection devised by Moon (1999), which identifies five stages of reflection:

- noticing (what specifically happened),
- making sense (why this might have happened),
- making meaning (how this relates to what they already know),
- working with meaning (how this links to theory and practice), and
- transforming learning (what you would do differently next time).

In engaging in reflective practice yourself, you may find you are able to model more effectively the process you are encouraging a beginning teacher to engage with (see also Chapter 10). This is important, as research (Standal and Moe, 2013) suggests that beginning teachers reflect best when engaging with others in the reflective process.

Therefore, as a mentor, you need to be able to demonstrate knowledge and understanding of, as well as skill in, the processes of reflection. You need to develop an understanding of different approaches to reflection as well as being able to reflect on your own teaching and mentoring. However, whilst knowing what reflection is and how to go about it is important, understanding how your ability to reflect changes over time is also important. Task 6.4 encourages you to consider how you feel your ability to reflect has changed over time.

Task 6.4 How does reflection develop over time?

Think about when you started as a teacher.

1. What was the focus of your reflections?
2. How detailed were these reflections?
3. How has the focus of your reflections changed over time?

Now answer the same questions in your role as a mentor.

When mentors are asked this question about their teaching, in general the response is that early reflections focused around behaviour management and organisation. They remember their reflections being very descriptive. However, as they gained experience, their reflections became much more focused and detailed. They developed their ability to make clearer connections between what they do and the impact it has on pupils' progress. This is supported by literature (Standal and Moe, 2013), which reinforces that over time, how and what we reflect upon changes. As we become more confident in the reflective process, behaviour changes, specifically in relation to moving away from focusing on our own behaviours towards the progress being made by the pupils, as well as decision-making.

Understanding how you engage within the reflective process on a continuing basis as a teacher and as a mentor, and how the depth of your reflections develops, allows you to differentiate your approach to mentoring, thereby acknowledging that over time a beginning teacher's ability to reflect evolves and develops.

In summary, a key aspect of mentoring is to know how and why we engage in reflection. Further, it is to develop appropriate skills to engage in the reflective process. Finally, it is to enhance understanding of how reflection can be used to support a beginning teacher to deepen their understanding of how their teaching impacts on the progress of the pupils they teach.

Having considered your own ability to reflect as a mentor, we now focus on the importance of understanding and supporting a beginning teacher as a learner.

Understanding and supporting a beginning teacher as a learner

As a teacher, you know that the ways pupils learn and develop are different. However, you also know there are strategies you can employ to support learners in your classroom to make progress. For example, you may apply Vygotsky's (1978) theory on the social construction of knowledge, through scaffolding learning activities, or you may use behaviourist theories of learning when looking at behaviour management. You might challenge your pupils through the tasks you set them as well as with whom they work. Working with a beginning teacher is no different. They come to you at different levels of development and learn and progress in different ways. Some beginning teachers need more support than others, whilst others might be able to offer support to other beginning teachers through sharing their knowledge of subject-specific content, for example. Seeing a beginning teacher as a learner allows you to consider the repertoire of skills you already possess as resources for supporting them in their individual development as a teacher. For example, as a teacher, you know that you need to set high expectations for your pupils and to reinforce these throughout each lesson. As a mentor, you need to set high expectations for a beginning teacher and look at how you reinforce these during the time you are mentoring them. Therefore, another key area of knowledge and understanding you use as a mentor relates to learning and learners. Task 6.5 asks you to apply your knowledge, understanding and skill as a teacher to your mentoring.

Task 6.5   Applying your knowledge, understanding and skill as a teacher to your mentoring

In this task, you are asked to look at what you already know and how you can apply this to mentoring in relation to using a range of appropriate strategies to support pupils' learning. In Table 6.1, the first column, 'Activity', identifies a number of strategies employed to enhance pupils' learning (these are taken from the Teachers' Standards (Department for Education (DfE), 2011a). You might want to identify further specific aspects of each of the broad headings as you feel appropriate (this has been done in Table 6.1a on the companion website for this book (www.routledge.com/9781138059658)), but you can use any appropriate list. In the second column, 'In my teaching', identify what specific activities you do within your teaching to demonstrate aspects of teaching. In the third column, 'In my mentoring', identify how the activities can be applied to your work as a mentor of a beginning teacher and what strategies you can use to support them. Some examples are included for you.

Table 6.1 How can my approaches to teaching support my approaches to mentoring?

Activity	In my teaching	In my mentoring
High expectations	e.g. Classroom routines	e.g. Deadlines for submission of lesson plans; Quality of planning; Organisation.
Promote progress and outcomes	e.g. Track pupils' progress Encourage pupils to reflect on their progress and what they need to do next	e.g. Monitor progress against the teachers' standards; Encourage reflection on progress and target setting to make further improvements.
Subject knowledge Planning Differentiation Use of assessment Behaviour management		
Wider professional responsibilities	e.g. Meet with parents to discuss pupil progress	e.g. Meet with appropriate colleagues to discuss progress of beginning teacher.

In order to support a beginning teacher, you need to adopt different approaches to mentoring.

Different approaches to mentoring

So far in this chapter, we have looked at how you reflect and how you can use the skills you already possess as a teacher to support a beginning teacher. We have considered how beginning teachers are learners in their own right. We now consider the importance of different approaches to mentoring in enabling you to effectively support a beginning teacher. Chapter 1 looked at some of the theory underpinning mentoring and also some of the recognised approaches to mentoring. The work of van Ginkel et al. (2016) identifies two approaches to mentoring: 'bifocal' and 'instrumental'. In bifocal mentoring, the focus is on beginning teacher learning development. The relationship between the mentor and the beginning teacher is reciprocal, built through collaboration and cooperation. In instrumental mentoring, the focus is on effectiveness and is more criterion based, suggesting that the mentor takes a more didactic approach. As a mentor, your capacity to consider the appropriateness of the mentoring approach you are adopting to enable you to support the needs of a beginning teacher is important. You may have a preferred approach(es) to mentoring, and it is important you are aware of this. However, it is also important that you know what alternatives are available, so that you are able to use these as appropriate.

Table 6.2 provides an overview of a range of mentoring approaches adopted by mentors. These are adapted from MinT approaches to mentoring (www.icre.pitt.edu/mentoring/docs/Tool_Mentoring_Styles.pdf).

Table 6.2 A range of mentoring approaches (MinT approaches to mentoring)

Style	Conversation
'Letting Go' Style	Gives time to let things develop.
	Waits for things to happen in a natural way.
	Avoids an over-emotional approach.
	Avoids rush and pressure.
'Active Listening' Style	Asks questions when things are unclear.
	Checks things by summarising.
	Is reserved in giving their own opinion.
	Gives space to the mentee.
	Shows that they understand the mentee.
'Advisory' Style	Gives suggestions for good problem-solving.
	Advises as an objective outsider.
	Gives alternatives so that the mentee can make a choice.
	Gives advice based on expertise.
'Prescribing' Style	Takes responsibility for solving the mentee's problems.
	Offers instructions on how to handle problems.
	Is convincing and persuading.
	Requires improvement, if necessary holding out the prospect of consequences.
'Cooperative' Style	Strives for a joint vision.
	Involves the mentee in problem-solving.
	Gives space to the opinion of the mentee.
	Appreciates equality in contributions.
	Is focused on cooperation.

It is important to acknowledge, though, that although each approach uses similar activities, the specific skills required in using each approach are adapted for that specific approach.

There are questionnaires available that enable you to identify your preferred approach(es) to mentoring; for example, http://liverpooluni.dualmedia.co.uk/Content/Catalogue/Docs/main/MentoringStylesSelfAssessment.pdf (viewed 10 January 2018).

Task 6.6 asks you to use one of these questionnaires to identify your own preferred approach(es) to mentoring.

Task 6.6   What is my preferred approach(es) to mentoring?

Complete the Mentoring in Teaching (MinT) questionnaire using the link provided (www.icre.pitt.edu/mentoring/docs/Tool_Mentoring_Styles.pdf). Using Table 6.2, identify what you think is your preferred mentoring approach(es). Did the mentoring approach that emerged reflect what you would identify as your preferred approach, or were you surprised at what emerged from the questionnaire as your preferred approach to mentoring? Reflect on what this means for you as a mentor.

When we have used the MinT questionnaire with mentors, there have been some interesting results, with some mentors identifying that they have one preferred approach to mentoring prior to completing the questionnaire, only to find out that their responses to the questionnaire identify a different preferred approach. In most situations, a main approach emerges alongside two other approaches with similar scores, suggesting that most mentors use a range of approaches depending on the situation they find themselves in. However, in establishing your approach(es) to mentoring, you are starting to highlight your own values, attitudes and beliefs as to what the role of the mentor is. In Chapter 3 Task 3.3, you were encouraged to identify the knowledge, skills and personal qualities you feel are important to being an effective mentor. Take some time to consider the relationship between important skills and qualities you believe are required to be an effective mentor and your preferred mentoring approach(es).

For many mentors, the way they mentor reflects their experiences of being mentored, what they feel works well and how they prefer to be mentored. As a result, the skills they develop reflect these approaches. However, their preferred approach(es) to mentoring may not always correlate with the needs and expectations of the beginning teacher with whom they are working. van Ginkel et al. (2016) argued that mentors should be versatile in the approaches they adopt in order to try to meet the needs of a beginning teacher at different times; hence, they need to know something about the individual beginning teacher (see Chapter 7). Therefore, as you develop as a mentor, it is important that you continue to reflect on the effectiveness of your approach, what specific aspects of your knowledge, understanding and skills are strengths, and what you need to develop to ensure that your skill set evolves over time.

Summary and key points

In this chapter, we have aimed to encourage you to

- Think about the knowledge, understanding and skills you need to be an effective mentor. It is highly likely that you already possess most of these as a teacher, but how you might use these in your role as a mentor to support a beginning teacher may be slightly different.
- Consider how you engage in the reflective process, both as a teacher and as a mentor. This should enable you to understand how a beginning teacher is developing their ability to reflect and also your own strengths and the knowledge, understanding and skills you need to develop as a mentor.
- Understand and support a beginning teacher as a learner.
- Recognise your preferred mentoring approach(es), but also recognise the need to adopt different approaches to mentoring at different times to meet the needs of a beginning teacher. It is important to remember that every beginning teacher you work with is different. As a mentor, you exert a strong influence over a beginning teacher you mentor. Having a repertoire of skills is, therefore, important if you are to provide a positive mentoring experience.

Finally, in Task 6.7, you are encouraged to look at what you consider to be your key areas for development based on your engagement with this chapter.

Task 6.7   Mentor reflection: My next steps

Having read this chapter, consider what areas of development you need to work on; for example, developing an understanding of how adults learn.

Using the following template, identify how you will address each area for development, moving forward.

Area for development	Strategy to adopt
Developing an understanding of how adults learn.	Access literature regarding

---

Further resources

van Ginkel, G., Oolbekkink, H., Meijer, P.C. and Verloop, N. (2016) Adapting mentoring to individual differences in novice teacher learning: The mentor's viewpoint, *Teachers and Teaching* 22(2), 198–218.
This research article focuses on key strategies that can be employed to support the development of a beginning teacher. In doing so, it encourages you to reflect on what you are currently doing and what other approaches you might adopt.

Knowl Social Enterprise and MENTEE (2015) *Mentoring, Networking and Training for European Entrepreneurs: Competence Framework for key Mentoring Competences*, viewed 28 January 2018, from www.mentee-project.eu/docs/MENTEE_IO2_Report_Public.pdf
This project report, whilst focused on mentoring in a more business-orientated environment, identifies some key competences, skills, attitudes and characteristics of effective mentors. These can be used to review what skills you already possess and which areas you wish to further develop.

See also the companion website for this book (www.routledge.com/9781138059658).

You may also find it useful to refer to/use the text books written for student and newly qualified physical education teachers with the beginning teachers you are mentoring (see list on Page 4).

SECTION 3

What a mentor does

7 Developing a mentor-mentee relationship

Julia Lawrence and Jane Woolliscroft

Introduction

A significant influence on the success of mentoring is the relationship between a mentor and a mentee (Hudson, 2016). Hobson and Malderez (2013, p. 90) defined mentoring 'as a one to one relationship between a relatively inexperienced teacher (the mentee) and a relatively experienced one (the mentor) which aims to support the mentee's learning and development as a teacher, and their integration into and acceptance by the cultures of the school and the profession'. Further, according to van Ginkel et al. (2016, p. 198), 'novice teachers in successful mentoring relationships tend to develop more positive outlooks on teaching and tend to stay in teaching longer'. A good mentoring relationship is, therefore, very important to a beginning teacher's development. A mentoring relationship should be seen as a two-way process (Hudson, 2016), in which both the mentor and the beginning teacher (the mentee) have significant roles to play in the success (or failure) of the relationship.

This chapter focuses on establishing, developing, maintaining and sustaining mentor-mentee relationships. It also looks at how to deal with situations when the mentor-mentee relationship may not be working well.

Objectives

At the end of the chapter, you should be able to:

- Understand how a mentor-mentee relationship is established, including establishing clear ground rules for an effective mentor-mentee relationship;
- Understand how to develop, maintain and sustain a mentoring relationship;
- Deal with the situation when the mentor-mentee relationship is not working well.

Before continuing any further, complete Task 7.1.

Task 7.1 Mentor reflection: Mentoring relationships

Using prior mentoring experiences, reflect on the following:

- What was the best relationship you had with a beginning teacher you were mentoring?
  - Why was it good?

- What strategies did you employ to establish, develop, maintain and sustain the relationship?
  - What strategies would you say were most successful?
- Did you have to modify your mentoring approach from previous experiences?

Establishing a mentor-mentee relationship

Hudson (2016) identified four key factors in establishing an effective mentor-mentee relationship. These include personal and professional qualities; skills and practices; environmental factors; and the selection process involved. We start by looking at the selection process.

The selection process

The allocation of a beginning teacher to a mentor varies. However, rarely are a mentor and a beginning teacher matched (Hobson et al., 2009; Hudson, 2016). The traditional approach in teaching is that you are identified as a mentor and allocated a beginning teacher. In most cases, this works effectively. However, it is becoming more common for a mentor to meet a beginning teacher prior to the start of the relationship, for example during the interview processes for some initial teacher education (ITE) routes or for a newly qualified teacher for their first post. Being in contact prior to commencing a formal relationship creates opportunities to start a conversation, to start to get to know a beginning teacher and to start to address any concerns they may have.

Meeting, and getting to know, a beginning teacher

Regardless of the allocation or selection process involved, in researching the development of mentor-mentee relationships, Hudson (2016) established that meeting with a mentee is an important part of establishing a meaningful relationship, as it encourages a dialogue, allowing basic social interactions to begin.

Beginning teachers come with different backgrounds and experiences and hence, are at different levels of development. Their background and prior experiences impact on their confidence and readiness to teach. Further, different beginning teachers present themselves differently in relation to their attitudes and expectations. Aderibigbe et al. (2016, p. 8) identified that a beginning teacher's 'expectations about learning to become a teacher may influence their expectations about their mentoring relationship'. Getting to know a beginning teacher allows you to begin to understand who they are and where they are coming from, and therefore, consider what strategies/approaches you might need to use to support them. Task 7.2 encourages you to look at getting to know a beginning teacher you are going to mentor. If you apply to establishing a working relationship with a beginning teacher what you already know as a teacher about how to develop positive working relationships with your pupils, for example getting to know something about them prior to meeting them and seeing them as individuals, you are probably approaching your role in a positive way.

Task 7.2   Getting to know a beginning teacher

Consider the last beginning teacher you mentored:

1. How was initial contact made? Was this before or as you met the beginning teacher?
2. What (if any) information did you receive about the beginning teacher prior to you meeting them?
3. If you received any information, how did you use this?
4. Would any other information have been useful?

Setting ground rules

Ground rules provide a framework for you and a beginning teacher to work from. They relate to, and support, the expectations you may have of a beginning teacher, and expectations they have of you. For example, they might relate to availability, for example when meetings will take place or times when you are contactable (or not), or they might relate to, for example, attendance at meetings, submission of lesson plans or other documentation. As in teaching, having clear expectations of each other's roles and responsibilities is important.

Whilst the temptation at times could be to get going and develop ground rules later (maybe as needed), establishing ground rules from the start limits opportunities for expectations to become blurred. One result of not setting ground rules could be that a relationship develops which you are not comfortable with. In Task 7.3, you are asked to think about what specific ground rules you will set. But remember, they will only be effective if both parties sign up to them.

Task 7.3   Setting ground rules

- From your own experience as a mentor or as a mentee, what do you feel are key ground rules in mentoring a beginning teacher?
- How do you involve a beginning teacher in the development, agreement and dissemination of these rules?
- What strategies would you consider if ground rules have been established but are not being followed?
- Identify any ground rules expected of you by others in working with a beginning teacher; for example, expectations of you and a beginning teacher from an ITE provider or your school.
- Discuss with other mentors what ground rules they establish and why.

In completing Task 7.3, you should have started to consider a range of potential areas in which you need to clearly articulate your expectations as ground rules. However, you should also have started to consider how you might work with a beginning teacher to jointly create and share ground rules.

As a teacher, you are undertaking a number of different roles, including that of mentor. Making time to undertake the role of the mentor alongside your many other roles takes organisation and self-discipline. It requires both you and the beginning teacher to understand that the role is one of many and that, although the mentoring role and relationship with the beginning teacher is important, at times it will not be your only priority. You need to work together to ensure the mentoring role does not take over other priorities. Meeting the needs of a mentee is a frequent issue raised in research studies (for example, Aspfors, 2015) relating to the mentoring process; establishing the expectations for both parties jointly may help alleviate such difficulties.

Being available to a beginning teacher is a key issue; however, emotional and psychological wellbeing for both parties must be a consideration. A beginning teacher may demand your time above and beyond what you are able to commit to. One common recurring expectation of beginning teachers is the availability of their mentor. Comments such as 'they are already available for me' or 'they respond to my emails almost immediately', whilst positive, require you to question specifically what it is you are or should be offering to a beginning teacher. Whilst your role is to provide support and guidance, you are not required to be available all the time. Thus, ground rules are important.

Providing a timetable of availability is a good starting point. This might include, for example, how many days in advance of a lesson the plan is required; within what time frame of receipt of the plan feedback will be given; and when the mentoring conversation will take place before and after a lesson observation (see Chapter 15 for pre- and post-lesson observation discussions).

Thus, you are looking at balancing expectations with reality. You need to work with a beginning teacher to ensure that what they are expecting from you is realistic.

Developing, maintaining and sustaining a mentoring relationship

In order to consider how you can go about developing, maintaining and sustaining a mentoring relationship, complete Task 7.4.

Task 7.4   How do I develop, maintain and sustain a mentor–mentee relationship?

Consider a mentoring relationship you have had as a mentor.

1.   Having established your ground rules, what do you look for in an effective mentoring relationship?
2.   What strategies did you use to develop, maintain and sustain this relationship?
3.   What strategies worked well?
4.   What might you do differently next time?

Over many years of working with mentors, when they are asked question 1 in Task 7.4, key aspects such as trust, respect, openness, collaboration and patience are frequently identified. In the next section, some of these are considered in more depth.

Building trust

Normore (2006) identified that being a mentor, and in particular being seen, at times, as the person assessing the progress of a beginning teacher, can place demands and pressures on a relationship. A relationship based on openness and trust is important in developing, maintaining and sustaining a successful mentoring relationship (Hudson, 2016). Trust is a concept that is built. It does not happen immediately. It is also two-way. You may well find it beneficial during one of your early mentor meetings (see Chapter 16) to discuss with a beginning teacher what you both see as trust.

One of the key components of developing, maintaining and sustaining trust throughout a relationship is that you do what you say you will do; for example, maintaining the ground rules you have set, especially in relation to availability. Communicating effectively with a beginning teacher is another important aspect in building trust. Being open and honest with a beginning teacher is important. If, for example, something comes up that impacts on your ability to do what you said you would, let the beginning teacher know, and try to instil the same approach as an expectation of a beginning teacher.

Hobson and Malderez (2013) described a mentor as an educator, a modeller, the provider of support to access the profession, and a psychological crutch whereby a beginning teacher can release their emotions. All these are high-level investments and have the potential to impact on you and a beginning teacher both personally and professionally. Knowing that the details of a conversation held between you and a beginning teacher will not be spread around the school, or that neither of you will talk about each other 'behind each other's back', is the basis for a successful relationship. You will know of occasions where this has not happened and the consequences in terms of the working relationship. Many a mentoring relationship has been ruined through a conversation with others outside of the pair, either formally or informally.

Relationships are organic. They need to be tended carefully to avoid them breaking down. Therefore, it is important to remember that you may need to revisit the expectations you have of yourself and the beginning teacher throughout the duration of the relationship.

In the extreme, a beginning teacher (especially one on an ITE programme) may have to change their mentor, or even school, because of a breakdown of the mentoring relationship. In many instances, this is a result of a breakdown in trust between the mentor and the beginning teacher. Here, it is probably important to consider the influence that social media, such as Facebook, Twitter and WhatsApp, can have on a mentoring relationship. Do you really want to 'friend' a beginning teacher or be part of a WhatsApp group? If you do, what are the rules governing behaviours? As one example, in an attempt to offer additional support to beginning physical education teachers whilst on placement, a WhatsApp group was set up. The purpose was to allow them to share ideas, concerns and questions. However, early on it became clear that there was a need to re-establish the purpose of the group and its membership in relation to what type of comments were being made.

Conversations, feedback and target setting

As a mentor, you support a beginning teacher in developing their competence as a teacher. When taking part in conversations, giving feedback and supporting a beginning teacher in setting targets, it is important to be aware that what you say and how you convey any guidance may be interpreted in different ways, which potentially could affect not only their confidence but also your working relationship (Korthagen et al., 2006). You may, therefore, need to work with a beginning teacher to understand how they interpret any feedback, to ensure they see it as developmental and given to support progress (some beginning teachers can interpret any feedback as personal criticism) and hence understand how best you might give feedback to support their development.

For mentors working with a beginning teacher on an ITE course in some countries, there is an expectation that they will make judgements about the beginning teacher's progress. Whilst there is much discussion surrounding whether a mentor should make such judgements (Hobson and Malderez, 2013; Hobson, 2016), there is little dispute that when someone is observed, one of the first things they want to know is how the observer has viewed the lesson. Realistically, the person being observed is seeking some form of reassurance on what they have done. Challenging a beginning teacher to reflect on their own feelings about a lesson allows them to draw out their strengths and areas for development. Their reflections may reflect the observations you yourself have made, and the ensuing conversation has the potential to provide both parties with an opportunity to discuss developments in pedagogy (Hobson et al., 2009). However, it is also important to consider how such conversations are structured, how you put over the points you want to make and the potential impact this might have on emotional wellbeing. Remember, a beginning teacher is likely to remember what you said in a mentor meeting long after you have forgotten it. Hence, the way you say something may have long-lasting consequences.

Working with a beginning teacher to enable them to understand that the support and guidance you are giving is there to scaffold their development, to understand how you can best give support and feedback and how it can be used to support their progress, is important (Chapter 13 looks at pre- and post-lesson observation discussions). This reinforces the need to review your working practices with a beginning teacher on a regular basis in order that the support and feedback you provide remains relevant and enables you to remove or add additional support, or increase/decrease the level of challenge you place upon them, as appropriate. In turn, this helps to maintain the mentor–mentee relationship.

Emotional resilience

Teaching is a challenging profession. A beginning teacher may experience emotional strains relating to the transition to becoming a teacher, including strains due to workload. A beginning teacher with whom you are working may be making a career change, trying to run a household, be returning to study, or be in their first job. What they bring to the mentoring relationship, and how they are able to cope with working in a different context, varies. Understanding emotional aspects of being a beginning teacher is important. It is important not to respond with 'we've all been there'. On the other hand, it is important to avoid asking a beginning teacher to do things just because you were asked to do them.

The emotional wellbeing of a beginning teacher has a major influence on how they feel about themselves and their levels of motivation (Schatz-Oppenheimer, 2017). In turn, this can impact on the mentor-mentee relationship. On many occasions, we have found our-selves engaging in a post-lesson observation conversation, only to find we are having to work through emotional reactions of the beginning teacher. Thus, it is important to consider the range of ways emotions might manifest themselves, as well as how you can support a begin-ning teacher to understand their own emotions. Taking time to talk to a beginning teacher about how they are coping, where they feel any pressure points are, and what strategies they can adopt to reduce any stresses is often time well spent. It is, therefore, important to under-stand the empathetic aspect of the role.

Approaches to mentoring

As individuals, how we relate to different people varies. Sometimes we just click with another person, whilst another relationship develops over time, and in other cases a relationship starts off well and then breaks down. The mentor-mentee relationship is no different. Each relationship is unique, as each beginning teacher has a different personality, background and experiences and arrives with different expectations. Therefore, understanding how you approach being a mentor and the strategies you adopt is an important aspect of a complex activity.

The MinT questionnaire (see Chapter 6) is designed to enable you to identify your mentoring approach or, more likely, two or three approaches you adopt. If you have not read Chapter 6 or reflected on your mentoring approach(es), you may consider looking at that now. For many of us, the approach we adopt reflects the experiences we have had in the past. However, it is important to acknowledge that whilst one approach might have been effective for you, it does not mean that it will be as effective for others. Whilst you have a preferred approach to mentoring, it is important that you get to know a beginning teacher in order to adapt your approach to meet their individual needs. Your ability to adapt your approach to reflect the needs of the beginning teacher with whom you are working is key (van Ginkel et al., 2016). As with teaching, having knowledge and understanding of a beginning teacher as an individual and as a learner and being able to modify and adapt your practice to meet their needs may ensure that you are able to sustain the relationship over a period of time. If you have not already done so, you may want to undertake Task 6.4 to find out your preferred mentoring approach(es).

Spend some time now looking at case study 7.1 and complete Task 7.5 to reflect on how you currently think about the mentor-mentee relationship.

Case study 7.1 A mentoring relationship

Jess is a beginning teacher working in a large physical education department. She is keen to make progress towards becoming an outstanding teacher. She is well organised and submits her lesson plans in plenty of time to receive feedback and make changes. Jess's mentor is an experienced teacher and head of department. She is keen to support Jess, but has limited time to provide feedback on lesson plans prior to the teaching of the lesson and frequently rushes off at the end of observations. When feedback is provided the mentor tends to lead, with little opportunity for Jess to make any reflections about what she thinks is going well and what she can do to make improvements. The quality of the feedback is limited, with most conversations focusing on what the mentor would have done. Whilst Jess tries to remain confident and focused on making improvements, over time she becomes frustrated and despondent.

When Jess started working with her mentor, they seemed to get on well. Jess was able to ask questions and feel that she was making progress. More recently the mentor-mentee relationship has become strained. Jess has become more distant from her mentor and is starting to seek advice and guidance from other staff within the department.

Task 7.5   How feedback impacts on the mentoring relationship

Having read case study 7.1, consider the following:

1.   As a mentor, what challenges do you see emerging from the situation described?
2.   If you were in Jess's situation, how do you think you would feel? What advice might you give to Jess in relation to talking to her mentor about the relationship?
3.   As a colleague, what strategies would you suggest the mentor looks to adopt to ensure a more effective working relationship?

Now reflect on your own mentoring relationships.

1.   As a mentor, how do you go about considering how the relationship is working between you and a beginning teacher you are mentoring?
2.   If you were aware that there was a potential issue, what would you do about it?

It is clear that Jess's experience as a mentee in case study 7.1 was not productive, which impacted on the relationship between Jess and her mentor. Whilst it is clear that expectations had been set in relation to submission of lesson plans and provision of feedback, these were not enacted by the mentor in the way agreed. There was a mismatch between Jess's expectations in relation to feedback and the practice of the mentor. There appeared to be an issue in relation to the time the mentor was able to give to the process. This may not be related to the value they placed on the mentoring relationship, but to the support they were receiving from within the school to undertake the role. The challenge, then, is how the situation could be resolved. It may be that just talking through the issues to establish a clearer understanding of expectations and also the impact the situation is having on both Jess and the mentor is all that is needed (how often do we really consider the impact of what we are doing on others?). However, it may be that other action is needed. For example, does the mentor need to draw on support from other colleagues? Or does the mentor need to speak with more senior staff to look at how they can support them to provide additional support? It is important to appreciate that no relationship is perfect; all relationships have highs and lows. However, there are strategies that can be used to manage challenging situations.

Dealing with conflict: What happens when a relationship breaks down?

At times, relationships do break down. This may be for a number of reasons. In working with beginning teachers over many years, the main reasons for a breakdown in a relationship include differences in expectations (including professionalism; for example, attendance at meetings), a breakdown in trust, and personality clashes. How you manage a breakdown in a mentoring relationship is important to ensure that you and the beginning teacher can continue to work together. Two examples, with possible solutions, follow.

Planning

A beginning teacher lacks initiative and continually relies on you to provide the materials for lessons or to give excessive feedback on planning, or is unable to submit lesson plans as requested. They come up with excuses as to why they have not submitted the lesson plan, and in extreme situations do not end up delivering the lesson at all.

In this scenario, the beginning teacher may not be demonstrating the professionalism expected. The lack of planning is impacting on the progress of the class, and you are finding you are spending more time than you would expect having to sort things out. This is causing frustration and additional pressure and is affecting your relationship with the beginning teacher.

The challenge is to understand why planning is a problem and to work with the beginning teacher to model the process and then gradually remove the support you provide. However, you also need to review expectations and look at how these are more closely monitored to ensure that the beginning teacher is aware of their responsibilities in relation to professionalism and to maintaining a positive working relationship.

Disagreement

A beginning teacher disagrees with what you say and/or challenges your teaching. After observing one of your lessons, they tell you how they would have taught the lesson or discuss your teaching with other staff.

This scenario reflects a potential breakdown in trust. Whilst you welcome feedback on your teaching, it is how this feedback is articulated that might be the issue. Your challenge is to try to avoid taking it personally, to try to understand why the beginning teacher might be making the comments they are and to look to establish clear boundaries. If possible, try to talk to the beginning teacher directly to get a better understanding of what they are thinking and why they are thinking that way (or talking to other staff about it) – it may be that they have seen something that you had not previously considered. Alternatively, consider talking with a more senior colleague to discuss your concerns. Look at the guidance provided within your school to support you; for example, are there any mechanisms available to support the difficult conversations you may find yourself having? Re-establishing expectations may well be all that is needed, but if the situation cannot be resolved, you may need to consider how you extract yourself from the relationship completely. It is important to recognise that in rare cases, a relationship becomes so strained that it eventually breaks down.

Now complete Task 7.6.

Task 7.6   Reflecting on challenging mentoring relationships

Consider your most challenging mentoring relationship; it could be as a mentor or as a mentee yourself. Write down a description of why it was challenging, and how it made you feel. How did you deal with the situation? Was it successful? If not, what could you have done differently?

Summary and key points

- Establishing a good relationship is key to effective mentoring. Both parties need to participate in the process (Hobson, 2002). Further, the mentor–mentee relationship must be seen by both parties as a two-way process. As Hudson (2016, p. 41) stated, both the mentor and the mentee 'need to be aware of the personal-professional actions that can aid in forming a successful mentoring relationship'.
- Enabling a beginning teacher to grow and flourish is not without its challenges. If the relationship is one where both parties perceive they are engaged within a cooperative working environment, then challenges can be overcome and development ensues.
- As a mentor, recognising an effective relationship is vital; knowing when to intervene or support from the side is an important skill to ensure that a beginning teacher receives the support and guidance they need to progress in the profession.
- In reading this chapter, you should have begun to consider the approaches you adopt in establishing your mentoring relationship, and in particular what ground rules you establish to support the relationship as well as how you can develop, manage and sustain a mentoring relationship. However, it is also important to identify how you might deal with the situation when the mentor–mentee relationship is not working well.

Further resources

Garvey, B., Stokes, P. and Megginson, D. (2018) *Coaching and Mentoring; theory and Practice*, London: Sage.
Whilst not specifically focused on teaching, this text offers practical support to some of the challenges faced by those engaging in the mentoring process. In particular, chapter 9 focuses on multiple learning relationships, including the complexity of a mentoring relationship.

Hudson, P. (2016) 'Forming the Mentor-Mentee Relationship', *Mentoring & Tutoring:Partnership in Learning*, 24(1), 30-43.
This research paper explores mentors' understanding of forming effective mentor–mentee relationships. It strengthens the premise that for relationships to be effective, they must draw on characteristics of trust, respect, professionalism, expectations, collaboration and support.

See also the companion website for this book (www.routledge.com/9781138059658).

You may also find it useful to refer to/use the text books written for student and newly qualified physical education teachers with a beginning teacher you are mentoring (see list on Page 4).

8 Collaborative approaches to mentoring

Peter Mellor

Introduction

According to Brisk (2008) (in Tinker-Sachs et al., 2011, p. 70),

> in this standards-driven era of education, it is more critical than it ever has been for educators at all levels to resist individualism and isolationism and work together to create collaborative and supportive communities of practice in institutions of learning.

Collaborative mentoring in teacher education and development involves individuals, groups and agencies working together on shared goals of developing knowledge, practice and experiences through teaching. In a collaborative mentoring relationship, 'knowledge of teaching is mutually generated, supporting change and innovation' (Richter et al., 2013, p. 168). In England, the Teaching Council's non-statutory national mentoring standards define a mentor as 'a suitably-experienced teacher who has formal responsibility to work collaboratively within the Initial Teacher Training partnership to help ensure the trainee receives the highest-quality training' (Teaching Schools Council, 2016, p. 7). In addition to collaboration between a mentor and a beginning teacher, there may be a range of other professionals and agencies involved in the mentoring.

Chalies et al. (2008, p. 562) believed that 'physical education classes are held in a context that is unique in teaching and that may well facilitate co-teaching'. Keay (2006, p. 286) highlighted physical education communities as appropriate settings for professional development through collaboration, citing 'working together, teacher influence, developmental groups and community acceptance' as examples. In other words, it is not just the professional development of a physical education teacher and beginning teacher that can benefit from collaboration, but also the actual teaching of physical education.

This chapter starts by clarifying the concept of collaborative mentoring and who is involved. It then considers examples of collaborative approaches to mentoring to support a beginning physical education teacher and considers the benefits and challenges of implementation.

Objectives

At the end of this chapter, you should be able to:

- Understand a range of collaborative approaches to mentoring, the nature of relationships and flow of information involved, and their benefits to the development of a beginning physical education teacher and to your practice as a mentor, as well as the pupils being taught;
- Identify individuals and groups who might be involved in collaborative mentoring;
- Consider examples of collaborative approaches to mentoring in support of a beginning teacher and the benefits and challenges of implementing these approaches.

Before you continue reading, complete Task 8.1.

Task 8.1   Mentor reflection: Knowledge and experience of collaborative mentoring

What do you understand by collaborative mentoring?

Reflect on your mentoring experience to date, both as a mentor and, where relevant, as being mentored. Identify any examples of collaborative mentoring you have experienced. How have these worked? What did you learn as a mentor or mentee? What were the benefits (above and beyond those of mentoring more generally)? Were there any challenges/issues/barriers to collaborative mentoring?

What is collaborative mentoring and what are the benefits?

Collaboration, on its own, is an action involving individuals, groups or agencies working collectively on a single shared goal. Collaborative approaches to mentoring in education, therefore, may involve groups of teachers working together with the aim of providing high-quality teaching for their pupils as a shared goal, for example.

Collaborative mentoring was defined by Cordingley et al. (2003, p. 2) as 'Programmes where there are specific plans to encourage and enable shared learning and support between at least two teacher colleagues on a sustained basis'. Sharing of knowledge and experience are key to this approach. For example, Kemmis et al. (2014, p. 160) highlighted shared self-development as 'assisting [beginning teachers] to become members of a professional community in which [they] participate as equals in professional dialogue, aimed at their individual and collective self-development'. For Carter and Francis (2001, p. 260), 'mentoring relationships that promote collaborative inquiry, cooperative practice and reflection are fundamental to workplace learning for teachers'.

The nature of relationships involved and the direction of flow of knowledge and learning is another key aspect of collaborative mentoring. For example, a mentor and a beginning teacher can work together through joint planning and teaching a lesson, with knowledge and learning passing both ways. The mentor and the beginning teacher are mutually involved, and both learn and develop. However, the relationship between mentor and beginning teacher is not truly collaborative if the mentor acts as an authoritative figure issuing instruction or psychological support and the flow of knowledge and learning is one directional (from mentor to beginning teacher).

Table 8.1 Perceived benefits of collaborative approaches to mentoring

Benefits of collaborative approaches to mentoring	Author
Opportunity for learning from different perspectives, including pupils and other members of school community.	Aderibigbe (2013)
Potential to support the development of sustained learning cultures in schools.	Sørenson (2014)
Positive impacts on pupil learning, a deeper learning and teaching culture in the school, professional development of experienced teachers, reduced feelings of professional isolation, increased job satisfaction and increased retention of teachers in the profession.	See Chapter 2
Significant contribution to teachers' commitment and confidence in influencing pupil learning and their abilities to match their teaching delivery to pupils' needs and outcomes.	Cordingley et al. (2003)
Reduced professional isolation for beginning teachers.	Hagger and Mcintyre (2006)
Growth of teacher efficacy, teaching enthusiasm, job satisfaction and retention of teachers by reducing emotional exhaustion.	Richter et al. (2013)
All parties involved in the process benefit in some way. Mentors report increasing confidence and purpose in their own teaching, shared knowledge and understanding, cooperation and focus on direction of professional development needs.	Hobson et al. (2009)
Beginning teachers are 'less likely to move to other schools and less likely to leave the teaching occupation after their first year of teaching' (Ingersoll and Smith, p. 681).	Ingersoll and Smith (2004) (see also retention in Chapter 2)
Schools become real agents of change to teaching and learning through the recruitment of teachers.	Feiman-Nemser (2012)

There is a distinction to be made between collaboration and cooperation. Individuals, groups and agencies are very often involved in supporting a beginning teacher, but in such a way that each is working towards separate goals. Shared goals usually involve developing teaching performance or pupil progress in lessons. They become more generic when more individuals, groups and agencies become involved in the process. Improvement is usually measured through inquiry using planning, teaching, evaluating and reflecting to develop knowledge, practice and experience.

Thus, knowledge could be something that both collaborators acquire at the same time or something that already exists and has to be acquired through experience. Other examples of collaborative practice include experienced teachers sharing with a beginning teacher a pedagogical problem they have not yet solved, which they try to solve together, or collaboration of peers, whereby two beginning teachers jointly plan a lesson, with knowledge and learning flowing in both directions and both being mutually engaged. Table 8.1 lists current research and information into the benefits of collaborative mentoring for all involved in the process.

Who might be involved in collaborating?

Collaborative mentoring can involve a range of people, groups and agencies sharing the same goal. Working together on issues can very often result in more effective solutions to problems, but in true collaborative relationships, shared goals of everyone involved in the process need to be identified. Other individuals and groups of professionals involved in the process may include staff in school (e.g. other physical education teachers, teachers from other subject areas, pastoral staff, head teacher, beginning teacher coordinator, staff development coordinator), staff working in a university partnership (including university tutor and subject specialist, teachers from other schools in the partnership) and/or other beginning teachers (student, newly qualified or early career). Task 8.2 looks at working collaboratively with a range of people to enhance the mentoring process.

Task 8.2   Working collaboratively with a range of people to enhance the mentoring process

First, consider how you work with a beginning teacher in a collaborative mode. How frequently do you do this? How effective is it? Ask a beginning teacher you are working with how they feel about working with colleagues on shared goals. What are the benefits to them? Are there any issues or challenges for them in this approach?

Now, consider the range of other people who might be involved in collaborative mentoring (see earlier). Outline how they might be involved in the process. Is the process truly collaborative, or cooperative?

Now, undertake the collaborative exercise looking at behaviour management in Table 8.2.

Having identified a range of people who might be involved in collaborative mentoring, the next section considers more approaches. There are some further examples of collaborative mentoring in Chapter 9.

Table 8.2 Collaborative exercise to undertake to support a beginning teacher

- *Arrange for a beginning teacher to observe practice in another teacher's classroom.*
- *Ask the beginning teacher to study the classroom (both when it is empty and during a session) and the behaviour of the pupils during the teaching session.*
- *After the lesson, discuss the classroom rules/code of conduct and your own approach to behaviour management.*
- *Support the beginning teacher in analysing the management of the classroom environment; this may include any instances of conflict between two or more pupils that occurred during the observation.*
- *Discuss the evaluation of the task with the beginning teacher and the other teacher. Ask the beginning teacher to consider the behaviour management they have observed in terms of their own development and practice.*
- *Ask the other teacher to observe a beginning teacher's lesson and feed back observations in relation to their own behaviour management protocol.*
- *Engage in a three-way dialogue between the beginning teacher, the classroom teacher and yourself to discuss behaviour management in different settings and influences of personalities/individuals on pupils and their learning.*
- *Consider the educational gains to all parties during this exercise (beginning teacher, mentor and classroom teacher).*

Range of approaches to collaborative mentoring

The approaches to collaborative mentoring covered in this section are: shared planning, teaching, reflection and evaluation (beginning teacher and mentor, of which lesson study and co-teaching are cited as examples); mentoring more than one beginning teacher in a class; collaborative self-development (peer group mentoring); and multi-agency working. The examples are arranged incrementally, from more commonly used approaches, which mentors can easily organise and implement in current practice, to more elaborate in-depth monitoring of beginning teachers involving a range of personnel in a variety of exercises and goals that are shared to develop everyone's knowledge, practice and experience, but which take more organisation and planning. Task 8.3 identifies some questions for you to ask yourself as you read about each of these approaches.

Task 8.3   Questions to ask about different approaches to collaborative mentoring

As you read each of the following examples, and in order to make each of the collaborative approaches a success, as a mentor, you need to determine how each of the approaches may work for all parties involved. Ask yourself the following questions:

Why would I engage in this approach?
What are the mutual benefits?
Are there links to professional development for all parties?
Are there any other questions that arise as you read each approach?

Shared planning, teaching, reflecting and evaluating (mentor and beginning teacher)

In this approach, mentor and beginning teacher collectively plan, teach, observe, reflect and evaluate on the teaching and pupils' learning with an emphasis on their collaborative engagement and the development of pedagogy. Cajkler and Wood (2016) described this as a lesson study approach to mentoring. A study in schools by Chalies et al. (2008, p. 561) found that this approach 'contributed to breaking down barriers between traditional training situations' where, traditionally, a mentor is seen as a critical colleague in a hierarchical relationship. Joint planning, teaching, reflection and evaluation help to encourage more engaging, professional, supportive relationships between mentor and beginning teacher. Further, Murata (2011, p. 2) believed that 'through multiple iterations of the process, [beginning] teachers [and their mentors] have many opportunities to discuss pupil progress and how their teaching influences it'.

Very often, a beginning teacher may have limited knowledge, experience and confidence to teach some areas of the physical education curriculum in comparison with experienced subject mentors and practitioners. An initial joint approach to planning, preparing resources, teaching, and reflecting on and evaluating the success, or otherwise, of a lesson can develop a beginning physical education teacher's knowledge and confidence in delivering unfamiliar material. It can also be useful for a mentor in evaluating why they teach in the way that they teach. Alternatively, it may be that a beginning teacher's knowledge of an activity area can contribute to a highly engaging lesson if a mentor can support them in areas such as managing pupils' learning.

However, this approach to supporting a beginning teacher does have some challenges. For example, a mentor will have to spend more time with a beginning teacher in joint planning, reflecting and evaluating on the outcomes of the lesson. Perry and Lewis (2009) reported that time and investment dedicated to the process is a significant barrier, considering mentors' current workload and the demands on their time. A sustained commitment from school leader, mentor and teacher is required, adding to an overcrowded school day. There is a fine line between a mentor directing the process and a beginning teacher feeling comfortable and confident in contributing their ideas and opinions. The teaching style, ideology and philosophy of two deliverers co-teaching may need rehearsal and consideration in the initial stages. A beginning teacher may feel less confident than their mentor in delivering parts of the lesson and may take less of a role in the teaching. The flow of the lesson may also be affected by a joint delivery, and so a beginning teacher may not develop an understanding of how to seamlessly move from one activity to another, how to engage with pupils, how to meet learning objectives, or what to do when the mentor is delivering their section of the lesson. The reflective process will also have to be managed carefully. A mentor must allow time for the beginning teacher to reflect on the strengths and areas to improve in the lesson. It must not become a one-sided conversation; both parties must engage in open dialogue in order for future planning to take place collaboratively again.

Mentoring more than one beginning teacher in a class

Another collaborative mentoring approach involves working with more than one beginning teacher in a class at the same time. This is more common in initial teacher education, where more than one student teacher might be allocated to a school. Collaborative team teaching and cooperative teaching are other descriptive models associated with this type of delivery.

Co-teaching offers a wide range of collaborative practice opportunities. Peer co-teaching may involve beginning teachers working in pairs (paired teaching), in small groups or even in subject-specific cohorts (team teaching). Tandem approaches may involve beginning teachers working with different classes but jointly planning and evaluating their lessons. Supportive teaching approaches focus on one beginning teacher taking the lead in the classroom with the other as support and assistance. Parallel teaching is where two or more beginning teachers split the class, with each being responsible for teaching similar or separate learning objectives to smaller groups. Scaffolding teaching may involve differentiated delivery of teaching material by a group of beginning teachers involved in one class. Beginning teachers may organise a carousel-style lesson in which all groups spend time at a learning station and then rotate round to the next station, with a beginning teacher at each station. In physical education, this method of collaborative work can be useful when differentiating activity groups by ability, so beginning teachers can work with groups requiring development in similar skills.

The key to the success or otherwise of these approaches lies in the organisation of the lessons. Plans have to be prepared equally, each beginning teacher's input discussed and agreed, objectives prepared and agreed, and interventions with pupils factored in to the planning.

The advantages in having more than one teacher in a class can be significant, particularly in physical education lessons. For example, two beginning teachers may complement each other in their subject content knowledge and pedagogy of a particular activity. This can provide a consistently higher quality of lesson compared with the two beginning teachers teaching separate lessons. Further, Sørenson (2014) believed that these approaches are an effective strategy for learning to teach and support more expansive and deeper learning through 'promotion of collaboration and dialogue, especially where attention has been given to the structuring of the placements and the role of the mentor or cooperating teacher' (p. 128). Further advantages include breadth and depth of content knowledge when working in pairs or small groups, and the development of a variety and quality of pedagogy and creativity through sharing ideas. Le Cornu (2005) explained that, whilst these approaches vary, the underlying assumption unifying them is that 'teacher learning is facilitated in collaborative cultures, as teachers learn with and from one another and feelings of isolation experienced by staff are reduced' (pp. 356-357).

As well as significant benefits, there are challenges. Mentoring is more complex when working with more than one beginning teacher at a time. Mentoring is different, but there are a number of different approaches that can be taken to supporting more than one beginning teacher at the same time. The nature of the collaborative practice needs to be determined. For example: Is everyone involved in sharing the same goals? Will the flow of knowledge be multi-directional? Will there be mutual engagement in planning, teaching and evaluating lessons, and will this contribute to everyone's professional development, including the mentors? The skills of observing, evaluating and reflecting on performance with several beginning teachers at the same time need developing. Task 8.4 focuses on mentoring more than one beginning teacher in a class.

Task 8.4   Mentoring more than one teacher in a class

Before you embark on mentoring more than one beginning teacher, reflect on any past experiences, how successful these have been and what you have learned from them. Then, identify strategies to implement the approach and, where appropriate, develop your practice from past experience. If you have no prior experience, you might liaise with another mentor to benefit from their experience. As you consider how you will work, ask yourself the following questions:

• How will you ensure the beginning teachers work together to produce the best possible outcomes for pupils?

- How will you manage beginning teachers with different values and beliefs (e.g. work ethic, responsibilities, motivation, personality etc.)?
- How will you work with the beginning teachers to ensure a shared workload (planning, delivery, reflection, generation of resources, marking work)?
- How will you meet to structure their personal development (individually, jointly)?
- How will you manage the feedback sessions (individual feedback individually, individual feedback collectively, shared collective feedback)?
- Will beginning teachers be allowed some time to plan and prepare solo lessons? If not, why not?
- How will you deal with contrasting performances by the beginning teachers?
- How are pupils responding?

Can you think of any other challenges involved in mentoring more than one beginning teacher in a class?

As you will have worked out from Task 8.4, mentoring more than one beginning teacher is far from straightforward, as each beginning teacher brings different values, ideas and perspectives. You therefore need to find ways to engage with beginning teachers' ideologies, philosophies and work ethics and to keep an open mind, maintain willingness to compromise and maintain shared goals. Table 8.3 looks at what you can do initially to develop a healthy, collaborative mentor–beginning teacher relationship.

As well as significant benefits to having more than one teacher in a class, there are potential challenges. These include, for example, the amount of teaching time each teacher gets, clashes of personality, parity of workload, unequal feedback and potential confusion for the class. You therefore need to heed these warnings when working with more than one

Table 8.3 Fostering a healthy, collaborative mentor–beginning teacher relationship from day one

- *Initial meeting with beginning teachers to discuss aims and objectives of the period of mentoring.*
- *Introducing beginning teachers to the school's aims and philosophies, policies and procedures, and culture and ethos.*
- *Induction procedure for beginning teachers: meeting staff, introduction to the physical education department, tasks relating to observing best practice in the school, such as shadowing a pupil for a day round school or observations of teaching physical education and other subject areas (see induction in Chapter 4).*
- *Further meetings to discuss experiences from tasks and observations. Chance to discuss ideology, motivation, philosophy and work ethic of beginning teachers.*
- *Open discussions around timetabling beginning teachers in collaboration, being flexible to take account of individual needs yet creative to provide maximum opportunities with regard to their teaching.*
- *Planning meetings structured in collaborative style, joint ownership, shared goals and agreements of all plans. Reflection meetings again open discussions around successes or areas for development.*
- *Regular meetings, one-to-one and open forum, to discuss progress. Beginning teachers to take responsibility for their progress, joint responsibility for agendas.*
- *Mentor to be open, honest, caring, able to model good practice where needed, trusting, supportive and conciliatory, yet offering guidance when needed.*

beginning teacher in the same class. In Task 8.5, you are asked to consider how you might address an issue that might arise.

Task 8.5   Dilemma to solve

There are two beginning teachers sharing a class. There has been a collaborative approach to planning, teaching, reflecting and evaluating a joint lesson; both beginning teachers have agreed to an equal share of the lesson and to provide feedback for each other after the lesson. You discover, however, that one of the beginning teachers has planned their share of the lesson in more detail than the other, but, during the teaching episode, the other beginning teacher dominates the delivery to the pupils and provides some negative feedback to the other beginning teacher on their lesson delivery.

How would you manage the situation to ensure both beginning teachers understand the issues at play and develop their skills positively in future lessons?

Mentoring as collaborative self-development (peer group mentoring)

A recognised collaborative mentoring approach to introduce beginning teachers into the profession involves a community of beginning teachers and their more experienced teaching colleagues and mentors working to the same outcomes of collective self-development (Kemmis et al., 2014). This approach differs from the previous models discussed by involving beginning teachers and established classroom practitioners, not necessarily from the same school or subject area. The aim is self-development through the promotion of professional dialogue and inquiry through established professional learning communities, to influence practice and to sustain professional growth throughout a teacher's career for all parties, including mentors. This supports a beginning teacher to develop professional autonomy and to better understand their own practice thorough an inquiry-orientated approach (Ovens and Fletcher, 2014).

Collaborative self-development involves meetings to share ideas, listen to issues, reflect on experiences and promote a sense of mutual professional development. Mentors are generally trained to ensure all members of the group engage in professional dialogue, share experiences and benefit from collective actions emerging for their own professional needs.

Brown (2011, p.19) believed that there are advantages to this approach, in that it provides 'context and real-world understanding for physical education teachers who feel disconnected by continuing professional learning'. Mentoring becomes synonymous with professional development, far removed from shared planning and teaching of lessons; rather, providing genuine partnerships of professionals working together for shared outcomes. Deeper collaborative relationships may emerge through working with beginning teachers and teachers from other schools and communities. Task 8.6 asks you to consider challenges of collaborative self-development.

Task 8.6   The challenges to collaborative self-development

As a mentor, consider how this approach to supporting a beginning teacher into the profession differs from other collaborative approaches to mentoring.

- How will you deal with a beginning teacher working in different schools in the group?
- How will you deal with a beginning teacher from other subject areas in the group?
- How will the group dynamics be affected by having established classroom practitioners present?
- How will you manage your professional development in the meetings?
- How will you promote theoretical and critical viewpoints to support professional development?
- How will you provide equal time for everyone in the group?
- How will you facilitate the emergence of deeper collaborative relationships?
- How will you monitor progress of everyone?

Multi-agency approach

Multi-agency working involves bringing together a range of professionals associated with, or who have a commitment to, the development of beginning teachers. Engaging with a range of professionals from, for example, universities, schools, other educational establishments, physical education governing bodies, and local sports associations pools expertise and experience, which provides you with advice to support one or more beginning teachers to become successful classroom practitioners.

Universities may take a lead role in supporting beginning teachers to develop content and pedagogical content knowledge. They may support research-informed practice and theories, so linking theory with practice. They may also support mentors in school whilst benefiting from the research informed practice through the shared goals.

Mentors may work with other senior staff in the school to provide a professional development package for beginning teachers. For example, senior leaders may provide workshops or support with behaviour management policy or school-based assessment procedures for beginning teachers to use. The pastoral team may lead professional development sessions on working with parents and carers, and outstanding teachers may support beginning teachers with teaching demonstrations and advice on teaching standards relating to planning and differentiating lessons. The school, in collaboration with mentors, may work with other schools locally to enable beginning teachers to broaden their experiences in a range of schools; for example, special educational needs and disability schools, different age phase schools, and schools with contrasting socio-economic, religious and ethnic circumstances. A mentor's role here would be to provide continuity for a beginning teacher in all schools, to collaborate with colleagues taking on the role of mentor in those schools, and to support with baseline expectations.

Early career teachers, and agencies engaged in the development of sport and young people, may also be invited into the group to engage in deeper professional dialogue to support beginning teachers' knowledge and understanding, contributing to a community of professional practitioners.

Collaborative mentoring with multi-agencies is a complex undertaking. It requires a wide range of professional skills developed over a longer period of time as a teacher and a mentor. Managing others and ensuring mutual benefit, promoting theoretical and critical viewpoints in support of professional development, monitoring progress, time management, and developing and sustaining shared goals through teaching are some of the challenges facing mentors. From the outset, all parties must engage in dialogue to establish shared goals of the exercise. Dialogue between a range of agencies and stakeholders becomes more complex with each addition to the group, and there may be increasing difficulty in maintaining clarity of outcome in a meaningful way. Resources and time need careful management to ensure that everyone is equally supported in the arrangement and everyone is aware of their role and the level of commitment required. The mentoring role takes on a greater organisational complexity, yet allows beginning teachers to receive high-quality input from specialists in the field. As a mentor, you need to ensure that there is procedural and ideological consistency in the programme of support between all agencies, that consultations take place regularly, and that supervision and competencies include developmental feedback.

Now complete Tasks 8.7, 8.8 and 8.9, all of which look at the collaborative mentoring approaches discussed in this chapter.

Task 8.7   Identifying truly collaborative mentoring that impacts on both the beginning teacher's and the mentor's professional development

For each of the collaborative mentoring approaches covered earlier (and any others you can identify), examine the patterns of collaboration, the nature of relationships involved, the direction of flow of knowledge and learning (one- or two-way) and mutual engagement. Which of the approaches demonstrate a truly collaborative partnership, and which may still provide a hierarchical approach (depending on how they are put into operation)? Identify the benefits of each approach. Discuss the approaches with others with whom you are likely to be working collaboratively.

Task 8.8   Reflect on collaborative approaches to mentoring

For each of the collaborative mentoring approaches considered earlier (and any others you can identify), consider exactly how they may be useful to both a beginning physical education teacher and a mentor. Consider the following questions:

- Why would you adopt this approach?
- What are the mutual benefits?
- Are there links to the professional development of all parties?

Task 8.9   Challenges to collaborative mentoring

Collaborative mentoring approaches provide challenges to a mentor. It is important that you consider these in relation to any approach you are going to adopt.

Identify one collaborative mentoring approach to try with a beginning teacher. What do you need to consider in order to organise this so that it can be implemented successfully? What are some of the potential challenges of the approach, and how do you plan to alleviate these?

Finally, complete Task 8.10.

Task 8.10   Mentor reflection: Knowledge and experience of collaborative mentoring

Return to the questions in Task 8.1 and reflect on your collaborative mentoring experiences (focusing on the approaches considered in this chapter). In light of your reading of this chapter, what have you done/will you do differently to enhance the learning from collaborative mentoring for both the beginning teacher and the mentor?

Summary and key points

The aim of this chapter was to support you in developing approaches to collaborative practice in mentoring. It reflected on the range of individuals and agencies involved, the nature of relationships, the flow of information involved, the need for shared goals, the benefits to a beginning physical education teacher and yourself, and the challenges of specific approaches.

- Collaborative mentoring involves a process in which all parties contribute significantly to the development of the commitment and confidence of a beginning physical education teacher and derive mutual benefit from the shared goals.
- In its simplest form, one-to-one collaborative mentoring using an inquiry-based model of shared planning, teaching, evaluating and reflecting through lesson study promotes engaging, professional, supportive relationships.
- Working with more than one beginning physical education teacher in a classroom and the promotion of co-teaching are effective strategies for more expansive and deeper learning, resulting in dialogue, the sharing of ideas, learning from one another, and reduced feelings of isolation.
- Self-development through collaboration with peers provides an opportunity for a beginning teacher to promote professional dialogue and inquiry through established professional learning communities, developing autonomy and sustained professional growth for a lifelong career.

- Multi-agency collaboration provides an opportunity for deep and meaningful partnerships and diversity of provision. It involves bringing together a range of professionals who have a commitment to the development of a beginning teacher through supporting the evidencing of competencies.

As a mentor, you are encouraged to engage in the process, irrespective of your level of experience. You will develop your knowledge, practice and experience and provide deeper understandings in real-world contexts, and a beginning physical education teacher becomes part of a more enriched and sustainable learning community. You become an 'agent of change' (Feiman-Nemser and Parker, 1993, p. 716).

Further resources

Kemmis, S., Heikkinen, H.L.T., Fransson, G., Aspfors, J. and Edwards-Groves, C. (2014) Mentoring of new teachers as a contested practice: Supervision, support and collaborative self-development, *Teaching and Teacher Education*, 43, 154-164.
This journal article studies mentoring practice for beginning teachers in different countries (Australia, Finland and Sweden). They observe the practice architecture and identify three distinct styles of mentoring - supervision, support and collaborative self-development - which are demonstrated in the different countries. The study explores why there are different mentoring styles and what influence they have on beginning teachers' identities entering the profession.

Richards, K.A.R. and Ressler, J.D. (2016) A collaborative approach to self-study research in physical education teacher education, *Journal of Teaching in Physical Education*, 35, 290-295.
This journal article highlights how self-study relates to wider research-informed teaching in the physical education community and teacher education. There are examples of best practice and lessons learned and discussion of the implications for future practice of collaboration in physical education.

See also the companion website for this book (www.routledge.com/9781138059658).

You may also find it useful to refer to/use the text books written for student and newly qualified physical education teachers with a beginning teacher you are mentoring (see list on Page 4).

SECTION 4

Supporting the development of beginning physical education teachers' knowledge, skills and understanding

9 What knowledge, skills and understanding do beginning physical education teachers need?

Will Katene

Introduction

Hattie (2009) argued that, after socio-economic status, the quality of the teacher is the most significant factor determining pupil outcomes. This chapter focuses on the knowledge, skills and understanding (KSU) needed by beginning physical education teachers in order for them to develop into high-quality teachers who teach effectively to support pupils' learning. The chapter first looks at different categorisations of KSU, then at how you, as a mentor, can work with a beginning teacher both to help identify strengths and areas for development and to support appropriate development of KSU. The chapter concludes by offering some guiding principles to consider when identifying, developing and measuring the KSU of a beginning teacher. The chapter includes case studies to help illustrate the KSU a beginning teacher might have that led them into a career in teaching, and hence, the range of KSU and values they bring with them. On the companion website for this book (www.routledge. com/9781138059658) there are five more case studies, which demonstrate the broad range of experiences beginning teachers have and/or which provide examples of the impact of a beginning teacher on a pupil(s). These demonstrate the need to treat each beginning teacher as an individual with different prior experience, KSU and values, which requires an individualised approach to their development.

Objectives

At the end of this chapter, you should be able to:

1. Understand that KSU can be categorised in different ways;
2. Understand how you, as the mentor, can work with a beginning teacher both to help identify strengths and areas for development and to support appropriate development of KSU;
3. Use some guiding principles for identifying, developing and measuring a beginning teacher's KSU.

Before reading further, complete the mentor reflection in Task 9.1.

Task 9.1 Mentor reflection: What KSU are needed for effective teaching?

- Based on your prior experience, what do you identify as the KSU beginning teachers need to develop?
- Ask a beginning teacher you are mentoring what KSU they identify as required for high-quality teaching (list up to 10).
- Both of you categorise or group these KSU, rank them in order of importance, and justify your reasons.
- Reflect on the implications of this for your practice as a mentor supporting a beginning teacher to develop their KSU.
- After reading the next section, return to this task and compare your categories of KSU with those of the beginning teacher and also with Shulman's (1987) categories of knowledge.

Knowledge, skills and understanding of beginning physical education teachers

There is widespread evidence that the quality of beginning teachers' subject knowledge impacts directly upon the quality of their pedagogical practices (Shulman, 1986; Turner-Bisset, 1999; Department for Education (DfE), 2011b; Coe et al., 2014; Capel and Whitehead, 2015; DfE, 2016e). For example, DfE (2011) stated that teachers should 'have strong subject knowledge, keep their knowledge and skills as teachers up-to-date …' (p. 10) and 'have a secure knowledge of the relevant subject(s) and curriculum areas, foster and maintain pupils' interest in the subject and address misunderstandings' (p. 11).

Although many beginning teachers focus, at least initially, on developing content, curriculum and pedagogical knowledge, these are not the only KSU beginning teachers need to develop in order to become high-quality teachers. What can be observed in the act of teaching (i.e. what goes on in the classroom or in the sports hall) can be likened to the 'tip of the iceberg'. Below that is the other nine-tenths of the iceberg: a wealth of different kinds of knowledge on which a teacher draws for effective teaching. The KSU needed for teaching is complex, as highlighted by Shulman (1987, p. 4): 'development … from a state of expertise as learners through a novitiate as teachers exposes and highlights the complex bodies of knowledge and skill needed to function effectively as a teacher'. Indeed, many mentors cannot explain what KSU they have that makes them an effective teacher, as it has developed over time and is just something they 'have'.

The next section looks at one categorisation of this complex body of knowledge.

One categorisation of knowledge, skills and understanding for teaching

Perhaps the most commonly used categorisation of knowledge needed for teaching is the seven knowledge bases identified by Shulman (1987):

1. *content knowledge* (the amount and organisation of knowledge per se in the mind of a teacher; the facts, principles and concepts contained within a subject/discipline);

2. *general pedagogical knowledge* (the broad principles and strategies designed to guide class instruction, organisation and management, such as how to settle a class, use of time and resources, etc.);
3. *curriculum knowledge* (the full range of programmes and materials designed for the teaching of a subject and topics, such as the physical education curriculum, as well as the wider curriculum);
4. *pedagogical content knowledge* (the blend of content knowledge and pedagogy, distinctively the province of the teacher; those regularly taught topics in a subject area and most powerful analogies, illustrations, examples, explanations and demonstrations, etc.);
5. *knowledge about learners and their characteristics* (knowledge of the characteristics of learners and of learning theories such as theories of child development);
6. *knowledge of educational contexts* (the educational settings where learning takes place, such as schools, classrooms, nursery settings, universities, colleges etc.);
7. *knowledge of educational ends, purposes and values* (the short-term goals for a lesson and long-term goals or ends of education which make teaching a purposeful activity).

Metzler (2011, p. 46) applied Shulman's (1987) categories specifically to physical education:

- content knowledge; subject matter
- general pedagogical knowledge; generic teaching methods
- pedagogical content knowledge; subject-specific teaching methods
- knowledge of learners and their characteristics; learning as a process
- curriculum knowledge; how content develops
- knowledge of educational contexts; how context impacts
- knowledge of educational ends, purposes and values; educational goals.

In this chapter, we use the knowledge bases identified by Shulman (1987) and applied to physical education by Metzler (2011).

It is important to remember that the different knowledge bases are not used in isolation; rather, effective teachers draw from different knowledge bases and use these in combination. Case studies 9.1 and 9.2 highlight this important point. Both beginning teachers have a range of KSU across the categories identified by Shulman (1987). This knowledge is based on their previous experiences and the values, attitudes and beliefs they have towards their subject area. However, both beginning teachers exhibit strengths and areas for development. Read the case studies and complete Task 9.2.

Case study 9.1 KSU of a beginning teacher (1)

The first beginning teacher is knowledgeable, confident and enthusiastic in a range of physical activities and specialist fields such as sport psychology (*content knowledge*) and values the rich and varied learning resources and teaching materials (including teaching assistants) to support her in enhancing physical education for pupils (*curriculum knowledge*). She is also familiar with theories of how children think and learn and about them as learners (*knowledge of learners*) and has an innovative way of teaching pupils that inspires and encourages them to do their best and achieve success

> (*pedagogical content knowledge*). She believes in the holistic development of children and preparing them for life (*knowledge of educational aims, purposes and values*) and values parents with whom she has developed an honest, trusting and supportive relationship (*knowledge of educational contexts*).

Case study 9.2 KSU of a beginning teacher (2)

> The second beginning teacher has a secure understanding of the National Curriculum for physical education in terms of expectations for pupils' learning at Key Stages 3 and 4, particularly the assessment of pupils at the end of Key Stage 3 (*curriculum knowledge* and *pedagogical content knowledge*). However, he lacks experience and has insecure knowledge of the skills and rules of the game of rugby (*content knowledge*). The beginning teacher has a very good knowledge and understanding of how learners learn (*knowledge of learners*) and a good grasp of a range of organisational and management strategies (*general pedagogical knowledge*). However, his methods of teaching rugby might ignore his wealth of knowledge of learners and how they learn, and of general pedagogical knowledge, by being based on his strong belief that the teaching of rugby should be targeted at boys only and that a skills-based approach to teaching rugby is the only way forward. He generally teaches by standing in front of the class and telling the pupils what to do rather than demonstrating and giving them the chance, both individually and in small groups, to think and make their own decisions or solve problems for themselves (*pedagogical content knowledge*).

Task 9.2   Strengths and areas for development in KSU

For both case studies 9.1 and 9.2, identify strengths and areas for development which you need to support each beginning teacher to develop.

It is important as a mentor for both you and the beginning teacher to know the beginning teacher's current level of knowledge about teaching.

Identifying and measuring the KSU of a beginning teacher

A common way of identifying a beginning teacher's KSU is through an 'audit'; a qualitative evaluation of KSU 'health'. It identifies strengths and areas for development or gaps between available KSU and what is needed to become an effective teacher. This enables effort and resources to be focused on improving KSU in areas for development through drawing up an action plan.

An example of a detailed 'KSU audit' is provided in Appendix A. Shulman's (1987) knowledge bases are used as the framework for this audit. The audit also allows the level of knowledge to be graded (e.g. 1 = outstanding/excellent, 2 = good, 3 = requires development).

Task 9.3 is designed to help you start identifying a beginning teacher's KSU.

Case study 9.3 highlights how one beginning teacher's previous experience helped develop her KSU for teaching to have a positive *impact* on a pupil's learning experience. Task 9.4 is then designed for you to support a beginning teacher to reflect on their own previous experiences and the impact on pupils' learning.

Case study 9.3 'The jewel in the crown' – life skills!

Over the course of the last year, I have been teaching a 16-year-old girl from Afghanistan how to swim. She had never seen the sport or been around a swimming pool and therefore had very limited knowledge of the sport. She had very limited opportunities in her home country to do sports and was lacking knowledge in the general area of sports. Due to her not being able to swim … I had '1-to-1' lessons once or twice a week across three school terms in an after-school extra curricula circumstance. Over the course of the year, she went from being a complete novice to being able to swim continuously on both her front and back and was able to perform three out of the four strokes to a good standard. She also learnt skills such as diving, submerging, picking up objects from the pool bottom and performing various rotations in the water. From teaching her these skills in the water, it impacted her learning of other sports that had similar movements and coordination. … From teaching her to coordinate her arms and legs in different movement patterns, she was able to develop body control and coordination. This allowed her to understand skills such as Dance and Gymnastics and how she needed to use body control to perform movements within these areas. As well as that she has access and the ability to participate in other sports involved in water such as Synchronised Swimming and Water Polo. Without my teaching of swimming, she would not have the opportunity to try out these sports which may be a sport that she pursues further in life. Finally, not only is this sport a good way to exercise and can have health benefits in the future, it is also a life skill that could not only save her life but others potentially as well. … From this experience, I have learnt to adapt to the situation and the individual needs. It is highly unlikely that I am going to be doing a '1-to-1' lesson on a regular basis and therefore I will need to take the whole class needs into consideration. I have learnt to create several goals, both short term and long-term to help keep my teaching on course, as well as it showing progress to both myself and those involved in the class. However, from this experience, I have also seen how much impact teaching smaller numbers can have on learning. Therefore, not only do I need to consider the needs of everyone in the class, but also think about breaking the group down into groups based on ability and giving them a focus relative to what they need to improve on. This helps to improve their learning as they are focusing on what is appropriate for the skill and ability. (Beginning physical education teacher, 2016-2017)

You might like to work with a beginning teacher to add which knowledge bases the beginning teacher is drawing on in this case study (as in case studies 12.1 and 12.2). Two points to highlight from this case study are:

1. the complex bodies of knowledge and skills a beginning teacher needs to function effectively and competently as a teacher;
2. that a beginning teacher should endeavour to interact and engage with Shulman's knowledge bases for teaching as they develop from less knowledgeable to more knowledgeable teachers.

Task 9.4   Impact of teaching on pupils' learning

The Office for Standards in Education (Ofsted, 2012, p. 29) stated that 'the key factor in judging the quality of teaching is the impact teaching has on the quality of learning'. Ask a beginning teacher to read case study 9.3 and reflect on the KSU brought to and developed in this situation and then what KSU was developed to bring into the teaching situation. Then, ask them to reflect on a successful teaching or coaching experience of their own in terms of young people's learning and how this was impacted on by their KSU, addressing the following questions:

- What impact did the teaching or coaching experience have on the learning experience of a particular pupil(s)?
- What KSU enabled you to be successful in this teaching or coaching experience?
- What did you learn to take into a (new) teaching situation?

You have identified strengths and areas for development in the beginning teacher's KSU through their audit and other means. As a mentor, you have a key role to play in supporting a beginning teacher to develop their KSU. This is explored in the next section.

Supporting the development of a beginning physical education teacher's KSU

One key purpose of auditing a beginning teacher's KSU is to inform the design and delivery of professional development opportunities to facilitate their learning. The outcomes of the audit provide the basis for a 'KSU action plan' (see Appendix B) in which steps, tasks and/or resources are identified to develop KSU to reach set/agreed targets, along with a timeline for when tasks need to be completed.

When completing an action plan, consideration should be given to all areas of KSU. In relation to content knowledge, whilst most beginning teachers focus on areas in which they feel they have less knowledge and are less confident, experience shows that many teachers who have more knowledge in a particular activity may struggle to deconstruct the activity to teach it at the level appropriate to the needs of the pupils. It is important that they are supported to consider different ways of teaching activities in which they perceive they are knowledgeable and confident (see, for example, Capel and Katene, 2000).

Task 9.5 focuses on supporting a beginning teacher to develop a KSU action plan.

Task 9.5 A KSU action plan

1. Refer back to Task 9.2 and discuss with a beginning teacher how you can support them to develop aspects of KSU that require further development as well as aspects identified as strengths. As a result of this discussion, ask the beginning teacher to complete the KSU action plan (see Appendix B).
2. Ensure that progress against these targets is included in your weekly discussion meetings (see Chapter 16).
3. Monitor this throughout their time with you so that they continue to develop their KSU for teaching.

Learning gain

By auditing at different points during the time you are mentoring a beginning teacher or the period in which their learning is to be measured (e.g., for initial teacher education (ITE), at interview, at the start of the course, at the end of the first term, at the end of the second term, at the end of the course), it is possible to measure the impact of particular learning activities or interventions on the improvement of their KSU. This enables the 'learning gain' to be measured. Learning gain is defined as the 'distance travelled' or the difference between the knowledge, skills, understanding, competencies and personal development demonstrated at two points in time (McGrath et al., 2015). In Task 9.6, the focus is on measuring learning gain and activities that supported this.

Task 9.6 Measuring a beginning teacher's learning gain and activities that support this

In order to measure a beginning teacher's learning gain, ask them to repeat Task 9.3 at the end of their time with you. Discuss with the beginning teacher any differences between the two audits, and hence in learning gain, between the KSU demonstrated by the beginning teacher at these two points in time. Discuss with them which activities helped them the most, as well as those which were not helpful.

Collaborative approaches to learning to support beginning teachers' development of KSU

Supporting a beginning teacher's development of KSU can include processes such as observation by the mentor of a beginning teacher's lesson, followed by feedback, and so on (Chapters 13 and 15). However, in this chapter, the focus is on some collaborative approaches to learning (between a beginning teacher and a mentor; between two beginning teachers alone or both with the mentor, e.g. a beginning teacher planning, teaching and reviewing lessons together with the mentor; two beginning teachers in one school working together to collaboratively plan, teach and review a number of lessons each week in a range of physical activities or topics; the mentor leading and the beginning teacher acting as a supporter, or vice versa, or, if two beginning teachers are working together, one leading and the other acting as the supporter). Collaborative learning is defined as the continuous interaction and dialogue of two or more people within and across disciplines, organised into a common effort, to share knowledge and expertise and solve or explore common issues (Herbert, 2005). Collaborative approaches to learning and mentoring are covered in greater depth in Chapter 8.

Collaborative learning has been based largely, although not exclusively, on Vygotsky's (1978) social constructivist theory. Vygotsky argued that individuals are introduced to new knowledge, new patterns of thought and new understandings by interacting and engaging in dialogue with others. Vygotsky stressed asymmetrical relationships in which one of the participants is more knowledgeable and expert than the other. He emphasised the Zone of Proximal Development (ZPD): the zone bounded by what the learner is capable of learning by him/herself and by the level achieved when solving problems in collaboration with an individual who is more knowledgeable and experienced. The helper is able to transform, reorganise, simplify, clarify and exemplify information to make it comprehensible to the learner (or less knowledgeable other). Vygotsky also claimed that the act of (the more knowledgeable and expert) helping improves cognitive processing in the helper by increasing attention and motivation towards the task, resulting in a review of existing KSU.

Research has shown both preference for and increased learning as a result of collaborative learning. For example, Katene et al. (2017) found a strong preference for active participation and collaborative learning by second-year exercise and sport sciences students, which contributed to learning gain in KSU. Likewise, Kooloos et al. (2011) discovered increased participation levels and higher learning gain in first-year medical and biomedical students as a result of working in smaller groups and through peer teaching (Chapter 8 looks at collaborative approaches to mentoring).

One physical education mentor (2011) highlighted the benefits of collaborative learning between two beginning physical education teachers as follows:

> Collaborative teaching encourages deep learning by allowing beginning physical education teachers to i) be 'critical friends' in the planning and evaluation of lessons, ii) improve subject knowledge via peer-to-peer learning and where the cycle of lessons allows, iii) review and re-deliver lessons in a short time frame. An ideal scenario is where each [beginning] teacher has a subject-based strength so that each can lead and each has an opportunity to increase subject knowledge. Guidance from the mentor is essential in setting 'ground rules' and overseeing the work of the beginning teachers to ensure equality of roles between them. Collaborative work can be seen as an additional burden but if all beginning teachers and mentors persevere, the benefits are enormous.

In order to be successful, as Jenkins (2002, p. 33) argued, 'implementing [collaborative learning practices] takes careful and extensive planning and involves the coordination of several individuals, all of whom must be educated in the process'. Further, as Williams (1996) stressed, the importance of clarifying the different roles, especially for beginning teachers who need to be aware of such things as authority shifts, must be communicated (e.g. a beginning teacher negotiating who will lead which parts of the lesson and what, if any, supporting role another beginning teacher or the mentor will take). In order to prepare for collaborative learning, beginning teachers could learn about the stages of group work (e.g. Tuckman's schema of forming, storming, norming and performing; see Further Resources) to help them see that the first phase is itself a point at which particular skills are needed.

Three examples of collaborative approaches to support the development of beginning teachers' KSU are given in the following subsections. All the activities can be undertaken either with one or two beginning teachers with the mentor or with two beginning teachers together. If there are two beginning teachers working together, it is very important to be alert to possible 'unequal contributions'; for example, the 'more knowledgeable other' beginning teacher takes the lead in the decision-making process and tasks (Bonanno et al., 1998; Brooks and Ammons, 2003; Nordberg, 2008). As a mentor, adapt these activities as appropriate for your situation. There are, of course, other activities that can be used (see Chapter 8; also, for example, Williams, 1996; Jenkins et al., 2002).

Demonstration and modelling

A beginning teacher(s) observes their mentor teach a whole lesson and then, using the same material, models all or parts of the lesson with another class. The important feature of this activity is that it is planned in advance and both the beginning teacher and mentor are clear about the learning focus of the teacher demonstration. The beginning teacher should make notes during the observation, keeping in mind the learning focus/foci. These notes can form the basis of discussion in a follow-up meeting and then inform their own teaching. Demonstration and modelling goes beyond the mere observation of classroom practice to include explanations and justifications of the methods employed. In this way, the mentor can assist the beginning teacher in thinking about teaching so that they become knowledgeable in the 'how' and 'why' of teaching and not just the 'what'. This will help to develop skills of reflective practice that will be invaluable to the beginning teacher throughout their teaching career (Chapter 10 covers the development of beginning teachers' reflection).

Linear sequence

1. Early in a mentoring relationship, the mentor and beginning teacher organise a lesson to enable the beginning teacher to demonstrate competence in a specific teaching skill which the beginning teacher has identified as needing practice (e.g. organising and performing accurate demonstrations, asking higher-order questions, organising pupils into groups). The beginning teacher then plans short teaching episodes focused on this teaching skill.

For example, Sarah-Jane chooses to focus on organising and performing accurate demonstrations. During a rugby lesson, she agrees with her mentor that she will plan to:

(a) set up and demonstrate a 3 v 1 (piggy-in-the-middle) learning activity, with the help of two 'more able' pupils, using a variety of passes, and explain to the class the purpose of this activity and a few key rules;
(b) allow the pupils to engage in this learning activity;
(c) observe pupils performing different types of passes (particularly the spin pass) in their groups of four;
(d) engage in a small group discussion with the pupils on types of passes performed (such as the spin pass, etc.);

(e)   with a pupil, lead a demonstration and explanation of the spin pass. Specifically, the beginning teacher shows pupils how to observe, analyse and give feedback to each other in small groups of three or four (one pupil acts as a 'teacher', another acts as a 'doer/performer' and the other pupil is the 'feeder'. The 'teacher' has a learning/task card comprising illustrations and brief explanations on the 'ready position', 'action' and 'follow through' of the spin pass). All pupils have an opportunity to experience all three roles;

(f)   ask pupils to return to the small-sided game/3 v 1 'piggy-in-the-middle'.

It was also agreed by the mentor that Sarah-Jane needs to consider (a) who demonstrates (boys, girls, more able, less able, beginning teachers); (b) where to position demonstrations for visibility and safety; (c) what key teaching points/assessment criteria they will emphasise to the rest of the class and what questions they will pose to the class to assess pupils' knowledge and understanding. Following the lesson, there is a discussion about the effectiveness of the demonstrations.

2. Two beginning teachers and the mentor plan a lesson together, beginning with SMART (specific, measurable, achievable, realistic, time) learning objectives. The mentor explains the purpose of each part of the lesson and how it is going to be introduced. The mentor and beginning teachers then negotiate which beginning teacher will lead which parts of the lesson and what the supporting role of the other will entail (e.g. observe specific aspects of the lesson, help a small group, assess pupils' performance/work).

For example, John and Becky have been asked to teach a Year 7 mixed dance class (30 pupils) who are working on a dance theme based on 'Traditional Cultural Dances'. John and Becky agree to teach the class a short motif based on a traditional New Zealand Maori haka or vigorous posture dance called 'Ka Mate'. Both plan the lesson thoroughly, clarifying who will be leading and who will be supporting from start to finish. They talk the lesson through in detail with the mentor, who agrees that they should proceed. The mentor acts as a facilitator and support mechanism for the two beginning teachers. By watching the motif and the finished routine develop, supported with feedback from each other and the mentor (during the post-lesson discussion/conference), John and Becky develop the KSU and confidence to tackle the same topic with another Year 7 class the following week.

3. One beginning teacher takes responsibility for distributing/managing equipment and other learning resources, whilst the second is responsible for explaining learning activities.

For example, two beginning teachers organise a 'circuit' of activities for a group of pupils. One explains the learning activities, starts and stops the activities, and gives positive, supportive and specific/corrective feedback after each. The other beginning teacher sets out equipment at each station before the lesson and checks that it is set up and cleared away properly and safely after each activity and that enough is ready for the next group. He or she also takes responsibility for putting everything away at the end of the lesson.

Class division

1. The class is divided into two or more groups; either the mentor and the beginning teacher or two beginning teachers teach half the class each, with the mentor supporting, for periods

ranging from parts of the lesson to the whole lesson. In this situation, the mentor is seen as an expert helper who can take on whatever activity suits the beginning teachers' needs, rather than an authority figure and critic. It also gives pupils opportunities that might not be possible with only one teacher present.

For example, Jim has a group of 30 Year 8 pupils for swimming, including six non-swimmers. He has a swimming Assistant Teacher's Certificate and current National Pool Lifeguard Qualification and is a very competent swimmer. Gemma, the other beginning teacher, holds a National Pool Lifeguard Qualification and can be described as a competent beginner. Jim works in the water, taking responsibility for the six non-swimmers, whilst both the mentor and Gemma teach the rest in two ability groups (intermediate and advanced). Five of the six non-swimmers are able to swim by the end of a half-term block.

2. A lesson with differentiated tasks is planned. The beginning teacher and the mentor plan a lesson that involves different groups being engaged on different tasks, making considerable demands on observation, organisation and management skills. The beginning teacher and the mentor teach the lesson together, with the beginning teacher introducing the learning objectives and explaining the tasks; then, once learning activities are under way, each is responsible for a specified number of groups. In subsequent lessons, the beginning teacher's responsibility for groups increases whilst the mentor's lessens.

For example, Alan has a mixed ability Year 9 group for gymnastics. Some pupils are quite 'able' and will want to continue with gymnastics as a GCSE practical option. Others lack confidence, although they can be motivated provided that learning activities and apparatus are developmental, progressive and differentiated to meet their diverse needs. Alan feels that setting the same learning activity and expecting a differentiated outcome has been successful up to a point, but that it is now only challenging the 'more able' at the expense of putting off some of the others. He does not feel he can keep an eye on everyone if they are all being asked to do different things. He therefore plans a lesson in which there will be a choice of six learning activities, making different physical demands and involving different kinds of apparatus. He looks after three groups and the mentor looks after the remaining three groups. (If there are two beginning teachers, the three teachers can each take responsibility for two groups in the first lesson, then for subse-quent lessons divide the groups equally between the two beginning teachers, with the mentor acting as support.)

3. A lesson could benefit from the presence of two (or more) teachers in the room due to safety considerations.

For example, one beginning teacher is helping to teach dance to an examination group. The pupils are interested in moves involving lifts and throws, but it is difficult to give everyone experience because of the need for the mentor to be there to support and ensure safety. The mentor and beginning teacher agree to each work with half (or one-third if there are two beginning teachers) the class to allow sustained practice so as to enable the whole group to reach a point of competence and confidence at which they can use the moves learned in the future when there is only the mentor in the classroom.

These types of activities help beginning teachers develop and improve their knowledge, skills, concepts or ideas, principles, facts and confidence (as reflected in the work of, for example, Springer et al., 1999; and Stiles and Katene, 2013). They also provide space for the beginning teacher (and mentor) to try things out, to develop critical and creative skills, and to innovate (Jenkins, 2002; Meirink et al., 2007). They also allow a beginning teacher to take risks and learn without fear of their attempts being assessed (taking risks is covered in Chapter 17). Task 9.7 looks at using collaborative approaches to mentoring.

Task 9.7   Using collaborative approaches to mentoring

With a beginning teacher you are mentoring, identify collaborative approaches (either those above or others you identify) to help them with a specific aspect of their KSU development.

Use this in a lesson and discuss how the approach supported their development.

When the beginning teacher completes their KSU audit, ask them to look at the learning gain in this particular area of development.

The next section of the chapter looks at some principles for mentors and beginning teachers interested in identifying, developing and measuring beginning teachers' KSU.

Guiding principles to consider when identifying, developing and measuring a beginning teacher's KSU

Identifying KSU

1. Be familiar with Shulman's (1986, 1987) Knowledge Bases for Teaching Model, which has been used as a framework for designing the KSU audit.
2. Understand the educational theory, value and rationale of a KSU audit and KSU action plan.

Measuring KSU

1. Understand the *purposes of* measuring learning gain (don't be afraid to 'test the waters'); consider a pilot (e.g. compare and contrast KSU audit at entry and exit of an ITE course).
2. Consider using collaborative learning practices to increase beginning teachers' learning gain.

Developing KSU

1. Joint planning between a beginning teacher and mentor on how to develop aspects of KSU identified on the KSU audit and action plan. Allow quality time to plan and prepare for tasks.
2. Joint planning, teaching and post-lesson review between two beginning teachers (where possible) are 'relevant and valuable for the improvement of their own teaching practice' (Meirink et al., 2007, p. 146). In the post-lesson discussion/review, it is crucial to allow

beginning teachers to share their reflective comments about the lesson *before* they meet with their mentor. These might include review of issues such as justifying teaching decisions, suggesting alternative practices, emphasising/demonstrating important teaching points to aid pupil understandings, problem-solving and pupil-centred activities, giving reassurance and emotional support, and highlighting areas to develop (see Chapter 15).

3. It is important to value the means (or technical competence in a range of physical activities or 'how') and the educational ends, purposes and values of these activities (or 'why') in equal measure (see, for example, d'Arripe-Longueville et al., 2002). Be careful not to focus more on means, techniques and procedures and less on the ends in teaching (Chapter 17 focuses on development once a beginning teacher has developed the basics).

4. It is widely accepted that the development of a set of collaborative, collegial relationships amongst beginning teachers and mentors (or between beginning teachers), such as trust, support, sharing and reflection (Hargreaves and Dawe, 1990), combined with administrative leadership and facilitation, is needed to further the development of beginning teacher (and mentor) learning.

5. Understand the educational theory, value and rationale for collaborative learning practices. They can form one means of professional development, amongst a whole range, to support beginning teachers.

6. If a mentor works with groups of beginning teachers together, s/he should explain to them why it would be better (e.g. to develop social skills and teamwork as well as knowledge and understanding). When groups of beginning teachers are put together, it should be recognised that working with a group of friends is conducive to learning.

7. Whilst beginning teachers see working together as an opportunity to develop teamwork skills, they also see conflict as a disadvantage when working in a group.

8. The professional commitment and energy of beginning teachers, mentors and other relevant staff (e.g. other staff in the physical education department or other staff working in an ITE partnership) to work as a team, sharing good practice, are of paramount importance. As Henry Ford, the American industrialist and pioneer of the assembly line, succinctly put it: 'Coming together is a beginning, keeping together is progress, working together is success.'

The mentor reflection in Task 9.8 asks you to reflect further on beginning teacher KSU after reading the chapter.

Task 9.8   Mentor reflection: Reflecting on beginning teachers' KSU

Having read the chapter, reflect on your thoughts about beginning teachers' KSU, how to support its development and how to measure the learning gain.

Summary and key points

This chapter focused on better understanding, identifying, measuring and supporting the development of beginning teachers' KSU for teaching. The chapter concludes with three *wishes* that we believe are significant for beginning teachers to develop into quality teachers. We would like beginning teachers and mentors:

1.   to consider measuring the learning gain of beginning teachers to:(a) measure the development of beginning teachers' KSU at different stages of their learning; (b)inform future planning and delivery of content to facilitate their learning; (c)investigate the impact of particular teaching and learning interventions or practices.
2.   to adopt a genuine desire for improvement of KSU, which leads to constant re-shaping and re-thinking of teaching and a willingness to take risks, be creative and innovate (taking risks is covered more fully in Chapter 17).
3.   to take an approach to supporting the development of a beginning teacher's learning and professional development that is informed by the latest thinking and research in the field, be that, for example, collaborative practices or aspects of content knowledge, such as biomechanical principles of movement. The design of our practices could be, for instance, founded on Vygotskian principles of social and collaborative learning.

Further resources

Tuckman, B. (1965) 'Developmental sequence in small groups', *Psychological Bulletin* 63 (6), 384-399.
Tuckman's (1965) Forming, Storming, Norming, Performing Team Development Model suggests that as a group or team develops ability and maturity, relationships are established, and the leader changes leadership style from direct and coaching through to delegating and (almost) detaching. It's a very informative model for beginning teachers to understand and apply in their planning and teaching of pupils in small groups.

Williams, A. (1996) *Teaching Physical Education: A Guide for Mentors and Students*, London:David Fulton.
This book includes a useful and relevant chapter on 'Collaborative Teaching'; student teachers working together as a pair and with the teacher when teaching a physical education lesson.

See also the companion website for this book (www.routledge.com/9781138059658).

You may also find it useful to refer to/use the text books written for student and newly qualified physical education teachers with a beginning teacher you are mentoring (see list on Page 4).

Appendix A

Beginning physical education teacher knowledge and skills audit

NAME OF BPET:
NAME OF INSTITUTION/ORGANISATION:
YEAR OF STUDY:

AUDIT OF RECENT AND RELEVANT EXPERIENCES OF TEACHING (& RELATED ACTIVITIES)

(NB Please indicate below any relevant experience you have gained prior to applying for your ITT course. Responses will help inform your PE Tutors & Mentors of individual BPET background experiences at the beginning of the ITT course).

1. Classroom Observation (voluntary) and brief description of experiences:

2. Classroom Assistant (voluntary) and brief description of experiences:

3. Teaching Assistant (paid) and brief description of experiences:

4. Teaching Assistant (voluntary) and brief description of experiences:

5. After-School Club Assistant and brief description of experiences:

6. Group Leader (i.e. scouts, Girl Guides, Church groups etc.) and brief description of experiences:

7. Duke of Edinburgh (DoE) Award Scheme (Bronze, Silver, Gold) and brief description of experiences:

8. Sports Coach and brief description of experiences:

9. FE/HE Lecturer and brief description of experiences:

10. TEFL/Teaching overseas/summer camp work etc. and brief description of experiences:

11. List any sports you have played and at what level?

KNOWLEDGE AND SKILLS (*SUBJECT CONTENT KNOWLEDGE*) (*i.e. skills, techniques, concepts, principles, rules, factual information of a range of physical activities & topics such as physiology of sport & exercise*) **For each of the boxes below, rate your level of knowledge and skills using the following '3-point' Ofsted grading criteria**			
Grade 1 = Outstanding (O) Grade 2 = Good (G) Grade 3 = Requires Improvement (RI)	1 (O)	2 (G)	3 (RI)
Athletics: ☐ Track 'Endurance' Events (800 m, 1500 m): …………………………… ☐ Track 'Speed' Events (100 m, 200 m, 400 m): …………………………… ☐ Field 'Throwing' Events (shot-put, discus, javelin, hammer): ……………………… ☐ Field 'Jumping' Events (long jump, triple jump, high jump): ………………………			
Dance: ☐ Educational/creative: …………………………………… ☐ Other (jazz, ballet, tap, aerobic etc.) (please specify):………………………			

Games:
☐ Invasion Games (basketball, football, hockey, netball, rugby, water polo
    etc.): ……………………………
☐ Net/Wall Games (badminton, squash, table tennis, tennis, volleyball
    etc.): . ……………………………………
☐ Striking/Fielding Games (baseball, cricket, rounders, softball
    etc.):………………………………
☐ Target Games (archery, darts,
    golf):………………………………			

Gymnastics: ☐ Educational:……………………………………… ☐ Other (Olympic, rhythmic, acrobatics) (please specify):………………………			

Outdoor & Adventurous Activities:
☐ 'Water-based' Activities (canoeing, sailing, water-skiing, wind-surfing
    etc.):………………………………
☐ 'Land-based' Activities (abseiling, orienteering, rock-climbing, caving
    etc.):………………………………			

Swimming: ☐ Strokes (front-crawl):……………………………… ☐ Strokes (back-crawl):……………………………… ☐ Strokes (breast-stroke):……………………………… ☐ Strokes (butterfly):……………………………… ☐ Personal Lifesaving & Water Safety:………………………			
Any other Physical Activities (please specify): ☐ ……………………………………… ☐ ……………………………………… ☐ ……………………………………… ☐ ……………………………………… ☐ ………………………………………			

KNOWLEDGE AND SKILLS (*SUBJECT CONTENT KNOWLEDGE*) *(i.e. skills, techniques, concepts, principles, rules, factual information of a range of physical activities & topics such as physiology of sport & exercise)* **For each of the boxes below, rate your level of knowledge and skills using the following '3-point' Ofsted grading criteria**			
Grade 1 = Outstanding (O) **Grade 2 = Good (G)** **Grade 3 = Requires Improvement (RI)**	**1** **(O)**	**2** **(G)**	**3** **(RI)**
Subjects/Topics at GCSE and AS/A2 Level ☐ Anatomy & Physiology (e.g. Control of Blood Supply; Respiratory response to exercise): ☐ Biomechanics (e.g. Kinematic chain): ☐ Contemporary Studies (e.g. Physical & outdoor education; Towards a concept of sport): ☐ Exercise Physiology (e.g. Energy continuum; Ergogenic aids): ☐ Exercise & Sport Psychology (e.g. Emotional control; Group dynamics of sport performance): ☐ Historical Studies (e.g. Games in popular recreation; Development of popular recreation in the UK): ☐ Other (please specify):			
Other Vocational Qualifications in PE ☐ JSLA (Junior Sports Leaders Award): ☐ CSLA (Community Sports Leaders Award): ☐ HSLA (Higher Sports Leaders Award): ☐ Other (please specify):			

KNOWLEDGE AND SKILLS (*PEDAGOGICAL CONTENT KNOWLEDGE*) *(i.e. planning, teaching, learning resources, assessment)* **For each of the boxes below, rate your level of knowledge and skills using the following '3-point' Ofsted grading criteria**			
Grade 1 = Outstanding (O) **Grade 2 = Good (G)** **Grade 3 = Requires Improvement (RI)**	**1** **(O)**	**2** **(G)**	**3** **(RI)**
Knowledge and Skills (*Pedagogical Content Knowledge*): For this section, reflect upon the teaching generally (in a school; or educational setting) and rate the level of knowledge and skills overall in relation to pedagogical content knowledge.			
☐ Planning (e.g. 4-point plan - starter, development, plenary, homework): ☐ Teaching (e.g. teacher and/or pupil-led discussions, explanations, demonstrations, examples, illustrations, analogies & instructions; deploying a range of teaching strategies/models; interactive, differentiated & pupil-led learning activities; using analogies, anecdotes etc.): ☐ Learning resources (e.g. task/learning cards, ICT such as iPads etc.): ☐ Assessment (e.g. peer assessment, quizzes, practical performance tests, use of questions, verbal and/or written feedback to pupils etc.): ☐ Relationships with both pupils and staff (including support staff):			

KNOWLEDGE AND SKILLS (*GENERAL PEDAGOGICAL KNOWLEDGE*)			
(i.e. principles & strategies of managing & organizing a class/pupils, equipment/learning resources/ teaching space & time) **For each of the boxes below, rate your level of knowledge and skills using the following '3-point' Ofsted grading criteria**			
Grade 1 = Outstanding (O) Grade 2 = Good (G) Grade 3 = Requires Improvement (RI)	**1** **(O)**	**2** **(G)**	**3** **(RI)**
Knowledge and Skills (*General Pedagogical Knowledge*): □ Management and organization of pupils (e.g. following school & department policies): □ Management and organization of time: □ Management and organization of equipment/learning resources/ teaching space: □ Other (please specify):			

KNOWLEDGE AND SKILLS (*LEARNERS & LEARNING*)			
(i.e. Learners, child development and theories of how children learn) **For each of the boxes below, rate your level of knowledge and skills using the following '3-point' Ofsted grading criteria**			
Grade 1 = Outstanding (O) Grade 2 = Good (G) Grade 3 = Requires Improvement (RI)	**1** **(O)**	**2** **(G)**	**3** **(RI)**
Knowledge and Skills (*Learners & Learning*): □ Child Development (e.g. physical, intellectual, emotional, moral & social development): .... □ Theories of Learning (e.g. Skinner's behaviourist theory, Vygotsky's social constructivist theory, Piaget's constructivist theory etc.): .... □ Different types of learners (e.g. obese, gifted & talented, EAL, SEN/D, BME, disengaged or reluctant etc.):			

KNOWLEDGE AND SKILLS (*CURRICULUM KNOWLEDGE*) *(i.e. factual information of the PE curriculum, 14-19 accredited qualifications, syllabi, programmes, materials, resources, teaching packs etc.)* **For each of the boxes below, rate your level of knowledge and skills using the following '3-point' Ofsted grading criteria**			
Grade 1 = Outstanding (O) **Grade 2 = Good (G)** **Grade 3 = Requires Improvement (RI)**	1 (O)	2 (G)	3 (RI)
Physical Education □ 1. Purpose of study: .... □ 2. Aims: .... □ 3. Attainment targets:			
Subject Content: □ 1. Subject Content: Key Stage 1 .... □ 2. Subject Content: Key Stage 2 .... □ 3. Subject Content: Key Stage 3 .... □ 4. Subject Content: Key Stage 4			
GCSE Level PE: □ 1. AQA: .... □ 2. Edexcel: .... □ 3. OCR:			
AS/A2 Level PE: □ 1. AQA: .... □ 2. Edexcel: .... □ 3. OCR:			
Other Vocational Qualifications in PE (e.g. BTEC): □ .... □			
Information and Communication Technologies (ICT): □ **Basic word processing** (e.g. keyboard skills; font formatting; saving files etc.): □ **Advanced word processing** (e.g. tables; text wrapping; importing graphics etc.): □ **Desktop publishing** (e.g. using Microsoft Publisher etc.): □ **Email** (e.g. sending & receiving emails; using attachments etc.): □ **Internet** (e.g. accessing known sites; searching; saving text & images to files etc.): □ **Databases** (e.g. setting up & using a database etc.): □ **Spreadsheets** (e.g. using software such as EXCEL etc.): □ **Digital technology** (e.g. using, saving & editing digital images - video & still): □ **Presentation software** (e.g. PowerPoint etc.): □ **Web design** (e.g. designing web pages/sites, using FrontPage etc.):			

KNOWLEDGE AND SKILLS (*EDUCATIONAL CONTEXTS*)

(i.e. a range of contextual factors which affect a teacher's development & teaching performance, such as the catchment area of the school, the type & size of school, class size, feedback teachers receive on their teaching performance, quality of relationships within the school, expectations & attitudes of the head teacher etc.)

For each of the boxes below, rate your level of knowledge and skills using the following '3-point' Ofsted grading criteria

	1 (O)	2 (G)	3 (RI)
Grade 1 = Outstanding (O) Grade 2 = Good (G) Grade 3 = Requires Improvement (RI)			

Knowledge and Skills (*Educational Contexts*):

For this section,

(a) select one (1) school where you have worked (or are currently working) on a voluntary/paid and part-time/full-time basis (e.g. as a Teaching Assistant);

(b) answer the questions below (to the best of your recollection);

(c) provide an overall judgement on your level of knowledge and skills.

□ Type of school? (e.g. nursery, primary, secondary etc.):

□ Category of school? (e.g. faith, selective, independent, free, academy etc.):

□ Age range of pupils? (e.g. 3-7, 5-11, 7-11, 7-14, 11-16, 11-18, 14-19)

□ Gender of pupils? (e.g. mixed, all boys, all girls):

□ Number of pupils on roll? (total):

□ Date of the previous school Ofsted inspection?

□ What did Ofsted grade the school in the following categories? (below):

   1. Overall effectiveness?

   2. Achievement of pupils?

   3. Quality of teaching?

   4. Behaviour and safety of pupils?

   5. Leadership and management?

□ Were you given feedback on your teaching at all? If so, what overall grade would you give yourself for the 'quality of your teaching'?

□ What overall grade would you give yourself for your level of knowledge and skills for this section (educational contexts)?

KNOWLEDGE AND SKILLS (*EDUCATIONAL ENDS, PURPOSES & VALUES*)

(i.e. aims of education & aims of PE; knowledge of the DfE, 2011, Teachers' Standards)

For each of the boxes below, rate your level of knowledge and skills using the following '3-point' Ofsted grading criteria

	1 (O)	2 (G)	3 (RI)
Grade 1 = Outstanding (O) Grade 2 = Good (G) Grade 3 = Requires Improvement (RI)			
Knowledge and Skills (*Educational Ends, Purposes & Values*): □ Aims of Education .... □ Aims of Physical Education .... □ Teachers' Standards (DfE, 2011):			

KNOWLEDGE AND SKILLS (*EDUCATIONAL RESEARCH*) *(i.e. research knowledge & skills required for Master's level PGCE course)* **For each of the boxes below, rate your level of knowledge and skills using the following '3-point' Ofsted grading criteria**			
Grade 1 = Outstanding (O) **Grade 2 = Good (G)** **Grade 3 = Requires Improvement (RI)**	**1** **(O)**	**2** **(G)**	**3** **(RI)**
Research Literature: □ Ability to search the library databases: □ Ability to find relevant articles in electronic journals: □ Using the Harvard Referencing System: □ Writing a literature review: □ Ability to read critically:			
Research Methodology: □ Knowing how ethical considerations impact upon research: □ Collecting data: Observation schedule: □ Collecting data: Interview schedule: □ Analysing data: Quantitative analysis: □ Analysing data: Qualitative analysis:			
Research Writing/Presenting: □ Constructing an academic argument: □ Critical reflection: □ Using academic reading to support an argument: □ Creating and presenting a research poster and/or PowerPoint presentation:			

IDENTIFICATION OF BEGINNING PHYSICAL EDUCATION TEACHER'S *PRINCIPAL NEEDS*	
(NB Having considered your level of knowledge & skills in each of the categories/knowledge bases, specify those areas that were rated as 2 (Good) and 3 (Requires Improvement)	
KNOWLEDGE AND SKILLS FOCUS:	**REVIEW COMMENTS:**
KNOWLEDGE AND SKILLS (*SUBJECT CONTENT KNOWLEDGE*):	

KNOWLEDGE AND SKILLS (*PEDAGOGICAL CONTENT KNOWLEDGE*):
KNOWLEDGE AND SKILLS (*GENERAL PEDAGOGICAL KNOWLEDGE*):
KNOWLEDGE AND SKILLS (*LEARNERS & LEARNING*):
KNOWLEDGE AND SKILLS (*CURRICULUM*):
KNOWLEDGE AND SKILLS (*EDUCATIONAL CONTEXT*):
KNOWLEDGE AND SKILLS (*EDUCATIONAL ENDS, PURPOSES & VALUES*):
KNOWLEDGE AND SKILLS (*EDUCATIONAL RESEARCH*):

OTHER:	DATE ACHIEVED:
1.	
2.	
3.	
4.	
5.	

1st Review Date: **Signed:**
(Start of Autumn Term):

2nd Review Date: **Signed:**
(End of Autumn Term/Start of Spring Term):

3rd Review Date: **Signed:**
(End of Spring Term/Start of Summer Term):

4th Review Date: **Signed:**
(End of Summer Term):

Appendix B

**BEGINNING PHYSICAL EDUCATION TEACHER KNOWLEDGE AND SKILLS
ACTION PLAN**

NAME OF BPET:
NAME OF INSTITUTION/ORGANISATION:
YEAR OF STUDY:

ACTION PLAN					
1	2	3	4	5	
(at PGCE interview)				*(at end of PGCE year)*	

PRINCIPAL STRENGTHS IDENTIFIED IN KNOWLEDGE AND SKILLS AUDIT: *(i.e. any knowledge & skills rated as '1' – 'outstanding')*:

PRINCIPAL NEEDS OR WEAKNESSES IDENTIFIED IN KNOWLEDGE AND SKILLS AUDIT: *(i.e. any knowledge & skills rated as '2' – 'good' or '3' – 'requires improvement')*:

TARGET/S FOR IMPROVEMENT *(NB note the target/s below, state specifically how it/they will be achieved & timeline for tasks to be completed)*:	**DATE TO BE COMPLETED**

Signature (BPET):   Signature (Mentor):   Date:

(NB To be kept in BPET's PDP)

10 Supporting beginning physical education teachers to become reflective practitioners

Paul McFlynn

Introduction

The development of critical reflective skills is a fundamental aim for beginning teachers. According to Tabachnik and Zeichner (2002, p. 13), 'there is not a single teacher educator who would say that he or she is not concerned about preparing teachers who are reflective'. As a mentor, you can have a major impact upon a beginning teacher's reflective development. Facilitating the development of a beginning teacher's reflective skills is, therefore, fundamental to your role and is something you must work at on a daily basis. When starting to mentor a beginning teacher, it is important to gauge their current level of knowledge and understanding regarding the implementation of reflective practice, as this will help you shape how you support their further development. It is also important for you to be reflective about your teaching and your mentoring.

Due to the complex nature of mentoring and perhaps the more complex nature of reflection, the aim of this chapter is not to provide you with all the answers regarding supporting beginning teachers to develop reflective skills; but to equip you with a range of strategies to support a beginning teacher on their reflective journey. The chapter also aims to support you on your reflective journey.

The chapter begins by revisiting the definition of reflection and then proceeds to address the following reflective methods: lesson evaluations, journal writing, peer review and video. It is important to emphasise that these four methods are commonly used in the development of reflective skills. The methods display a developmental approach to improving beginning teachers' reflective skills, from basic individual lesson reflections to journal writing (both very individually based) to peer review and use of video (both involving the use of one's own and others' input to help develop reflection).

Objectives

At the end of this chapter, you should be able to:

- Identify a range of methods that help support the development of beginning physical education teachers' reflective skills;
- Have gained a deeper understanding of the important role you play in supporting the development of beginning teachers' reflective skills;

• Understand the importance of reflecting on your practice as a mentor (and as a teacher).

What is reflection?

As a mentor, you should have an appreciation of the role that reflection can play in your own and a beginning teacher's professional development, but before beginning to examine various reflective strategies, it is important to revisit what constitutes reflection. According to Black and Plowright (2010, p. 246), reflection is

> the process of engaging with learning and/or professional practice that provides an opportunity to critically analyse and evaluate that learning or practice. The purpose is to develop professional knowledge, understanding and practice that incorporates a deeper form of learning which is transformational in nature and is empowering, enlightening and ultimately emancipatory.

This view is supported by Boultona and Hramiak (2012), who argued that it is only when teachers critically explore why they do things, and when they begin to make links between learning theories they utilise and why they might or might not use them in future practice, that they move from evaluation to reflection. In order to progress, beginning teachers must begin to question and evaluate their educational beliefs in the light of alternative teaching methods (Hobbs, 2007). As a mentor, it is important to be aware that many beginning teachers have preconceived ideas as to what high-quality physical education should look like; therefore, it is important that you make a deliberate effort to understand their beliefs and attitudes so that you can begin to relate to their thinking and allow you to empathise with their views. Now complete Task 10.1.

Task 10.1   Investigating beliefs about physical education

1. Separately, both you and a beginning teacher you are mentoring write down what you each consider to be the three most important aspects of a high-quality physical education programme, and why.
2. Share this information with each other.
3. Discuss the beginning teacher's answers and probe beyond the information given. Encourage them to reflect on why they have given these answers. Where might these beliefs have come from? Consider the personal factors (e.g. gender, significant others, self-concept), situational factors (e.g. academic achievement, own participation in physical education and sport, socio-economic status). Have the beginning teacher record important points emerging in their professional development portfolio for future reference.
4. Write down what you have learned about the beginning teacher's beliefs.
5. Apply these same questions to your own responses. What have you learned about your own beliefs?

It will be important for both you and the beginning teacher to revisit these beliefs and discussion points at certain junctures throughout your mentoring relationship. Everley and Flemons (2015) emphasised the importance of reflecting critically on your beliefs and what this means for pupils' learning experiences. They also acknowledge that 'beliefs are not static but shaped over time' (p. 258). Therefore, it is important that both you and the beginning teacher are constantly aware of your beliefs and how these are shaping your pedagogical approaches. Revisiting your beliefs at various junctures helps you become aware of how these beliefs may be impacting your teaching and, consequently, the teaching and reflective practice of a beginning teacher (see Chapter 3 for more on beliefs). A beginning teacher must also revisit their beliefs at various junctures throughout the year and reflect on how these beliefs are evidenced in their practice and how they intend to change their pedagogical approach based on changes to their belief system.

Methods for developing reflection in physical education

Some beginning teachers may have experienced a very thorough approach and a range of methods for developing their reflective skills prior to you mentoring them, whilst others have experienced the very opposite. In terms of knowing what methods to employ with a beginning teacher, it is important to find out the exact nature of reflective work they have encountered thus far and then discuss how best to take their reflective work forward.

There are many reflective methods to choose from. In this section, we outline commonly used methods for supporting the development of reflective practice amongst beginning teachers. The methods are outlined in a definite order, beginning with less complex forms of reflection and continuing right through to more complex methods. Before we delve into each method, it is important to introduce Larrivee's Reflective Framework (see Figure 10.1). This can be used by you to monitor the quality of reflections of a beginning teacher, thus allowing you both to evaluate the effectiveness of the method(s) employed.

In order to be able to use these methods effectively with a beginning teacher(s), it is important that you familiarise yourself with the principles of each method and are clear about your role in each method. If you have already acquired considerable experience in utilising such methods, it is important to continue reflecting on their use, and likewise, if your experience is limited, it is important to embrace each method and reflect on how, as a mentor, you are able to use each method. Judging the effectiveness of each method in supporting the development of a beginning teacher's reflective skills is important for you, as this will allow you to develop your knowledge and expertise in relation to the employment of such methods. It must also be noted that there are other reflective methods available, which you may already use, such as case study workshops and collaborative online discussion forums. If you find these to be effective, then continue to use them, but it is hoped that by engaging with the methods described in this chapter, you will be comfortable in utilising a range of reflective methods with a beginning teacher.

Prior to working your way through the following sections on methods to support the development of reflection and the associated tasks, it is good practice to reflect on your current/most recent mentoring experience (see Task 10.2).

Pre-reflection: At the pre-reflective or non-reflective level, developing teachers react to pupils and classroom situations automatically, without conscious consideration of alternative responses. They operate with knee-jerk responses, attributing ownership of problems to pupils or others, perceiving themselves as victims of circumstances. They take things for granted without questioning and do not adapt their teaching based on pupils' responses and needs.

Surface reflection: At the level of surface reflection teachers' reflections focus on strategies and methods used to reach predetermined goals. Teachers are concerned with what works rather than with any consideration of the value of goals as ends in themselves. For this level, the term 'technical' has been most used. It has also been referred to as 'descriptive' (Jay and Johnson, 2002). The term 'surface' was chosen to depict a broader scope than technical concerns while highlighting that values, beliefs and assumptions that lie 'beneath the surface' are not being considered at this level of reflection.

Pedagogical Reflection: At this level practitioners apply the field's knowledge base and current beliefs about what represents quality practices. This level has probably the least consensus in the literature as to its composition and label. It has been variously labelled 'practical' (Van Manen, 1977), 'theoretical' (Day, 1993), 'deliberative' (Valli, 1997), 'comparative' (Jay and Johnson, 2002) and 'conceptual' (Farrell, 2004). The term 'pedagogical' was selected as a more inclusive term, merging all of the other concepts to connote a higher level of reflection based on application of teaching knowledge, theory and/or research. Teachers reflect on educational goals, the theories underlying approaches and the connections between theoretical principles and practice. They strive to understand the theoretical basis for classroom practice and to foster consistency between espoused theory (what they say they do and believe) and theory in use (what they actually do in the classroom).

Critical reflection: At this level teachers reflect on the moral and ethical implications and consequences of their classroom practices for pupils. Critical reflection involves examination of both personal and professional belief systems. Teachers who are critically reflective focus their attention both inwardly on their own practice and outwardly on the social conditions in which these practices are situated. They are concerned about issues of equity and social justice that arise in and outside the classroom and seek to connect their practice to democratic ideals. Acknowledging that classroom and school practices cannot be separated from the larger social and political realities, critically reflective teachers strive to become fully conscious of the range of consequences of their actions.

Figure 10.1 Larrivee's (2008) Reflective Descriptor Framework

Task 10.2   Mentor reflection: My current/most recent mentoring experience

Reflect on your current/most recent mentoring role by responding to the following questions:

1.   What were the main strengths of your mentoring with this beginning teacher(s)?
2.   How do you know that these areas were strong?
3.   What areas of your mentoring practice could have been more effective with this beginning teacher(s)?
4.   What evidence do you have that these areas could have been better?
5.   What strategies might you put in place to address these areas?

Day-to-day conversations

As a mentor, you have many conversations with a beginning teacher(s), some of which are in formal meetings and others are fairly informal, but nonetheless important. Early conversations between you and a beginning teacher can be some of the most important conversations you have, as they help to establish the nature of your working relationship. Portner (2003) argued that creating a positive working mentor–mentee relationship is of critical importance in order for a mentor to carry out their role productively. He stressed that a mentor–mentee relationship devoid of trust, honesty and respect leads to the development of an ineffective and perfunctory relationship (see Chapter 7 on mentor–mentee relationships).

Assisting a beginning teacher in the early stages of developing their ability to reflect is usually in the form of posing questions during both pre-lesson and post-lesson discussions (see Chapter 15). Getting a beginning teacher to explain the rationale behind their decisions about lesson activities and justify their approach begins the process of pre-lesson discussion. Developing the skill of allowing a beginning teacher 'thinking time' and avoiding the temptation of telling them how you would plan the lesson can be an effective starting point. Providing 'thinking time' during a pre-lesson meeting may simply be a matter of asking a beginning teacher to reread their lesson plan and consider what governed their decisions regarding lesson content and pedagogical strategies. This initial thinking exercise should take no more than five minutes. It provides the basis for the discussion that follows. Upon hearing a beginning teacher's lesson rationale, you can begin by posing open questions that generate dialogue. This may lead to lesson adaptations based on your ideas and experience; however, it is important that a beginning teacher arrives at this decision based on their reflection and the discussion that such reflection generates. Therefore, allowing appropriate 'thinking time' during discussion is vital, so that a beginning teacher can process the questions and have adequate space to think and reflect. It is important that you avoid answering your own questions but, through effective questioning, probe and prompt a beginning teacher to respond with their own thoughts.

The use of effective questioning post-lesson is often, perhaps, of more significance in helping to shape the reflective focus of a beginning teacher. As a mentor, it is important to prioritise the area(s) you wish a beginning teacher to reflect upon; they cannot address too many things at once. Allowing a beginning teacher some time to quietly reflect on the lesson before you begin questioning is essential, as this allows them to gather their thoughts. Asking them to identify three strengths and three areas for development is often an effective way of starting this process. From here, you can begin to question and probe areas identified for improvement. If a beginning teacher has failed to highlight an area for development which you considered to be significant, it is important to address this area with good questioning: questions that encourage reflection on this area (see Page 214 for sample questions).

Lesson reflections (often called evaluations)

Daily lesson reflections are extremely important for a beginning teacher, as they allow them to identify strengths and areas for development in their teaching, which can then be used to inform their next lesson. Lesson reflections can be undertaken immediately, the same day or the following day, but should not be left any longer before being completed. Zwozdiak-Myers (2015a) argued that taking a few minutes to reflect immediately after the lesson is crucial in facilitating the reflective process, as it allows a beginning teacher to establish what went well, what requires improvement and how they can attempt to bring about improvement, thus gaining insight as well as learning from mistakes. It is important that you establish this protocol with a beginning teacher from the very beginning. Because there are occasions when a beginning teacher has very little time between lessons, it is important that they focus on the main issues arising from the lesson, that is, the main strengths and main areas for development. Zwozdiak-Myers (2015a, p. 244) argued that lesson evaluations are the 'forerunner of documenting your reflection on your teaching', and she recommended that the following questions should be considered when conducting a lesson evaluation:

- What did the pupils achieve/learn or not achieve/learn?
- Why did they achieve/learn or not achieve/learn?
- How should I plan/teach in the next lesson to accommodate these findings?

It is important to note that the focus of the evaluation is on pupils' learning. Responding to these questions requires a beginning teacher to think about their teaching in a variety of patterns. In responding to the first question, they are engaged in evaluative thinking, whereby they consider the progress made by pupils in relation to the learning objectives/learning outcomes of the lesson. When a beginning teacher considers question 2, they are engaged in more analytical thinking, whereby they are likely to consider aspects of their planning and teaching and how these impacted pupil learning. In responding to question 3, a beginning teacher is taking the learning forward and using this to plan their next lesson, showing an awareness of the importance of reflection informing future practice. According to Zwozdiak-Myers (2015a), when responding to these questions, a beginning teacher is conducting reflection-on-action (Schön, 1983). Reflection-on-action after each lesson should be an expectation for all beginning teachers, as it allows them to gain insight into how effective or ineffective particular aspects of the lesson were. In addition to the three questions listed earlier, it will sometimes be appropriate to consider the following questions:

1. Was there any deviation from the lesson plan? Why did this occur?
2. Record any 'critical' incidents.

If a beginning teacher deviated from the lesson plan, it is important for them to reflect on why they did this, so that if a similar situation arises in future lessons, they can draw on this experience. If critical incidents occur in a lesson, it is vital that these are recorded as accurately as possible (see the 'Journal writing' section on how to reflect on critical incidents). Now complete Task 10.3.

Task 10.3   Supporting a beginning teacher to reflect on a lesson

Read the sample lesson reflection (Figure 10.2), completed by a beginning physical education teacher on a Postgraduate Certificate of Education course, then:

1. Using Larrivee's Reflective Descriptor Framework (see Figure 10.1), assign this sample a level.

2. Record the feedback you would provide to the beginning teacher regarding the quality of the reflection, and prepare questions you would pose to them as you aim to extend their thinking and approach to deepening their reflection.

This is usually the time when you get the opportunity to probe more deeply and ask the beginning teacher to reflect further on what they have written and for them to consider alternatives not noted in their reflections. It is important that, when conducting such a session, a beginning teacher takes accurate notes, which they should keep for future reference.

---

1. What did the pupils achieve/learn or not achieve/learn?
Pupils were successful in achieving two out of the three learning intentions. All pupils demonstrated the correct grip and stance used in hockey and all were able to recall the basic rules of hockey. The third learning intention was only partly achieved. All pupils could dribble by the end of the lesson, using the correct technique; however, not all were able to change the pace and direction they did this at.

2. Why did they achieve/learn or not achieve/learn? Why did this learning take place/not take place? Consider planning, teaching strategies, content, time etc.
The level of focus and engagement throughout the lesson was high; however, there were a few instances when pupils got distracted/lost interest. To combat this, it is crucial to plan activities that are exciting and maintain the attention of all pupils. Behaviour management was identified as a minor issue during this lesson. Some pupils' behaviour was negatively impacting the learning of others. Time management was an issue. Some of the activities lasted longer than I had planned for. Plenary was also too long.

3. How should I plan/teach in the next lesson to accommodate these findings? (What do I continue to do next time or what do I need to do differently to promote learning (e.g. differentiate more/better, provide more specific feedback etc.)?
Lesson pacing needs to improve. I must ensure that pupils don't spend too long on an activity but be careful not to rush through activities. I must be willing to move on to the next activity when I see that pupils have experienced and demonstrated success. Teach the pupils not the lesson plan! Warm-up needs to be more active and stimulating so that I can capture pupils' attention. I could perhaps allow the pupils to choose the warm-up activity? I will explore the use of small-sided games next week to ensure pupils get the opportunity to develop their decision-making and overall understanding of the game. Too much time spent on skill/drill work in this lesson. I will have a quiet word with the pupils who misbehaved so as to remind them of the importance of following rules and the need for their cooperation. I will also have different groupings so that certain pupils are kept apart.

Comments and targets for future lesson planning
• Behaviour management
• Time management
• More effective positioning whilst demonstrating
• Gaining and maintaining pupils' attention. Use a buzz word to capture attention.

Figure 10.2 Lesson reflection

Placing a word count on lesson reflections is not normally required. However, in some cases, when a beginning teacher judges their ability to reflect by how many words they write, it is important to monitor these entries and focus on developing quality reflection rather than quantity of words. It is also important to be aware that some beginning teachers have an excellent command of written English and may produce what can be categorised as a good reflective account, whilst other beginning teachers may not be good writers, and thus, their written lesson reflection is likely to be categorised at a lower reflective level. However, it must be noted that a more competent writer may not necessarily be more reflective than a less competent writer, but simply more effective at putting their thoughts down on paper. The true measurement of reflection is in the ability to translate what has been written into actual teaching practice, and, as a mentor, it is important that you help a beginning teacher monitor this process. Having a beginning teacher highlight these aspects in the next lesson plan is a very simple way of tracking this process and helps you when completing the next observation, as you will surely be focusing on these aspects.

It is possible that a beginning teacher has been using an already acceptable lesson reflection template, and if so, there may be no need to change this, but it is hoped that the sample in Figure 10.2 will provide further guidance in this area.

Journal writing

Mason and Klein (2013) emphasised that reflective journal writing is one of the most often used methods for developing reflection in initial teacher education, and whilst there are benefits to be gained from engaging in reflective journal writing, they emphasise that 'reflective thinking and writing are skills that require scaffolding, guidance and practice' (p. 210). Pavlovich (2007) supported this view by emphasising that journal writing can be a powerful mechanism for a beginning teacher to develop their reflective skills, but emphasised that a rigorous and structured approach is required in order to facilitate and extend their reflective abilities (see Figure 10.3). Pavlovich (2007) argued that journal writing is a very personal journey and that it is particularly challenging 'because of the unfamiliar use of the personal voice, so divergent from the usual passive voice and densely referenced text familiar in academic writing' (p. 284). Crème (2005) argued, however, that journal writing requires more than the personal voice, as we are asking a person to be very open when writing about personal experiences, which therefore requires honesty. Varner and Peck (2003) emphasised that journal work often reveals sensitive information, which some beginning teachers may not want others to read. Taggart and Wilson (2005) argued, however, that mentors or instructors are best placed to help identify and promote the connections between theory and practice, and that they should have access to a beginning teacher's journal work. Therefore, if you read sensitive and personal information, it is important that you are not judgemental but that you are always supportive and professional.

The expectation for a beginning teacher should be that they complete a weekly journal account which provides a critical overview of their week's teaching and pupil learning by reflecting on critical incidents that occurred. 'A critical incident is one that challenges your

- Topic: identify the critical incident that occurred and why you selected this incident.
- Description of the critical incident: what happened? where? and when?
- Emotional response: how did you feel during this incident? Have your feelings changed since the incident?
- Analysis: analysing the reasons why this incident occurred. Consider planning, teaching strategies, classroom management, environment.
- Learning and changed actions: what have you learned from this incident and subsequent reflection? How has experience of this incident changed your approach to teaching and learning?

Figure 10.3 Reflective journal structure

own assumptions or makes you think differently' (McAteer et al., 2010, p.107). It is, therefore, an incident that a beginning teacher views as having a very positive or negative impact on the lesson and pupil learning.

As with lesson reflections, placing a word count on journal entries is not appropriate. The choice of critical incident(s) is entirely a beginning teacher's decision.

Figure 10.3 provides an example of a journal template that can be used with a beginning teacher. This example has been taken from the work of Pavlovich (2007), who created the journal template based on an extensive analysis of literature related to reflection as a method.

It is important to note that a beginning teacher should reflect on two or three critical incidents only for each weekly journal entry, and even if they identify five or six incidents, it is important that they choose what they consider to be the most critical.

Most debates regarding whether journal work should be read centre around grading and assessment. As a mentor, you should not be grading a beginning teacher's journal accounts, but you should be reading with a view to highlighting issues you wish them to explore further.

Having reviewed the weekly journal entries, it is best to sit down and discuss issues emerging with the beginning teacher. Discussion of a weekly journal entry requires tact, ensuring that you ask questions that allow deeper reflection by the beginning teacher but that you avoid being judgemental, particularly when it concerns their feelings. Critical incidents, by their very name, are significant; therefore, it is important that the changed actions/targets emerging from this reflection are a main focus for the following week's teaching. These targets should be identified in lesson plans/resources so that you can track progress/development in these areas. (See case study 10.1 for a sample journal entry.)

Case study 10.1 Sample journal entry

> During my second gymnastics lesson with my Year 9 class, one girl stormed out of the lesson, informing me that she hated physical education. I selected this incident because it had a detrimental impact on my teaching and the pupils' learning.

> I was about 25 minutes into my lesson on vaulting when pupils were exploring various vaulting exercises. I had spoken with this pupil on two occasions about her unwillingness to participate and emphasised the importance of paying close attention to her and others' safety. On the third occasion I raised my voice and told her to swap groups, to which she replied, 'I hate PE' and she stormed out.
>
> I was in complete shock when this incident occurred and my initial reaction was to feel increased anger and frustration at how this pupil had behaved and treated me. I also became frustrated with the other pupils, some of whom enjoyed the drama that this incident created. I tried to progress with the lesson but I could feel that my confidence had taken a battering. I could feel my heart pumping faster and I was beginning to feel stressed. Since the incident my feelings have changed as I now recognise how I could have handled the situation better.
>
> On reflection it was obvious that I did not feel entirely comfortable with teaching vaulting and as a result I was very uptight regarding pupil safety. This impacted my approach with the class and resulted in the employment of a very didactic teaching style. There was also a considerable lack of differentiation in the lesson particularly for the more able pupils who were at times bored with the activities. I could also have managed this pupil in a more positive manner by utilising less intrusive methods as there is no doubt that my overly direct approach made this pupil feel angry and frustrated.
>
> I have learned that I need to know my subject content much better – I need to do more research in this area. I also need to cater for all ability levels by utilising a wider range of teaching strategies that help to deliver appropriate content for all pupils. I must also not let my insecurities impact how I deal with disengaged pupils. It is important not to escalate the situation by dealing with the pupil's behaviour in a much more positive manner.

Peer review

According to Buchanan and Stern (2012, p. 38), 'there are many different forms and approaches to peer review and consequently it is difficult to provide a precise definition of peer review'. Van Zundert et al. (2010), cited in Buchanan and Stern, 2012, p. 270), argued that peer review is 'a process whereby students evaluate, or are evaluated by their peers' (p. 270). Yiend et al. (2012, p. 1) supported the use of peer review by emphasising that 'formative peer observation is considered by many to be a powerful tool for providing feedback to individual teachers, disseminating disciplinary good practice and fostering a local evaluative enhancement culture'.

Beginning teachers can benefit greatly from the process of peer review. As a mentor, you have responsibility for ensuring that this process develops in a supportive and non-threatening manner. You play a supervisory role in establishing the protocols surrounding this process, thus ensuring that both teachers are clear as to how the process works. Peer review may be, for example, between two student teachers in the same or different schools or two newly qualified teachers in the same or different schools. If a beginning teacher is working with a peer in a neighbouring school, it is imperative that you and the mentor in the neighbouring school have an agreed protocol surrounding this process so that the experience for both beginning teachers is equitable. For example, you review a beginning teacher's lesson plan and ensure that targets from the previous lesson are highlighted and that the reviewer receives a copy of the lesson plan. Establishing observation protocols is important: for example, emphasising to the peer reviewer that when acting as an observer they want to portray themselves in the least intrusive manner possible, thus helping the teacher and pupils to relax.

In the post-lesson feedback discussion, it is important that roles are established. Providing effective feedback post-lesson is vital to help beginning teachers engage with the reflective process. Winson and Wood-Griffiths (2010) argued that the majority of teachers prefer feedback immediately after the lesson, but emphasise that from the cohort they sampled, many acknowledged the need for some delay between lesson conclusion and the feedback session. This allows a beginning teacher the opportunity to reflect on their teaching. Further, asking them to write their own evaluation of the lesson prior to the feedback session 'can be advantageous and can create a richer ... conversation' (p. 55). Upon receiving feedback from the peer reviewer, it is important that a beginning teacher records what the reviewer says by adding these points to their initial reflection. The sharing of this information inevitably generates discussion, which should be in a shared and dialogic manner. Portner (2003) argued that the reviewer's role during the feedback session is to probe with open-ended questions phrased in positive rather than negative language (see sample questions in Figure 10.4). Posing open-ended questions allows a beginning teacher to think more deeply about the issues highlighted.

A beginning teacher will have already completed their initial reflection as well as having received the peer reviewer's feedback; therefore, they will have considered some of the questions in Figure 10.4, so the peer reviewer only selects questions that focus on areas that have not previously been highlighted or explored in appropriate depth.

How do you think the lesson went?

Why do you think the lesson progressed in this way?

How can you be sure that those were the contributing factors?

What factors did you consider when planning activity X?

I could see that you amended your lesson plan during (activity X). Why did you do this? Do you think this worked?

What did the pupils learn? How do you know?

How did you assess pupil learning? Were the methods effective? How do you know?

How did you manage transitions between activities? Could this have been more effective?

If you were to teach this lesson again, what might you do differently?

Why?

Overall, what have you learned from teaching and reflecting upon this lesson?

What targets would you set for yourself?

Figure 10.4 Example of questions that can be used to stimulate positive and constructive dialogue between a peer reviewer and a beginning teacher

Video

Welsch and Devlin (2012) argued that one of the most promising practices in developing reflective practice involves the use of video. They believed that video can be used to enhance teachers' reflective skills and provide a medium whereby they can observe and interpret their practice. Danielowich and McCarthy (2013) argued that engagement with this type of reflection can help reduce resistance to regular peer observation and discussion. They continued that such a process increases beginning teachers' self-efficacy, creating the situation where a beginning teacher not only accepts feedback but quite often seeks feedback from peers and uses it to inform their daily practice. According to van Es and Sherin (2002), video allows beginning teachers the opportunity to distance themselves from classroom practice. This view was supported by Greenwalt (2008), who believed that the creation of this more objective distance allows them to deal more effectively with their subjective apprehensions of their world as a teacher. Cummins et al. (2007) argued that the use of video teaching evidence helps create conflicts in their minds, so that they examine their pedagogical decisions. Danielowich and McCarthy (2013, p.266) believed this approach helps them to analyse their 'intentions and actions and triggers change-directed thinking to resolve the conflicts'.

As a mentor, the use of video can be of value in helping to develop a beginning teacher's reflective skills. The use of video allows a beginning teacher an opportunity to replay their lesson and identify particular issues they may not have highlighted under normal post-lesson reflection protocol. Harford et al. (2010, p. 59) argued that video 'captures the immediacy of the classroom, offering detailed and rich data on the teaching and learning process'. It is important to note that the use of video-recorded sessions is also a sensitive issue, and permission to do so must be sought.

The decision to utilise video depends on whether you consider a beginning teacher to be ready to engage with such an open and transparent approach. For many beginning teachers, observing themselves on video can be, at first, a daunting and exposing experience, and to use this method with a beginning teacher who is not developmentally ready for such close scrutiny can be counter-productive. Recognising that reflective skills and abilities develop at different rates is important, and the time will come when you realise that a beginning teacher is developmentally ready and has the confidence to engage with this reflective process.

It is also best to use video-recorded sessions over a period of time rather than one or two isolated lessons throughout the year, as you become much more comfortable in assisting a beginning teacher through the review process, and they are also likely to become a much more willing participant in this process, thus hopefully leading to better outcomes. Leading by example can often be the best strategy in moving this process forward, where you organise for your teaching to be videoed and you complete the same steps (1–6) listed in Task 10.4. Task 10.5 asks you to look at a post-lesson observation feedback session. Such a process allows you to demonstrate that you are continuing to develop as a physical educationalist and also permits a beginning teacher to observe good practice, which they will have the opportunity to review more than once.

Task 10.4   Video-assisted reflection

1.   Arrange for a beginning teacher to have a lesson video recorded.
2.   After the lesson, allow the beginning teacher time to complete their initial reflection before observing the video, and then have them share their reflection with you.
3.   Watch the lesson, with both of you recording what you see (this may not be possible directly after point 2 has been completed, but should be completed as soon as possible).
4.   Share your recorded notes with each other and compare the similarities and differences. Try to find out why the differences occurred. Have the beginning teacher compare their initial reflection with the information they have now recorded.
5.   Observe the video again with a specific observation in mind; for example, how effective was the positioning of the beginning teacher? Were the learning objectives achieved and to what extent? How much time did the pupils spend being active? Otherwise, it is likely that you will focus on an aspect of their teaching that has been previously identified and is a current target for development.

NB: It is good practice for you to video record the post-lesson feedback session so that you have the opportunity to replay and reflect upon the effectiveness of this session (see Task 10.5).

Task 10.5   Mentor reflection: Reflecting on the post-lesson observation feedback session

1.   Observe the post-lesson feedback session.
2.   How effective was your questioning? Did you challenge the beginning teacher appropriately?
3.   How supportive were you?
4.   Did you provide sufficient and appropriate praise?
5.   Did this session provide further stimulus to assist with the beginning teacher's reflection? How?
6.   Upon reflection, how well did you perform during this post-lesson session? Outline your strengths and areas for development.

The unreflective beginning teacher

For the majority of beginning teachers, the methods and strategies outlined above will be of huge benefit in their development as a reflective practitioner. However, as a mentor, at some time you are likely to encounter a beginning teacher who could only be described as 'unreflective'. As Hobbs (2007) pointed out, there are teachers who value reflection and consider it worthwhile but simply do not have the depth of understanding required to reflect on their teaching, whilst there are some who are capable of reflecting but simply dislike it and see it as a waste of time. How might you, therefore, support both types?

Supporting a beginning teacher who values reflection but is incapable of reflecting requires the use of basic strategies that encourage them to think about their teaching. You could arrange a reflective practice workshop whereby you explore reflection in a teaching context and its value. The use of sample reflective accounts can be very useful, whereby you ask a beginning teacher to read a range of reflective journal entries that include some weak reflective accounts and some good reflective accounts. Ask the beginning teacher to grade these accounts in terms of quality, from the most reflective account to the least reflective account. This process exposes the beginning teacher to what reflection looks like and helps them to begin the process of understanding reflection. You could progress to having the beginning teacher complete a reflective exercise using the sample lesson reflection template in Figure 10.2, whereby they reflect on a critical incident outside of teaching. The reason for including this exercise is that sometimes beginning teachers find it easier to reflect on an event/topic of which they have more knowledge or in which they have acquired a greater depth of experience. The next step would be having the beginning teacher reflect on a lesson. These beginning teachers require very close guidance and support, and your ability to extend their thinking with effective questioning during the post-lesson feedback sessions will be crucial to maximising their reflective potential.

Supporting and guiding a beginning teacher who is capable of reflecting but does not value reflection is difficult. As a mentor, you are aiming to convince them of the value of reflective practice and the important role it must play in their development. Perhaps the best approach to begin with is having the beginning teacher observe your teaching, asking them to record their observations, focusing on strengths and areas for development in the lesson. Once the lesson is completed, you should complete your initial reflection, aiming to identify strengths and areas for development with possible reasons as to why certain aspects did not go as well as you had anticipated. Share your reflection with the beginning teacher, and then ask them to share their observations with you. The sharing of this information will generate dialogue, and it is important for you to highlight the areas of your practice you aim to improve in your next lesson as well as to identify how you intend to address these areas by explaining your pedagogical approaches. Leading by example and demonstrating to the beginning teacher that you place value on reflection is crucial if you are to change their attitude. Ensuring that the beginning teacher observes the next lesson is important, as this allows them to witness how you have transferred your reflection to actual practice. Establishing the importance of transferring reflections into actual practice is critical; otherwise, this particular beginning teacher will fail to see the connection and value.

Summary and key points

- Developing beginning teachers' reflective skills is a complex task and, as a mentor, you support them on a daily basis through day-to-day conversations, daily lesson reflections, journal writing, peer review and video-recorded lessons
- It is important for a beginning teacher to record their reflections in a journal or portfolio so that they keep a permanent record. This information is also very beneficial for you as a mentor, as it allows you to track their progress
- Just as a beginning teacher reflects on their teaching, it is important that you reflect on your teaching and your mentoring practice in order to identify strengths and areas for development. Recording your reflections in a journal helps you track your development as a mentor
- Developing clear protocols for pre-lesson, observation and post-lesson feedback is important, as this helps to establish consistency of approach (see Chapters 13 and 15)
- Each beginning teacher develops at a different rate, and as their mentor, it is important you stay alert to when they need to begin using more complex reflective strategies
- When using video, always ensure that permission has been granted from the school and parents
- Some beginning teachers appear 'unreflective' and therefore require greater support and encouragement

Further resources

Gibbs, G. (1988) *Learning by Doing: A Guide to Teaching and Learning Methods*, Oxford: Oxford Further Education Unit.
The reflective learning cycle presented in this book outlines how teachers can link theory and practice through engaging in a cyclical sequence of activities: describing, feeling, evaluating, analysing, concluding and action planning. This model is very useful for those who are new to reflective work, as the clearly defined sections allow beginning teachers to structure their reflective accounts.

Larrivee, B. (2008) 'Development of a tool to assess teachers' level of reflective practice', *Reflective Practice*, 9(3), 341-360.
This article outlines Larrivee's Reflective Assessment Framework. It provides guidance on how to effectively assess a teacher's level of reflection and therefore serves as a vehicle for facilitating the development of practices to mediate higher levels of reflective thinking.

Winson, A. and Wood-Griffiths, S. (2010) 'Chapter 4, Reflective practice: The mentoring conversation', in Wright, T. (2010) *How to be a Brilliant Mentor: Developing Outstanding Teachers*, Abingdon: Routledge.
This chapter offers very clear advice regarding the initial stages of the reflective process and some very useful practical tips and strategies to help develop your approaches to developing reflective skills amongst beginning teachers. It addresses key areas such as motivating a beginning teacher; how to help a beginning teacher set appropriate targets; as well as advice on how to deal with a beginning teacher who does not appear to be engaging with the process.

See also the companion website for this book (www.routledge.com/9781138059658).

You may also find it useful to refer to/use the text books written for student and newly quali-fied physical education teachers with a beginning teacher you are mentoring (see list on Page 4).

11 How to mentor beginning physical education teachers through the lesson planning process

*Jon Binney, Deb Barrett, Simon Green,
Lucy Pocknell and Warren Smart*

Introduction

Good planning is at the heart of successful teaching and learning. The process of writing a lesson plan helps to clarify what the pupils will learn, how they will learn, and how the teacher and the pupils know learning took place. There is no doubt that in the initial stages of learning to teach (usually during initial teacher education), planning is time consuming and may sometimes seem laborious. However, as they gain teaching experience, a beginning teacher develops their ability to reflect when evaluating lessons, which results in the process becoming much more time efficient and easier.

This chapter aims to give you, as a mentor, guidance to assist a beginning teacher (normally a student teacher) to develop their ability to plan lessons. The first part of the chapter looks at why lesson planning is important. The next section details key components of a good lesson plan to enable you to advise and guide a beginning teacher through the intricacies and complexities of effective lesson planning. The chapter then offers insight into student teachers' experiences with lesson planning during school-based placements, and then looks at some issues associated with lesson planning. Finally, the chapter provides guidance about what you can do as a mentor to support a beginning teacher to develop their ability to plan.

Objectives

At the end of the chapter, you should be able to:

- Effectively assist and guide a beginning teacher with lesson planning;
- Understand the detailed information included on a lesson plan and why it is included;
- Understand a range of strategies to help a beginning teacher plan and evaluate their lessons effectively;
- Understand student teachers' experiences with lesson planning and issues associated with lesson planning.

Before progressing any further, reflect on your views about lesson planning in Task 11.1.

Task 11.1   Mentor reflection: Your views about lesson planning

Use the following questions to consider what you feel the value of planning is and what your expectations of a beginning teacher are.

- How has your approach to lesson planning evolved as you have acquired greater experience of teaching?
- What do you perceive to be the potential barriers for a beginning teacher with limited practical experience within certain activities?
- What strategies could you implement to support them with planning lessons in which they have limited prior experience and subject content and pedagogical content knowledge?
- What aspects of planning would you consider essential for a beginning teacher to focus on first? Why?

The next section of the chapter focuses on why a written lesson plan is important.

Why is a written plan important?

There follow a few reasons why we believe a written lesson plan is important.

Lesson planning is an essential learning process: planning is considered by many teachers as one of the most important processes to understand, more so than subject content expertise or charismatic delivery. Good planning underpins a teacher's security in the classroom, continuity of pupil learning and good behaviour. It is important that various complexities of curriculum requirements and logistical 'every day' matters, such as how many bibs, balls or worksheets are needed, are considered.

Lesson planning serves as a mental rehearsal for the lesson: it encourages a teacher to 'visualise themselves in the lesson'. For example, they need to think about how they will explain key skills and ideas, break down tasks into manageable steps and safely organise pupils in the teaching space.

Lesson planning provides evidence of a beginning teacher's knowledge and understanding: it allows the mentor to offer formative guidance on content and pedagogy; for example, aspects of progression, teaching points and assessment for learning (AfL) strategies. Planning can also provide a source of evidence, for example for the award of qualified teacher status, such as against the Teachers' Standards in England (Department for Education (DfE), 2011a) or the requirements of a specific professional body.

Lesson planning provides a beginning teacher with a record/resource to be used on future occasions: keeping good-quality lesson plans, which can be revisited, adapted and updated, is a worthwhile and sensible strategy.

Task 11.2 asks you to consider reasons why lesson planning is important.

The next section considers the components of a good plan.

What are the key components of a good lesson plan?

In order for a beginning teacher to become confident with the lesson planning process, it is essential that the structure and components of a good lesson plan are fully understood. As a mentor, one of your roles is to work with the beginning teacher to understand not only the 'what' and 'how' of lesson planning, but also the 'why'.

This part of the chapter breaks down the components of a lesson plan and explains what is required in each section. A lesson planning template standardises the process. In this chapter, one template is used (see Figures 11.1–11.4) (examples of the completed template are on the companion website for this book (www.routledge.com/9781138059658) (Figures 1a, 2a, 3a,

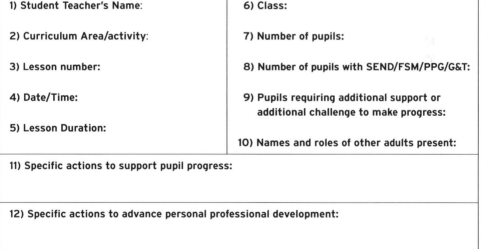

1) Student Teacher's Name:	6) Class:
2) Curriculum Area/activity:	7) Number of pupils:
3) Lesson number:	8) Number of pupils with SEND/FSM/PPG/G&T:
4) Date/Time:	9) Pupils requiring additional support or additional challenge to make progress:
5) Lesson Duration:	10) Names and roles of other adults present:
11) Specific actions to support pupil progress:	
12) Specific actions to advance personal professional development:	

Figure 11.1 Lesson planning template for essential information

4a). The lesson planning template you use may be different, or this one can be adapted according to personal preference. Other examples of lesson plan templates are given on the companion website for this book (www.routledge.com/9781138059658). However, similar information should be included on any template to support a beginning teacher to think through all aspects of the lesson, that is:

- Essential information
- Achievable and realistic learning objectives
- Specific and measurable learning outcomes
- Within the main body of the lesson plan there should be evidence and a description of

  - The actual activity
  - The teaching points associated with this activity
  - The organisation and safety points associated with this activity
  - The lesson plan evaluation and targets/action plan for the forthcoming lesson

(Stidder and Hayes, 2016)

Essential information

Quite a lot of essential information is included at the beginning of most lesson planning templates. If a beginning teacher understands the reasons for including this specific essential information, they can see its importance and relevance. They need to understand that this information is designed to remind them of specific factors they need to consider about the target lesson and target group as well as to create the context, framework and building blocks within which they can plan purposeful and appropriate activities. It also enables them to begin visualising what they want pupils to achieve from the lesson. The rationale for inclusion of essential information in Figure 11.1, which can be explained to a beginning teacher, is:

- *Beginning teacher's name*: establishes ownership for future reference.
- *Curriculum area/activity*: provides clarification of the general lesson content to follow. It allows a beginning teacher to focus on a specific activity appropriate to the current unit of work. This could be a named activity, a set of skills or ways of thinking, or a concept which is the context for learning.
- *Lesson number:* highlights the context of the lesson regarding previous, current and future learning for pupils. It allows what has been taught previously to be considered, and activities based on current understanding and possible future content to be planned.
- *Date and time:* helps with overall time management and organisation. Placing a lesson in a specific place on a specific date and time stimulates consideration of possible issues with facilities or other teaching groups which may happen on specific days or at specific times.
- *Lesson duration:* outlines the time available for content to achieve the desired learning. It allows consideration of how much content is realistic in the actual teaching time available after arrival, changing and lesson transition time.
- *Class:* ensures that planning is suitably tailored for a specific group. Previous lessons' evaluations with this group help inform subsequent planning.

- *Number of pupils*: supports planning and organisation of the equipment, space, grouping and activities. Alternatives should also be considered in case numbers are affected due to attendance, injuries and so on.
- *Number of pupils with special educational needs and disabilities (SEND), having free school meals (FSM), with English as an Additional Language (EAL) or who are gifted and talented (G&T):* encourages identification and investigation of the specific needs of these pupils. This may include seeking advice from colleagues and reference to specific strategies and individual education plans (IEPs). This facilitates the consideration of any adaptations to planning for the educational benefit of pupils within the context of the lesson.
- *Pupils requiring additional support or additional challenge to make progress*: builds on the initial identification of numbers and helps to focus on specific learners within the group. This includes those who struggle to access the learning and those who are of higher ability in this context. Due to safeguarding and confidentiality, specific pupils should not be identified by name on the plan.
- *Names and roles of other adults present*: for example team-teaching colleagues, learning support assistants (LSAs), technicians, parents and any other adults who support pupils' learning. Being clear about the role of these supporting adults allows the opportunities afforded through this support to be considered to aid the planning of learning activities.
- *Specific actions to support pupil progress*: The previous lesson evaluation for the group should be considered, and key information regarding the effectiveness of teaching strategies and potential responses to these findings should be detailed here. This reflective and reflexive practice aids in identifying and employing appropriate actions to aid pupil progress.
- *Specific actions to advance personal professional development*: a beginning teacher should be setting themselves weekly targets in terms of their own development and should look to identify their current focus on their lesson plan. It is important that these actions are specifically related to the current lesson context and are not generalised targets.

Whilst essential information focuses a beginning teacher on the general structure and organisation of the lesson, the next section focuses on the learning that will take place during the lesson.

Achievable and realistic learning objectives (see Figure 11.2)

This part of the lesson planning process requires a beginning teacher to answer the most important and fundamental question: 'What do I want pupils to learn?'

Beginning teachers often struggle to know where to start when writing learning objectives (Illeris, 2007). As a mentor, you can guide them to consider what pupil learning is required in the forthcoming lesson. For example, will the pupils be learning a new skill, or some compositional principles, or the ability to offer corrective feedback?

You can help a beginning teacher to understand that physical education-specific learning objectives can be related to:

- Performing: skill and technique development, gaining confidence and competence and mastery of the body in a broad range of contexts.
- Planning/Creating: the application of ideas, knowledge, skills or the creation of something new. It requires imagination and the ability to problem solve.

- Evaluating/Appreciating: making informed judgements in order to bring about improvements, or critical, interpretive comments.

(Curtner-Smith, 1999)

Many beginning teachers focus their plans on performance and do not plan for pupils planning/creating and/or evaluating/appreciating. Once a beginning teacher knows the type of learning that will be the focus of the lesson, they can select key verbs that can help them form achievable and realistic learning objectives. Table 11.1 provides some examples of verbs for writing objectives.

Table 11.1 Verbs for writing learning objectives in lesson plans

Stage of learning	Performance	Planning and creating	Evaluating and appreciating
Pupils will learn how to	perform	select	identify
	refine	explore	discuss
	adapt	experiment	describe
	develop	create	express
	practice	test	observe
	show	devise	analyse
	demonstrate	plan	interpret
	compete	choreograph	reflect
	rehearse	compose	justify
		improvise	criticise
		apply	comment
		link	explain
		modify	recognise
			coach
			compare
			consolidate

(Nevid, 2013)

		Learning Objectives	Differentiated Learning Outcomes		
		What do I intend the pupils to learn? **(Knowledge, understanding, values attitudes and skills)**	**Working towards... Pupils will...**	**Achieving... Pupils will...**	**Beyond... Pupils will...**
	LO1				
	LO2				
	LO3				

Figure 11.2 Learning objectives and differentiated learning outcomes

Table 11.2 An example of how learning objectives and associated tasks may be written

Learning Objectives	Differentiated Learning Outcomes		
What do I intend the pupils to learn?	Working towards …	Working at …	Working beyond …
'Pupils will learn how to observe and improve a partner's performance and provide appropriate feedback on the use of dynamics'.	Notice obvious areas for improvement when prompted by teacher. Provide short generic suggestions offering limited guidance.	Identify and comment on aspects of the solo phrase where dynamics require greater contrast. Use appropriate words to describe dynamics, such as tension, rigid and smooth. Offer suggestions for improvement in a positive and helpful manner.	Offer a detailed explanation about how to improve. Use a range of ways to help their partner, for example demonstration, physical manipulation and constant verbal feedback.

Having set achievable and realistic learning objectives, as a mentor, you will need to support the beginning teacher in identifying what the learning will look like written in identified learning outcomes.

Specific and measurable learning outcomes (see Figure 11.2)

There must be a clear relationship between a learning objective and the associated outcome as a beginning teacher predicts pupils' responses to the learning objectives. In the outcomes, the knowledge, understanding and skills outlined in the objective should be 'unpicked'. The learning outcomes are a key source of evidence for a beginning teacher to use to demonstrate learning has taken place. Outcomes should generally be *observable* and *measurable*. The aim should be to keep the language positive by focusing on what the pupils can or are attempting to do (Collins-Brown, 2015).

Further, it is important that a beginning teacher plans for the varying levels of achievement within a class. Whilst they should be encouraged to plan for individual pupils in a mixed ability class, it is helpful and, at least initially, more manageable for them to think about the class as progressing and achieving at three different levels: those *working at* (the level that the majority will achieve), those *working towards* (below the level that the majority will achieve) and those *working beyond* (above the level that the majority will achieve). It may be helpful to identify and consider three pupils in the class who typically represent each of the three levels and consider how they might respond differently. It may be helpful for a beginning teacher to write the 'achieving' outcomes first and in detail, as the majority of the class will be working towards this outcome. Having done this, they then need to identify differences between what they expect most to achieve and what those working towards and those working beyond will be doing.

Characteristics that distinguish pupils who are 'working towards' may be:

… with support … with teacher guidance … show moments of … made some attempt to …

Characteristics that distinguish pupils who are 'working beyond' are, for example:

> ... to consistently demonstrate ... shows precision and control when ... original and sophisticated response to ... can analyse in detail ...

You may want to use with a beginning teacher the example in Table 11.2 of how learning objectives and associated tasks may be written.

Task 11.3 is designed to enable you to support a beginning teacher to plan for different levels of achievement in a class they are teaching.

Task 11.3   Differentiating learning outcomes

Ask a beginning teacher the following questions in relation to a lesson they have just planned:

- If learning has taken place and the objective(s) have been met, how will you know this?
- What will you SEE, HEAR or READ from the majority of pupils? (*Working at*)
- How will this look different for those pupils who have not made so much progress? (*Working towards*)
- How will this look different again for those pupils who have progressed further than the majority? (*Working beyond*)

So far, you have worked with the beginning teacher to consider the nature of the class, the learning they want to take place and how this learning will be evidenced. The next part of the chapter explores the information detailed in the main body of the plan.

The main body of the plan

Once the essential information and learning objectives/outcomes have been established, the lesson content can be planned to facilitate pupil progress and achievement within the context of knowledge, skills and understanding to be taught. To enable this process to be as user friendly and effective as possible for a beginning teacher, the main body of the suggested lesson plan is split into five columns, as illustrated in Figure 11.3. You should encourage a beginning teacher to keep things simple and avoid long, overly descriptive sections of text. They should instead aim to summarise, divide, bullet point and illustrate throughout the main body of the plan. This helps to provide a clear overview of what they plan will happen in the lesson and thus avoid the need to 'double plan' by making a simplified version for 'actual' use (Stidder and Hayes 2016).

Time and learning objectives
In this column, a beginning teacher breaks down the overall amount of time available for the lesson and details the amount of time allocated to each phase of the lesson (they may divide their lesson into four or five phases, e.g. introduction, warm up, development, conclusion and plenary). Alongside this information, the learning objective(s) addressed in each phase should be presented. This is a useful reminder for them to ensure that adequate time is allocated to each objective to realistically enable progress and achievement.

Time & Learning Objectives	Pupil learning activities	Teaching points/ strategies / teacher role	Organisation and risk assessment	Assessment for learning strategies
	What learning activities will pupils be engaged in? How will you differentiate these activities so they are achievable for all pupils?	*What teaching points will you provide in order to support and progress the learning of all pupils?*	*What will you need to consider in organising and managing the learning environment effectively?*	*How will you use the outcomes of assessment to inform ongoing teaching and learning? How will you monitor, assess and evaluate the progress of all pupils?*

Figure 11.3 Main body template

Pupil learning activities

In this column, a beginning teacher covers what pupils will be doing during the different phases of the lesson and what strategies they are using to differentiate and support different pupils' needs. They should design the activities with achievement of the learning objectives in mind. Tasks should be clearly outlined, with attention given to how pupils will learn through the planned activities (e.g. copy, practice, watch, listen). Strong lessons often involve a range of teaching and learning strategies that are presented in a package of exciting, engaging and enjoyable activities relevant to the lesson focus. It is good practice for a beginning teacher to plan any questions they may use to focus, challenge and illustrate the learning activity and facilitate pupil progress. They should add these to this column with predicted responses and correct answers, as appropriate.

Teaching points, strategies and teacher role

In this column, a beginning teacher provides the specific information or terminology required to support pupils in achieving the learning objectives. This may be a description of the technique when performing a skill (including safety points), specific terminology to describe a tactic or game strategy, or prompts to guide pupils' exploration in a creative activity. It is important that a beginning teacher researches and provides accurate teaching points so that pupils can make maximum progress against the learning objectives. They should align this information with the appropriate learning activity in the previous column.

Organisation and risk assessment

In this column, a beginning teacher should present a plan showing the organisation and management of the teaching and learning environment. It should address the organisation of groupings, the use of the space available, the transitions between activities, and the distribution and collection of equipment and other resources. Weather implications should be considered if the lesson is due to be taught outside, and logistical considerations regarding sharing of space and routines at the start and finish of the lesson should also be presented. Health and safety issues must be carefully considered here, particularly when moving equipment and teaching higher-risk activities. A beginning teacher may find the use of diagrams particularly helpful in this section.

Assessment for learning strategies

In this column, the AfL strategies a beginning teacher plans to use to gauge pupil progress and achievement against the learning objectives are identified. A beginning teacher should ask themselves how they will assess, monitor and track progress formatively and summatively, and how these assessments will inform their teaching in both the current and subsequent lessons. It is a vital component of the plan in identifying whether pupils are ready to move on or whether further work is still required. They might use a range of strategies during the lesson, such as question and answer, self-assessment, observation and peer assessment episodes. Once identified, these strategies should be stated and described in this column, accompanied by a supportive rationale detailing why they are being used.

Figure 11.3 presents an example of how a lesson plan main body may be completed, and Task 11.4 asks you to jointly plan a lesson with a beginning teacher.

Task 11.4   Working with a beginning teacher to complete a lesson plan proforma

- Using the lesson plan proforma in Appendix A (one you normally use or another one), jointly plan a lesson with a beginning teacher. Discuss the information to be included and reasons why.
- Once planned, team teach the lesson being taught. Agree who will lead specific phases, tasks and so on.
- After the lesson, find time to reflect together on why key aspects of the plan were successful and consider aspects of the lesson that could have been planned differently.

The lesson plan evaluation

Numerous models of reflection and evaluation have been developed since the seminal work of Dewey (1933) and Schön (1987). Many of these models (such as Kolb's (1984) cycle of experiential learning) are cyclical in nature and highlight that the process of developing knowledge, skill and understanding is an ongoing one. Such models facilitate a beginning teacher inferring meaning from their experiences and improving the quality of their subsequent practice (Bolton, 2014). Critical evaluation is a vital component in the process of learning and, therefore, a key element in the development of a beginning teacher's practice (this is covered in greater depth in Chapters 10 and 12). A beginning teacher must, therefore, afford the process of evaluation and reflection the time and importance it deserves if the practice is to be purposeful and effective. They should move beyond a simply passive endeavour such as internal reflection and incorporate constructive dialogue between beginning teacher and mentor. Clutterbuck (2014) recognised that an immediate emotional response to the lesson is likely to occur, which can inhibit the quality of any immediate reflective dialogue. As a mentor, therefore, you should adopt a more non-directive role in any immediate post-lesson discussion/evaluation and focus on listening to allow a beginning teacher an opportunity to express and process these emotions. Bolton (2014) then recommended returning to the evaluation some time after this initial emotional response has been voiced in order to achieve a deeper level of reflection. It should be recognised, however, that postponing the evaluation process for too long can lead to issues with accuracy and effectiveness of reflection. A beginning teacher should formalise the process by writing their findings, feelings and interpretations (using a lesson evaluation template) to allow effective reflexivity to occur (Bolton, 2014).

Initially, some beginning teachers may struggle to see the importance of the formalised evaluation process and look at it as 'additional' work. However, you should insist on a thorough evaluative process, as failure to do so will often result in brief and ineffective evaluations that can compromise beginning teacher development. The evaluation is also an important source of evidence for post-lesson conversations (see Chapter 15) and weekly meetings (see Chapter 16). By making the evaluation process a regular and systematic part of their routine, a beginning teacher is more likely to think deeply and critically, and the process will become a normalised and accepted aspect of their development.

It is important that a beginning teacher reflects upon pupils' progress against the learning objectives of the lesson, the progress they make personally against their professional development targets, and the effectiveness of any specific strategies they plan and execute. Borton (1970, p.95) offered a simple model of how a beginning teacher may approach lesson evaluation in an attempt to reduce negative perceptions and facilitate engagement in it. This model is shown in Figure 11.5.

A beginning teacher should initially consider the 'What?' of their lesson by describing their experience. The second question challenges them to dig deeper and interpret the events in order to develop their understanding and see what can be learned ('So What?'). The final question invites a beginning teacher to reflect on how they can improve in light of the experience. This can be used to assist in their subsequent planning to aid the progress of their pupils and to address areas for their own professional development ('Now What?'). A beginning teacher should then make these evident in the essential information on the subsequent lesson plan. They should repeat this three-step process for each of the three sections of the evaluation: that is, evaluating the extent to which the learning outcomes have been achieved in relation to the learning objectives; evaluating pupil progress, including the impact and outcomes of the actions previously identified; and evaluating their own professional development, including the impact and outcomes of the actions previously identified.

Lesson evaluation	
1) To what extent have the learning outcomes been achieved in relation to the learning objectives?	
LO1	
LO2	
LO3	
2) Reflect upon your professional development including the impact and outcomes of the actions previously identified	
3) Reflect upon pupil progress including the impact and outcomes of the actions previously identified	

Figure 11.4 Lesson evaluation template

Figure 11.5 The What, So What, Now What process
(Source: Borton, 1970, p. 93)

Figure 11.4 provides an example of a lesson evaluation template. As with the plan itself, you may use a different format with a beginning teacher, this one can be adapted, or the evaluation can be presented in any format according to personal preference. Task 11.5 is designed to enable you to support a beginning teacher to evaluate lessons.

Task 11.5   Evaluating a lesson

Following the lesson taught in Task 11.4, ask the beginning teacher to evaluate the lesson using the proforma provided (or one you use in your school), paying particular attention to the progress made by the pupils. Evaluate the lesson yourself, and then meet with them to discuss the lesson and how pupils' learning and beginning teacher progress can be developed in future lessons.

This section has focused on the detail required in a lesson plan (an overview of the lesson plan is given in Figure 11.6 on the companion website). The next section of the chapter focuses on some common issues experienced by student teachers in planning and offers some strategies you could employ to assist them.

Commonly occurring issues with student physical education teachers' lesson planning and suggested mentor strategies

In order for mentors to better assist with their lesson planning, a sample of Year 4 student teachers on their final teaching placement were questioned about commonly occurring issues they associated with lesson planning. The key themes are highlighted in the following subsections.

Time-related issues

The most common occurrence cited was 'spending too much time planning'. Examples included 'staying up beyond 23.00 in the evening planning for the next day due to the depth and detail required'. Some student teachers suggested that they would spend 'well over' an hour planning for an individual lesson. Some highlighted that they would spend this time planning and then would also make separate notes from the plan, which they would then use in the lesson as prompts. This was due to feeling anxious that they might forget elements of the lesson whilst teaching. This highlights a disjointed view of planning, as a lesson plan should be a usable document that a student teacher can follow within the lesson. It should not be a lengthy and onerous task which has a detrimental effect on their teaching.

Mentor strategies
Getting student teachers to be concise and schematic, with diagrams of the practical activities, is beneficial to them, as they can glance at the plan throughout the lesson to ascertain what they should be doing next or what possible questions/prompts they should be using to check learning within the lesson.

Adaptability

For some student teachers, time spent planning was considered to be demotivating, partly because spending significant time in the evenings preparing made them feel fatigued for the next day. Further, having spent significant time planning a lesson made it challenging for them to adapt to changes that often occur within a PE environment or to deviate from the plan in the lesson. If a lesson had to dramatically change due to reasons such as absenteeism, weather, changes in resources available and so on, they felt they had wasted time in the initial planning.

Mentor strategy
It is advisable to collaboratively plan and teach with a student teacher (see earlier and Chapter 8). This allows them to feel able to move away from the plan when required, as this is what they are likely to see from an experienced practitioner.

Knowledge of the class

A regular point made by student teachers was that at the start of any teaching experience, they found it particularly daunting with regard to planning for specific groups, because they did not know the pupils, as they had not taught and developed a rapport with them, even though they used the information available to them, for example school information management system (SIMS) data, to inform their planning. For example, they either planned lessons that were pitched at too high a level or vice versa, making the lesson delivery challenging – particularly if they were anxious about deviating from their plans.

Mentor strategy

Early on in the relationship, it is particularly important for a student teacher to collaboratively plan with the mentor and other department members to confidently ascertain the level at which to pitch lessons. In this process, they should be supported by analysing SIMS data to contribute to their planning.

Developing experience

Many student teachers felt that, over time, they became more relaxed with their planning and became more concise in including the key detail required. They became more comfortable with moving away from the plan if the lesson required this, partly because the time investment was lower. Further, being more concise allowed them to adapt more, for example to a change in the environment. It also allowed them to adapt to the needs of the group with regard to differentiation. However, they could do this because they understood the importance of detail earlier on, for example with regard to including detailed questions and possible answers from pupils as prompts. Therefore, with more experience, this would occur organically, as they had laid the groundwork on planning earlier.

Mentor strategy

When student teachers are able to implement consistently the detail within plans that meets the requirements they are working within, this can be the point at which they can experiment with different approaches to planning that are more schematic and concise.

Other issues with lesson planning

Other issues with lesson planning include:

Failure to accurately predict the learning outcomes: lesson planning is about being able to predict what learning will look like for all pupils. However, this can be problematic, particularly if a student teacher lacks content knowledge. Weak content knowledge can impact on the ability to plan tasks which are progressive and developmental to enable the predicted learning outcomes to be achieved (Chapter 8 looks at supporting beginning teachers to develop content knowledge).

Writing poor and overly descriptive evaluations: it is important to evaluate teaching for two distinct reasons: first, to improve pupil learning and second, to improve a teacher's practice. Student teachers need to learn how to reflect on their experiences in order to plan how they might improve; experience alone is not enough – it is the reflection on and learning from that experience that is important. If the evaluation is to be of any value to the planning process, it needs to go beyond a superficial description of the lesson. Student teachers should be encouraged to admit their mistakes honestly. Understanding why things might not have gone as planned is important to support future planning

Quality of formative feedback from mentors: broad and overly descriptive feedback from the mentor serves merely as a 'running commentary', as opposed to feedback that is specific and targeted towards a student teacher's current development needs. In attempting to accelerate a student teacher's professional practice, mentors can be quick to offer 'top tips' ... or an 'I would have done it this way' approach to their feedback, as opposed to encouraging the student teacher to think and reflect autonomously.

Overemphasis on description: often a plan includes elaborate description, for example of an activity. This is impossible to glance at during the lesson, and hence, the plan becomes unworkable in the teaching environment. The plan must be a usable document. Early on, a mentor can assist a student teacher in making activities more visual so they can clearly be understood and used within a lesson.

Lack of specifics within objectives and outcomes: the language of objectives and outcomes needs to be clear. It is important for the student teacher to know what differentiated outcomes looks like; for example what those achieving, working towards and working above should achieve, what a skill should look like, or what the pupils should say or do to show understanding. Mentors should always look at plans prior to the lesson and question a student teacher on their objectives and outcomes. For example, do they reflect to an observer what the skill would look like? Could they observe the group and identify those pupils achieving, those working towards and those working beyond from what is suggested in the outcomes?

Failure to link outcomes to teaching points: from the previous point, do student teachers link outcomes to teaching points within the lesson? Are the AfL strategies in the planning, and does the subsequent feedback being given in the lesson relate to the learning objectives and outcomes? Mentors should check that the outcomes correlate with the teaching points in the plan whilst further checking that these are implemented within the lesson.

Failure to clearly address differentiation within the lesson plan: by not using previous assessment information, student teachers limit their ability to use differentiation within their planning and subsequent lessons. It is essential that they use assessment data to consider the differing levels and specific needs of pupils. The mentor can show the student teacher how to use SIMS data to inform planning, and provide support. In the lesson, the mentor can observe whether the student teacher steps back and observes. Do they create a learning environment that allows them to observe and circulate in order to make adjustments (are they thinking on their feet?)? How often do they take a step back and observe their pupils? The mentor can then question and support the student teacher in developing pupil-centred strategies and activities which enable them to make changes to suit pupils' needs, thus leading to greater pupil progress. Now complete Task 11.6.

Task 11.6   Issues in lesson planning

As part of a weekly meeting, encourage a student teacher to think of two contrasting lessons, one negative and one positive. Can they articulate which of the commonly occurring planning issues were present within the two lessons?

The next section identifies some strategies you can employ as the mentor to support a student teacher in developing their ability to plan.

How a mentor can assist with good planning

Listed in this section are some tried and tested strategies used by mentors to support student teachers during their early experiences of lesson planning. Whilst this is not to be seen as a definitive list, it offers some suggestions with guidance on how student teachers can be best supported with planning.

Micro planning

This involves a student teacher planning specific parts of a lesson, supported and monitored by the mentor (based on their current development needs); for example, the warm up, devising a reciprocal sheet, a mini plenary and so on. This builds a student teacher's confidence in the early stages, as planning for a whole lesson can be a daunting prospect (Clutterbuck, 2014). In this process, the mentor is able to offer specific and targeted feedback, which is then fed forward into subsequent planning.

Establishing confidence

In addition to micro planning, an effective strategy is for mentors to initially request that student teachers plan lessons in areas in which they already have greater content knowledge and expertise (Bolton, 2014). This strategy serves two purposes. First, strong content knowledge reduces the need for a student teacher to research the activity and means they can often articulate differentiated learning outcomes with greater confidence. Second, the mentor can focus explicitly on supporting a student teacher with developing their underpinning pedagogy. This is often realised through planning tasks that demonstrate clear progression and unpick and differentiate learning outcomes.

Collaborative planning

Experienced mentors can make planning and teaching look very easy. Whilst this is aspirational for a student teacher, they gain most insight when they are able to co-plan with the mentor. A critical component of collaborative planning is when the mentor and student teacher actively engage in a discussion about effective planning with a focus on pupil progress. This should explicitly relate to what pupils should have learned by the end of the lesson. This strategy also permits the mentor to empathise with the student teacher's current concerns and issues with the planning process (Grout and Long, 2009). Co-planning seems to typically happen only in the initial stages of the time a student teacher spends with a mentor (e.g. at the start of a teaching placement). However, it is most beneficial when it is ongoing, as the demands and expectations of the lesson plan become increasingly pupil centred.

Focused feedback/shared responsibility across the department

In the early stages of a student teacher's professional development, there is a tendency to feed back on all aspects of the lesson plan; to try to improve everything at once. For some student teachers, this quantity of feedback can be both overwhelming and unmanageable. Best practice would suggest that feedback that is specific and is targeted on the most important aspects for development is of far more value, as it highlights key issues for the student teacher to focus on (Illeris, 2007).

Targeted feedback might focus explicitly on:

- organisation of resources (e.g. video, reciprocal sheets, gym mats)
- planned opportunities to give praise and constructive feedback
- planning clear and concise teaching points
- clear progression and layering of tasks that relate to the learning outcomes

Feedback needs to acknowledge where a student teacher is at in terms of their professional development. For example, student teachers often need support in the early stages with organisation of equipment, space, groupings, resources and so on, but over time, and as these things become more embedded, they need support with planning for differentiation and inclusion, which would be beyond their capacity in the early phase of learning to teach. Targeted feedback that encourages deeper thinking and reflection helps student teachers develop pedagogy, and, as a consequence, learning is often accelerated (see Chapter 10 on reflection). Now complete Task 11.7.

Task 11.7   Mentor reflection: Supporting a student teacher to write lesson plans

Having read this chapter, do you have any thoughts about how your support and expectations of the student teacher's lesson planning may evolve over time? How might your expectations differ for a student teacher on their second placement as opposed to their first, or even a newly qualified teacher? What different types of support might a student teacher require from you on their second placement?

Summary and key points

- Planning is one of the most important aspects of successful teaching and learning. A student teacher with a clear plan is focused on what needs to be done, how it will be done and when it will be done in order for the desired learning to occur.
- For many student teachers, lesson planning can appear on the surface to be a laborious and time-consuming process, which keeps them away from what they truly love doing; standing in front of a class and delivering high-quality lessons.
- As a mentor, you should aim to instil or encourage a new perspective and approach to lesson planning. The process of creating and selecting what the pupils will learn and participate in should be fun and where the enjoyment begins. Merely getting them to reproduce a mentor's previous lessons, or heavily prescribed activities from departmental units of work, will only add to a student teacher's lethargy towards lesson planning. If they have direct ownership of the lesson content, are given the freedom and flexibility and are encouraged to create, refine, experiment and play with lesson content, then the planning process suddenly becomes exciting and rewarding, creating a safe environment where content and activity can be explored, selected and refined, leading them towards a secure and confident position in relation to planning their lessons. Allowing a student teacher to create and design innovative, creative and outstanding lesson content should be a characteristic of an outstanding mentor.

Further resources

Arthur, J. and Capel, S. (2015) 'How planning and evaluation support effective learning and teaching', in S. Capel and M. Whitehead (eds.) *Learning to Teach Physical Education in the Secondary School: A Companion to School Experience*, 4th edn, London: Routledge. This book combines underpinning theory and knowledge with suggestions for practical application to support student physical education teachers in learning to teach. This particular chapter covers lesson planning.

Hayes, S. and Stidder, G. (eds.) *The Really Useful Physical Education Book*, 2nd edn, London: Routledge.
This book offers support, guidance and practical ideas for effective, innovative and imaginative physical education lessons. It is especially useful for student physical education teachers. With an emphasis on inclusive physical education, it highlights ways in which schools can re-design the curriculum to ensure maximum enjoyment for all pupils. Key topics covered include lesson planning, organisation and management.

See also the companion website for this book (www.routledge.com/9781138059658).

You may also find it useful to refer to/use the text books written for student and newly qualified physical education teachers with a beginning teacher you are mentoring (see list on Page 4).

12 Supporting beginning physical education teachers to deliver and evaluate their lessons

Sophy Bassett, Mark Bowler and Angela Newton

Introduction

This chapter is designed to help you support a beginning physical education teacher to teach and evaluate the success of the lessons they have planned to promote pupil learning and development. Chapter 11 looks at supporting a beginning physical education teacher to plan a well-structured lesson.

The chapter starts by looking at important teacher personal characteristics (the 6 Cs), which assist a beginning teacher in maintaining a positive learning environment that enables all pupils to achieve their potential. It then looks at a range of basic teaching skills, including self-presentation, organisation and safety, movement and positioning, use of voice and instructions, use of praise and use of demonstration, which you need to support a beginning teacher to develop. The third section of the chapter focuses on enabling you to support a beginning teacher to develop teaching approaches further once they have mastered the basics. In particular, we discuss the important role that differentiation, teaching strategies and assessment *for* learning play in supporting pupil learning, and how you might support a beginning teacher's practice in these areas. The final section provides some strategies and ideas to help you scaffold a beginning teacher's evaluation of lessons they have taught.

It is worth noting that the approaches included in this chapter can be applied to various developmental stages of teaching. For instance, a beginning teacher may be teaching collaboratively (team teaching) or independently, parts of lessons, whole lessons or a series of lessons. As a result, your role may change according to the stage of a beginning teacher's development (see examples in Chapters 1 and 4), and you should use your judgement and knowledge of a beginning teacher to select the most appropriate approaches discussed in this chapter.

Objectives

At the end of this chapter, you should be able to:

- Support a beginning teacher in developing characteristic behaviours that underpin effective teaching;
- Support a beginning teacher to develop basic teaching skills in order to teach well-structured and progressive lessons;

- Support a beginning teacher to develop their teaching approaches further once they have mastered the basics, to enable them to teach lessons to support pupil progress;
- Support a beginning teacher in evaluation of their teaching and pupils' learning.

Before proceeding, in Task 12.1 you are asked to reflect on teaching and evaluation of lessons.

Task 12.1   Mentor reflection: Teaching and evaluation of lessons

What does a good physical education lesson look like?

How do you know it is good? What would you expect to see in a good physical education lesson? What would you not expect to see?

What would you expect of a beginning teacher in terms of their behaviour, skills and teaching approaches in a good physical education lesson?

How could you support a beginning teacher to recognise a good lesson as opposed to an average lesson?

How do you work with a beginning teacher to think about teaching the lessons they have planned to promote pupil learning?

Return to these questions as you support a beginning teacher in developing their ability to teach high-quality lessons to enhance pupil learning.

Stages of development as a teacher

Leask and Moorehouse (2005) identified three phases of beginning teacher development, connected to their main concerns during each phase. In the first phase, *self-concern*, the teacher is focused on self-presentation and group management, pupil compliance and the material planned. The second phase is *class-concern*, where there is a shift to concerns about pupils but on a group needs basis. The final phase is *individual-concern*, where each pupil's individual progress is the key feature. As a mentor, you should look to develop an awareness of each phase, and more specifically, the phase that a beginning teacher has reached. This will impact their focus and their ability to, plan, teach and evaluate a lesson (and, hence, the support you provide, including the questions you ask in pre- and post-lesson discussions (see Chapter 14)). Indeed, your role may change according to the stage of a beginning teacher's development (see example in Chapter 4).

Characteristic behaviours of effective teachers

There has been much written on the characteristic behaviours of effective teachers across a range of subjects. They have variously been referred to as attributes (Lowe and Redfern, 2016), qualities (Stronge, 2007) or styles (Lawrence, 2014). Physical education is different from other curriculum subjects; pupils are asked to perform difficult, challenging and sometimes potentially dangerous activities in surroundings in which they may not feel comfortable, with others with whom they would not necessarily choose to work. Consequently, as a mentor working with a beginning teacher, you should support them to understand their role as an ambassador, to sell the subject to their pupils. To do this effectively, you need to support them in developing characteristic behaviours to enable a positive and productive classroom climate. As a starting point, we have selected six characteristic behaviours (the 6 Cs):

Calmness: Pupils often reflect emotions, so if the teacher is calm, the class are more likely to be calm. The teacher avoids displaying strong emotions through voice and behaviours.

Clarity: The teacher sets high expectations, giving information or instructions which are concise and focused on the desired outcome. This is likely to result in a more immediate, desirable behavioural response.

Consistency: The teacher knows and adheres to established routines and policies to maintain expectations for all pupils. They make prompt and decisive interventions to address pupil responses which do not meet these expectations. They use repeatable teacher behaviours that the pupils recognise and trust.

Confidence: The teacher is confident and knowledgeable in the content, pedagogy, structure and intentions of lessons. They use positioning, movement and demonstration to show this confidence. They have a presence in other contexts at school. They are not overtly confident to the point of arrogance.

Commitment: The teacher is dedicated to high-quality teaching for learning and pupil progression. They seek professional development opportunities, recognise the school as a community and engage fully in all aspects of school life.

Care: The teacher has a strong desire to teach high-quality lessons for high-quality learning. They recognise pupils as individuals and are sensitive to pupils' needs and aspirations. They show interest and support for pupils in school and out-of-school contexts.

Task 12.2 focuses on identifying and supporting a beginning teacher to improve these characteristic behaviours.

Task 12.2   Identifying and improving characteristic behaviours

1) Review the characteristic behaviours provided in the 6 Cs and reflect on whether you believe they are a comprehensive representation of the characteristics of an effective teacher. If not, what would you add?

2) Discuss the importance of these characteristic behaviours (and any you have added) with a beginning teacher you are mentoring (expectations identified by the Professional Statutory or Regulatory Body (PSRB) to which a beginning teacher is working may be a useful guide to help focus discussion on what the characteristic behaviours mean for teaching lessons).

3) Discuss which characteristic behaviours are current strengths and those which require further development.

4) Support a beginning teacher to create an action plan for improving any characteristic behaviours identified as areas for development, including what support you can give for their development.

5) For each characteristic behaviour, discuss situations in which it might be demonstrated. Identify a range of situations in which you and a beginning teacher can evidence how these have been demonstrated, as well as any areas for further development.

Basic teaching skills

There are many suggestions as to the types of skills which make teaching effective (Kyriacou, 2014; Capel, 2015; Haydn-Davies, 2011; Hay McBer, 2000) to enable pupils to learn. A good starting point with a beginning teacher is to support them to develop basic teaching skills (see Task 12.3 and Figure 12.1) so that they can be effective in teaching lessons. At this stage, a beginning teacher is focusing more on their own teaching competence than on pupils' learning when they are teaching. Early mentor observations of a beginning teacher might focus on one or more of the basic skills. Similarly, if any of the skills are identified as requiring development, a beginning teacher could be set a task to observe an experienced physical education teacher teaching. The focus of their observation might be one or more of the basic skills. Other strategies to support a beginning teacher could include a focused observation of them using one or more basic teaching skills, or video recording their teaching and collaboratively evaluating their effectiveness. Once these basic skills are established, a beginning teacher can be supported to adapt them to suit different contexts.

Task 12.3 focuses on supporting a beginning teacher to develop their basic teaching skills.

Task 12.3 Supporting a beginning teacher to develop basic teaching skills

Use Figure 12.1 with a beginning teacher to identify and reflect on their basic teaching skills.

1)   Consider the list of basic teaching skills. Do you agree with the list? Are there any other skills you consider are basic for effective teaching? Add any further examples under each basic teaching skill or under another sub-heading.
2)   Encourage the beginning teacher to highlight/underline/add current strengths in the left column.
3)   Collaboratively identify targets for development (with possible actions) in the right column.
4)   Identify a range of opportunities for the beginning teacher to develop skills highlighted as areas for development.
5)   Provide opportunities for a beginning teacher to observe good practice and identify how these basic teaching skills are used by an effective teacher.
6)   Collaboratively with the beginning teacher, reflect on the achievement of specific basic teaching skills.

Note: it is important for a beginning teacher not to try to develop a number of skills at the same time; rather, help them to identify the most important and concentrate on developing that before identifying another skill to develop.

Skill (strengths highlighted/underlined/added)	Targets and actions to be agreed in mentoring conversation
Self-presentation, e.g.	Targets for development and associated actions for completion:
Dress appropriately; maintain a relaxed stance; move with confidence around the space; use open hand and arm gestures when talking; maintain good posture; show facial expressions; use gestures as signals for gaining attention; maintain eye contact with individuals or scan/monitor the whole class (see Whitehouse et al. (2015) for further information) *Other:*	
Organisation and Safety, e.g.	Targets for development and associated actions for completion:
Develop organisational routines; give explicit instructions to control all activities and ensure work is done properly; have an awareness of working space and risk assessment to ensure that it is safe and fit for purpose; teach pupils how to set up, use and store equipment safely; consider pairings and groups; have smooth number transitions, e.g. 2s ⇒ 4s; 3s ⇒6s; give non-performers a set task; plan use of time to ensure efficient, safe transitions (see Lawrence and Whitehead (2015) and Chappell (2015) for further information) *Other:*	
Movement and Positioning, e.g.	Targets for development and associated actions for completion:
Stand where the whole class can see/hear you and you can see them during equipment collection, teaching and monitoring the class; be aware of external distractions such as sun, wind, slope, proximity of other groups; move around the whole teaching space and teach from different places; when working with one group doing group work, position where the rest of the class can also be monitored (see Killingbeck and Whitehead (2015) for further information) *Other:*	
Giving Instructions and Use of Voice, e.g.	Targets for development and associated actions for completion:
Use a clear, concise, audible tone, pitch and modulation which are enthusiastic and varied: a quiet voice for focus and intrigue, a loud voice for attention and instruction in large spaces; never shout. Keep instructions brief so pupils are not overloaded with information (see Zwozdiak-Myers (2015a) for further information) *Other:*	

Figure 12.1 Six basic teaching skills and how they might be developed

Skill (strengths highlighted/underlined/added)	Targets and actions to be agreed in mentoring conversation
Use of Praise, e.g.	Targets for development and associated actions for completion:
Say what you mean, and mean what you say; sound convincing, with well-chosen words appropriate to the level of effort/achievement, accompanied with positive facial expressions and body language; avoid disingenuous comments; be specific with what is being praised; avoid over-praise as it becomes meaningless; make sure praise is earned (see Whitehouse et al. (2015) for further information) *Other:*	
Use of Demonstration, e.g.	Targets for development and associated actions for completion:
Decide which method of demonstration to use (teacher, pupil or resource) and the purpose of the demonstration, e.g. to organise a task; show a skill; apply a tactic or sequence; interact safely with equipment; set standards or a challenge; evaluate performance; recognise good work. Decide where the demonstration is to take place. It is important to position observers and remind them of the focus of the observation. Other considerations: The speed of the demonstration can be slowed down to allow observation or performed at full speed to emphasise quality in context. Movement can be modelled by using strategies such as freeze frame, reset or repeat (see Zwozdiak-Myers (2015a) for further information) *Other:*	

Figure 12.1 (Cont.)

Whilst focusing on basic skills in teaching lessons, a beginning teacher is focusing on the development of their own competence rather than on pupils' learning. It is important that once they have mastered basic teaching skills, you support them to develop further, con-centrating on teaching approaches which enhance pupil learning; that is, they change from teacher-focus to pupil-focus.

Supporting a beginning teacher to develop teaching approaches to support pupil progress

Teaching approaches that support pupil progress include differentiating work to include all pupils in the lesson, developing teaching strategies to achieve intended learning outcomes, assessment for learning, grouping strategies, using information and communications technology (ICT) effectively, and using pedagogical models, amongst others. This section considers how you can support a beginning teacher to develop the first three of these important approaches. The approaches you use to support a beginning teacher to develop these three areas can then be applied to supporting a beginning teacher to develop in other teaching approaches to support pupil progress.

Differentiation

As a beginning teacher moves from self-concerns to class-concerns and ultimately individual-concerns, it is important to help them to identify approaches that will help all pupils to improve. The most important of these is to differentiate their teaching. Differentiation can be achieved in a number of ways, but for a beginning teacher, a good method is to focus on the STEP (space, task, equipment, people) process (Training and Development Agency for Schools (TDA) 2009). You can use Task 12.4 and Figure 12.2 to support a beginning teacher to apply and reflect on the STEP process to develop their ability to differentiate.

Task 12.4 Supporting a beginning teacher to apply the STEP process

1) Ask a beginning teacher to read and reflect on Figure 12.2 in relation to their experiences to date.
2) Support them to record instances from practice (their own or observed) of the STEP process in action.
3) Ask the beginning teacher to identify additions to the STEP process (left hand column) (in collaboration with you and other colleagues).
4) Ask the beginning teacher to identify in their lesson plans examples of each of the STEP processes that will be used in a series of lessons they are going to teach. Following lessons (some of which you may have been able to observe), discuss the effectiveness of each STEP process in promoting learning for all pupils.

Process to be used	Examples from practice
Space (where is the activity happening?) Smaller/larger activity areas Smaller/larger or higher/lower targets/goals Participants further apart/closer together *Other:*	
Task (what are the participants doing and how can this be varied?) Simplify or make harder Give pupils different roles in the task Vary rules for some pupils *Other:*	
Equipment (what is being used?) Vary size of implement/equipment used Vary the type of equipment, e.g. ball, by size/ weight/texture *Other:*	
People (what grouping will be used?) Mixed or same ability Size of groups/individual work Overloads in games play Buddy systems *Other:*	

Figure 12.2 Differentiation using the STEP process

Teaching strategies

Another approach to teaching to enable pupils to achieve appropriate intended learning outcomes which you can support a beginning teacher to develop is the use of a range of teaching strategies (Mosston and Ashworth call them teaching styles). You can refer the beginning teacher to Blair with Whitehead (2015) for more information about teaching strategies. A good starting point is Mosston and Ashworth's (2008) eleven landmark teaching 'styles' that can be readily applied to physical education lessons.

Task 12.5 focuses on supporting a beginning teacher to use a range of teaching strategies to enable pupils to achieve intended learning outcomes.

Task 12.5   Designing teaching strategies for pupils to achieve intended learning outcomes

1) Discuss with a beginning teacher their understanding of the importance of teaching strategies to support pupil learning. Mosston and Ashworth's (2008) Spectrum can be used to develop their knowledge and understanding if needed.
2) Challenge the beginning teacher to plan lessons focusing on the use of a variety of teaching strategies. Review the lesson plan(s) prior to teaching, asking the beginning teacher to justify their choice of strategy/ies in relation to the achievement of the intended learning outcome(s).
3) Observe the lesson(s) if you can.
4) Following the lesson(s), discuss the effectiveness of the strategy/ies in relation to the achievement of the intended learning outcome(s) and what they can do to develop the effectiveness of the strategies.
5) Subsequent discussions with the beginning teacher could highlight their confidence in using different strategies and the suitability of specific strategies for different groups, levels of attainment and activities/tasks.

Chapter 10 is concerned with supporting beginning teachers to plan good lessons and may be of use to you in supporting them to develop their range of teaching strategies.

Assessment (assessment for learning)

As a mentor, you will know that assessment is not only an essential part of effective teaching and pupil learning, but is also a complex process to get right. Supporting a beginning teacher to use assessment effectively to evaluate not only the progress of pupils they are teaching, but also the effectiveness of their teaching, is a challenging task for you as their mentor and may require a different focus or level of support at different stages of development. For example, a starting point might be to support a beginning teacher to develop formative assessment (assessment *for* learning) strategies to help all pupils to learn and make progress. Once a range of assessment *for* learning strategies is mastered, your role might evolve to supporting the beginning teacher to assess summatively (assessment *of* learning) for the purposes of grading, diagnosis or formal reporting.

Spackman (2002) identified five assessment *for* learning strategies used in physical education: shared intended learning outcomes; questioning; feedback; peer assessment; and self-assessment. Information on the use of assessment *for* and *of* learning to support a beginning teacher to develop each of these approaches is in Newton and Bowler (2015) and Bowler et al. (2014) and on the companion website for this book (www.routledge.com/9781138059658).

Task 12.6 focuses on assessment and planning for action to support a beginning teacher to make productive use of assessment.

Task 12.6   Establishing an awareness of assessment and planning for action

During an early meeting with a beginning teacher, discuss their current level of understanding of assessment *for* learning processes and the approaches to assessment they have used in their teaching up to this point. Review this against the assessment terminology word cloud included in Figure 12.3 in order to prioritise some short and longer term targets for development of their ability to use assessment effectively.

Identify actions you might take to support the beginning teacher to develop their understanding and practice. These might include, for example, a beginning teacher observing you or another teacher to develop their understanding of assessment, employing a particular approach to assessment with a class supported by you observing and/or asking pupils for their feedback on a particular approach to assessment in helping them to progress.

Task 12.7 focuses on supporting a beginning teacher to develop productive assessment *for* learning practices.

Task 12.7   Developing productive assessment *for* learning practices

Work with a beginning teacher to reflect on the assessment *for* learning strategies identified by Spackman (2002) (shared intended learning outcomes, questioning, feedback, peer assessment and self-assessment).

1) Consider with the beginning teacher whether/how they currently use each of these strategies and, for each one, identify how its use could be modified or varied for more productive use. If a strategy/ies are not used, how could they be used? Consider activities you could undertake with the beginning teacher to develop their ability to use each of these strategies.

2) Discuss with the beginning teacher ways in which pupil learning and development could be more effectively evidenced within a single lesson, and across several lessons, using each of the assessment *for* learning strategies and any other strategies you can identify.

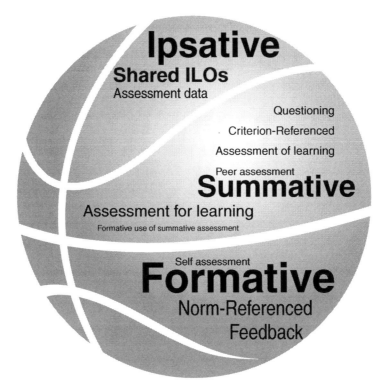

Figure 12.3 Assessment terminology word cloud

Task 12.8 focuses on one of these strategies: supporting a beginning teacher to provide effective feedback to pupils.

Task 12.8   Improving teacher feedback

To support a beginning teacher's effective use of feedback:

1) Video record them teaching a section(s) of a lesson where feedback will be given.
2) After the lesson, review the video material together, identifying good practice and areas for development in relation to effective feedback. A key area for discussion should be the crucial importance of different types of feedback for pupil motivation (the beginning teacher can be referred to Zwozdiak-Myers (2015a and b) for further information on feedback).
3) Help the beginning teacher to create an action plan, identifying areas for development in relation to their ability to give effective feedback.
4) Repeat the process, ensuring that the beginning teacher leads the review of the video footage, identifying their own strengths and areas for development.

You can follow similar processes to support a beginning teacher to develop their ability to use assessment *of* learning effectively. This can be linked to lesson evaluation.

Evaluation of lessons

Effective evaluation of lessons is an essential skill for any teacher. As a mentor, you support a beginning teacher to evaluate as they progress towards becoming a reflective practitioner (see Chapter 10 for further information). The next section provides ideas of how to scaffold a beginning teacher's progress in evaluating their lessons through focused questions.

Lesson evaluation at different stages

In the early stages of their development, a beginning teacher may be asked to take on responsibility for short phases of a lesson (episodes), especially if they are in initial teacher education. When evaluating these episodes (as well as evaluating early whole lesson experiences), a beginning teacher is likely to focus on self-presentation and class management; for example whether pupils responded quickly to teacher instructions or how quickly equipment was collected and placed in position. In discussing their evaluations, your questions should therefore focus on the beginning teacher's behaviours identified in the personal characteristics and basic teaching skills mentioned earlier in the chapter.

In order to help them progress into the class-concern phase of teacher development and then into the individual-concern phase, it is necessary to ask more pupil-focused (rather than teacher-focused) questions. Figure 12.4 identifies examples of questions that can be included in a lesson evaluation proforma (and which you can then discuss in the post-lesson discussion (see Chapter 15)). Further questions are in Figure 17.7 on the companion website for this book (www.routledge.com/9781138059658). Reflection by the beginning teacher on these questions can contribute to the summative assessment of pupils (assessment *of* learning).

Questions that can be used to move a beginning teacher from phase one (self-concern) to phase two (class-concern).
• To what extent did the class achieve the intended learning outcomes?
• What evidence do you have that the class achieved the intended learning outcomes?
• What points must you consider when planning your next episode with this class?

Questions that can be asked to move a beginning teacher from phase two (class-concern) to phase three (individual-concern).
• Did all pupils achieve the intended learning outcomes? (If yes, was the work too easy?)
• What prevented some pupils from meeting the intended learning outcomes? (Were the tasks suitable? Was the strategy the right one?)
• How can you find more information about the pupils to help their progress?
• What points must you consider when planning your next lesson?

Note: In chapter 10 three questions are identified that could be used as suitable alternatives to these questions.

Figure 12.4 Examples of questions to support beginning teachers' evaluation of lessons

Use of data to support planning, teaching and evaluation

In order to support a beginning teacher in finding information about pupils to help their progress, you need to ensure that they have access to relevant school data, such as data on pupils with specific needs or varying levels of achievement, particularly pupils with English as an Additional Language (EAL) or those from underachieving groups. Both benchmarking data and data concerning value added should be considered.

As the mentor, and in relation to the stage of development of the beginning teacher, you may need to work collaboratively to highlight specific considerations and appropriate curricular targets for these pupils. Subsequent planning (and evaluation) can then make reference to appropriate support and differentiated activities used in a lesson.

Task 12.9 considers the use of data to plan for individual needs.

Task 12.9   Using data to plan for individual needs

Ask a beginning teacher to select three pupils from a new class who require some additional support. (These might be pupils with EAL, Special Educational Needs and Disabilities (SEND), those not meeting expectations or achieving beyond expectation, or who need to be challenged individually). Provide appropriate access to pupil data to support the process. Review the individual needs of these pupils and collaboratively plan with the beginning teacher differentiated activities to meet the pupils' needs in the first lesson. Repeat the process for the following lesson after a review of the success of the activities planned. Repeat as necessary and withdraw support gradually once a beginning teacher is confident with the process.

As well as assessing pupils in an individual lesson, a beginning teacher needs to assess pupils against the unit objectives (see the companion website for this book (www.routledge.com/9781138059658) for further information).

Task 12.10 asks you to look at supporting a beginning teacher to assess unit objectives.

Task 12.10   Assessing unit objectives

1) Ask a beginning teacher with whom you are working to select a unit of work they are teaching. Challenge them to identify three unit objectives and create a TAB criteria grid as shown in Figure12.5 (on the companion website for this book (www. routledge.com/9781138059658).
2) Discuss the suitability of their criteria for the age and development of the pupils.
3) Ask the beginning teacher to plan opportunities for pupils to engage with and be assessed against the criteria. This should include encouraging pupils to reflect on what they have achieved, what they need to improve on and how they will

achieve this. Alongside this, the beginning teacher should be making their own judgements to corroborate the pupils' decisions.

4) At the end of the unit, discuss with the beginning teacher the merits and potential issues with involving pupils in the assessment process.

Now complete Task 12.11.

Task 12.11 Mentor reflection: Teaching and evaluating lessons

Having read this chapter, reflect on whether you have changed, or can change, the way you work with a beginning teacher to support them to better teach and evaluate their lessons to promote pupil learning.

What are your strengths and areas for development in providing this support? How can you improve your areas for development?

Summary and key points

This chapter has identified ways to support a beginning teacher in teaching lessons they have planned by developing characteristic behaviours that underpin a positive learning environment; embedding basic teaching skills in order to teach well-structured lessons; developing further teaching approaches, such as differentiation, teaching strategies and assessment for learning, to enable them to teach lessons to support pupil progress; and helping them to evaluate these lessons effectively.

Key points from the chapter are:

- Teacher characteristic behaviours (the 6 Cs) are critical in maintaining a positive learning environment.
- Effective combined application of the characteristic behaviours and basic teaching skills should improve the structure and quality of lessons to enhance pupil learning.
- Helping a beginning teacher to develop further teaching approaches, such as differentiation and the use of a variety of teaching strategies, will support effective pupil learning.
- A beginning teacher also needs support to use assessment *for* learning productively to support pupil progress, as well as to assess summatively and to assess against unit objectives.
- As a beginning teacher progresses through the three phases of teacher development (self-concern, class-concern and individual-concern), the focus of their teaching and their evaluation changes. Questions have been suggested to help you to move their practice forward.

Further resources

Capel, S. and Whitehead, M. (2015) *Learning to Teach Physical Education in the Secondary School: A Companion to School Experience*, 4th edn, Abingdon: Routledge.

Chapter 1 focuses on starting out as a physical education teacher, whilst chapters 4 to 13 consider a range of teaching and learning issues that beginning teachers can develop in order to support pupil learning and progress.

Kyriacou, C. (2014) *Essential Teaching Skills*, 4th edn, Cheltenham: Stanley Thornes.
This provides an accessible text for a beginning teacher, covering the development of teaching skills, planning and managing lessons, assessment and evaluation.

Newton, A. and Bowler, M. (2015) 'Assessment for and of learning in PE', in S. Capel and M. Whitehead (eds) *Learning to Teach Physical Education in the Secondary School: A Companion to School Experience*, 4th edn, Abingdon: Routledge, pp. 140-155.
This chapter considers the purposes of assessment; validity and reliability in assessment; approaches to assessment for learning; approaches to assessment of learning; and building assessment into your planning.

See also the companion website for this book (www.routledge.com/9781138059658).

You may also find it useful to refer to/use the text books written for student and newly qualified physical education teachers with a beginning teacher you are mentoring (see list on Page 4).

13 Observing beginning physical education teachers teaching

Julia Lawrence, Karen Low and Joanna Phan

Introduction

Observing a beginning teacher teaching is one approach used to identify progress and to support development of their teaching in order to enhance pupils' learning. However, there are also other observations of a beginning teacher, such as observations made outside the classroom setting, for example in relation to professional conduct around the school. Observation can also be used for other purposes; for example, as a way of measuring attainment against predetermined criteria (for example, teaching standards). Therefore, in order for observations to be effective, it is important to be clear about the purpose of any observation you are undertaking.

Beginning teachers commonly raise concerns over the heavy workload they are expected to manage, so you should consider how observations impact on an already stretched beginning teacher. Observations must be seen as adding value to their development as a teacher. This is more likely if an observation is not seen as 'being done' to the beginning teacher; rather, it is a two-way process, whereby both the mentor and the beginning teacher are active participants in discussions around the planning of an observation and reflection against the outcomes of the lesson.

Each observation should have a clear focus, which both the observer and the beginning teacher agree on and are clear about. It is important to plan and prepare for each observation and to learn from the observation. Hence, each observation starts prior to the lesson and finishes after the lesson, with pre- and post-lesson preparation and follow-up activities, normally with pre-and post-lesson discussions (see Chapter 15).

Therefore, the aim of this chapter is to support you in undertaking observation. It looks at the importance of observation, the process of observation, and how observation can be used effectively to support a beginning teacher's development.

Objectives

At the end of the chapter, you should be able to:

- Understand why you are observing a lesson and how such observation supports a beginning teacher's development;
- Understand the observation cycle, from pre-lesson preparation to post-lesson follow up;

- Engage in effective and meaningful observations that focus on teacher performance and pupils' progress.

Before reading further, complete Task 13.1, which encourages you to think about your current approach to lesson observation.

Task 13.1   Mentor reflection: Your current approach to lesson observation

Reflect on a series of lesson observations you have undertaken. The following questions act as a guide, but do ask yourself other questions as appropriate.

1.   Why do you observe a lesson? Is the reason the same for every lesson?
2.   What are you looking for when observing a beginning teacher?
3.   What pre-observation preparation do you engage in?
4.   How do you record your observations?
5.   How do you use your observations with the beginning teacher?
6.   What post-observation follow up do you engage in?
7.   What impact do you think your observations have on the beginning teacher?
8.   What do you feel are the advantages/disadvantages of lesson observations?

Purpose of lesson observation in supporting a beginning teacher's development

Observation is commonplace in the teaching profession. As a teacher, you will have been observed on many occasions for a number of reasons, through which your own practice will have grown and developed. The most common reason for observing is to support a beginning teacher's development. It can, for example, help a beginning teacher to shift from surviving to learning, to be better prepared and more confident, or help improve their teaching to enhance pupils' learning. In order to achieve this, there should be a clear focus for the observation, agreed by the beginning teacher and observer, related to the beginning teacher's current strengths and areas for development. Such an observation may also provide a snapshot that can be used as evidence of a beginning teacher's competence in the classroom, for example against achievement of the Teachers' Standards (Department for Education (DfE), 2011a).

The observation cycle

Observing teaching is a process; therefore, you need to consider the constituent parts and how they each contribute to an end product. The process of observation is realistically broken down into a cycle comprising three stages, as shown in Figure 13.1.

Each of these three stages of the observation cycle is considered in more detail in the following sub-sections.

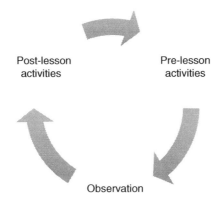

Figure 13.1 The stages of the observation cycle

Pre-lesson activities

Activities undertaken prior to the lesson being taught should aim to make a beginning teacher feel comfortable about the observation in supporting their development. This is best achieved either by a beginning teacher taking the lead, or by the mentor and the beginning teacher agreeing the focus of the observation and how it will be carried out. The approach adopted should reflect the developmental stage of the beginning teacher (see, for example, Chapter 12), including how comfortable and confident they are in taking the lead.

Task 13.2 asks you to consider what activities you currently undertake prior to a lesson observation.

Task 13.2   Pre-lesson observation activities

Based on your current experience of observing lessons, reflect on the following questions.

1. How do you engage with a beginning teacher prior to the lesson?

    a. Do you arrange a meeting prior to the observation to discuss the lesson plan and focus of the observation?
    b. What information do you ask for? A copy of the lesson plan? Information about the previous lesson?
    c. Anything else?

2. What are the purposes of the activities detailed in 1?
3. How do you use these activities to support your observations?

Activities undertaken prior to a lesson observation usually include a review of the lesson plan, and a conversation about the learning objectives and intended learning outcomes for the lesson and any concerns a beginning teacher might have about the lesson. It is an opportunity for you to encourage the beginning teacher to reflect on, for example, why they have chosen to deliver the activities they have planned and what they are expecting to see by the end of the lesson. They also include establishing a focus for the lesson observation. Following the discussion, time should be given for the beginning teacher to reflect on the conversation and to make any changes they feel appropriate for the lesson (Chapter 15 looks at pre-lesson conversations).

However, it is also important that you consider what you already do in preparation for your observations and to reflect on why and how you do them. You may consider that what you have done in the past has worked, so why consider changing? Whilst it is important not to change what works for the sake of it, it is important to consider whether there are better ways you can do things, or alternatives. For example, do you ask the beginning teacher how they might like the process to be undertaken? Have you considered how they feel during the process? Have you considered how you could change your approach to better reflect the needs of the beginning teacher? How are you using the information you ask for to support a beginning teacher? Do you use all the information, and therefore, do you need to ask for it all?

Recognising subjectivity and reliability of observations

It is important to consider that all observations are subjective. For example, the observer's viewpoint in relation to the observation focus will inform what the observer thinks they should see/should be happening. Further, the reliability of observations can also be questioned. For example, we all know of instances when someone performs better when being observed than they might do normally, and vice versa.

Hence, in order to reduce the subjectivity of an observation, it is important to be clear about exactly what you are looking for. One way of doing this is to consider what good teaching looks like and, hence, what you are looking for. This also makes your expectations and what you are looking for clear to the beginning teacher. Proper planning, subject mastery, monitoring progress and providing feedback, establishing a conducive learning environment and commitment to continual professional development have been commonly identified as important aspects of good teaching (see, for example, Manross and Templeton, 1997; Danielson, 2011; Rovegno and Bandhauer, 2013; The National Board for Professional Teaching Standards (NBPTS), 2016) (on the companion website for this book these are described in more detail, summarised in Table 13.3; what makes a good physical education lesson is covered in Table 13.4 (and Task 13.7) (see www.routledge.com/9781138059658)).

The lesson observation

The lesson observation

Task 13.3 asks you to consider how you currently undertake your lesson observations.

Task 13.3   Undertaking lesson observations

Using a recent mentoring experience, reflect on how you engaged in lesson observations:

1. Identify specifically what you were looking for in lesson observations.
2. Did what you look for change over time and if so, how?
3. How did you record your lesson observations?
4. Did the way you recorded your observations change? Did you use a range of strategies to support these?

A lesson observation provides an opportunity to collect evidence to support the development of a teacher's competence. It should be a constructive process, in which you are an extra pair of eyes for the teacher. An observation may be made against set criteria, for example teachers' standards or set school foci, but should consider how a beginning teacher is demonstrating characteristics of effective teaching, particularly in relation to enhancing pupils' learning. Importantly, a lesson observation should have an identified focus, not be generalised; the depth and specificity of the observation are important, not the breadth. The identified focus of what specific behaviours you might be looking for should have been agreed with the beginning teacher in the pre-lesson activities. If you think about your knowledge of teaching, in the mentoring context you are identifying your learning objectives (what you are wanting to achieve) and your success criteria (what it will look like in practice).

As with reflection, what you focus on during your observation also changes over time, moving from a teacher-centric focus, where observations focus on the teacher's skills, to a more pupil-centric focus, where observations focus on the impact of the teacher on pupil learning (Sherin and Han, 2004; Towers, 2007). It is important, therefore, to consider how the focus of lesson observations is identified and managed and evolves over time, and how this is shared with the beginning teacher.

So, what specifically are you looking for when undertaking an observation? What specific behaviours do you identify? Task 13.4 encourages you and a beginning teacher to review a lesson to establish similarities and differences in what you highlight in your observations.

Task 13.4   What are you looking for in a lesson?

Working with a beginning teacher, identify a key focus for a lesson observation; for example, behaviour management. Then record the lesson visually. Both then independently review the recording, thereby allowing both you and the beginning teacher to highlight specific aspects of behaviour management in the lesson. Discuss each other's observations and identify:

- Any similarities in the behaviours focused on.
- Any differences in the behaviours focused on.

  Consider why you think there were similarities and differences.

  After a few weeks, repeat the process to identify whether there have been any changes in what you and the beginning teacher focus on when observing.

In completing Task 13.4, you may well have identified differences between yourself and a beginning teacher in what you highlighted. Although you have a specific focus for the observation, it is the specific behaviours you might identify that may differ. For example, with behaviour management, you might identify activities occurring before an incident, whereas the beginning teacher may focus purely on the incident itself. Alternatively, although you might both focus on organisation, your observations might be pupil focused, whilst the beginning teacher focused on themselves. Research (Standal and Moe, 2013) has suggested that a person's ability to reflect develops over time, and the behaviours they base such reflections on also vary over time. So, it is not surprising if you have seen differences, or that you have focused on different behaviours.

How do you record your observations?

In Task 13.3, you were asked to consider how you currently record your observations. Recording lesson observations is an important skill. Your school, a university or other provider of initial teacher education courses with whom you are mentoring a beginning teacher may well have clear documentation to complete when undertaking lesson observations. This might be, for example, a proforma that focuses on specific school requirements regarding what good teaching looks like, or a more open-ended proforma that allows you to write down key points. For some lessons, it might include completing a proforma focused on a specific aspect of teaching; for example, the amount of learning time (ALT) in the lesson (examples of lesson observation proforma for observing ALT and other aspects of teaching are available on the companion website for this book (www.routledge.com/9781138059658), as well as on other websites). Alternatively, it could be subject specific, thereby drawing out key aspects of high-quality physical education. One example of this is an observation tool that focuses specifically on the seven key practices that facilitate effective delivery of quality lessons (called PELOT), developed by The Physical Education and Sports Teacher Academy (PESTA) in Singapore (Ministry of Education, 2013) (see www.youtube.com/watch?v=tNU1ns5sqB4). During an observation, behaviours specific to the practices on the observation schedule are noted and then used to support post-lesson discussions.

Rather than completing a formal document during the lesson, you may prefer to make notes against the agreed focus of the lesson and then write them up. Sources of information you use to formalise these notes might include comments made on the lesson plans before and during the lesson when you identify something that requires further clarification, or if there is a point you wish to address during your post-lesson conversation. They might also include noting key questions you might ask during a post-lesson conversation. When observing, you may have made a note of the key focus for the lesson and what sort of behaviours/outcomes you might be looking for. During the lesson, you add comments relating to these and then write prompts to use later with the beginning teacher to support your discussions with them and to guide them to reflect on what was happening during the lesson. An example of these notes is provided as Figure 13.2.

Whatever format/approach you choose to use, it is important not to focus so much on recording information that you are missing important aspects of the observation. Taking time after the lesson to develop notes can allow you to provide more focused feedback on the observation in the post-lesson conversation. Tables 13.1 and 13.2 look at two further examples of observation notes; Table 13.1 is an example of a basic set of observation notes, made during the lesson, and Table 13.2 is an example of more detailed observation notes, developed after the lesson.

The two examples in Tables 13.1 and 13.2 both provide focused feedback to the beginning teacher, but the comments in Table 13.2 provide more prompts from the mentor for the beginning teacher to consider. As a mentor, this also allows you to start considering some of the questions you might ask during the post-lesson discussion. How feedback is used to support the progress of a beginning teacher is important (see, for example, Chapters 5 (the Clean Feedback Model), 7 and 10 and the companion website for this book (www.routledge.com/ 9781138059658)). Even when recording your own observations, take some time to consider how your comments might be interpreted. Now complete Task 13.5.

Task 13.5   Mentor reflection: Providing feedback

Using the examples in Figure 13.2 and Tables 13.1 and 13.2, consider how and when you are currently making notes in relation to your observations.

How do you share this feedback with a beginning teacher?

The use of digital recording to support observations

The use of visual recording is becoming more common in observing beginning physical education teachers. Marsh and Mitchell (2014) identified that the growing use of video within the classroom can enhance observational practice. Whilst issues around permissions to record pupils and access to resources to record with might arise (you will, of course, need to sort these out prior to using any digital recording to support observations), it provides a more permanent record of the lesson.

If you have ever had a lesson recorded and then observed your own teaching, you will know that it is a very powerful tool for learning. It allows you to watch closely your own behaviours, and it gives clearer meaning to the feedback given by the person who has undertaken the observation. Sometimes it is easier to see what you are doing, rather than have someone describe it to you. I know that when I have watched myself teach, issues around organisation, positioning and personal mannerisms become very evident.

It is not the recording itself that is important; rather, it is how the recording is used that has the most impact. It allows observers to 'deconstruct' a lesson (Brophy, 2004), and hence

Teacher Education PGCE Secondary 2017-18

LESSON OBSERVATION FEEDBACK FORM – SECONDARY PGCE

Trainee:	School:
Observer(s):	Lesson Observed:
Date: Time: Subject: Agreed focus for observation:	Year Group:

Evaluation of Teaching and Learning [please link your comments to specific standards where possible]

Focused question as going out
Activity levels - its cold get them moving
Purpose of the activity? How could you have developed this to be more games specific (TS3)
Purpose of the progressions? (TS4)
Organisation of equipment? (TS4)
What was the focus of the lesson? (TS4)
Objectives were obviously explored but not clear how and when
Could the gate activity have been done earlier? Maybe as the warm up?
How are you challenging the more able?
Was skill level appropriate for the 3 v 1 activity?

Reflections: focuses on negatives some around activity Need to expand answers	You need to be more confident in your delivery. At the moment you are adopting a more coaching approach rather than teaching. Be clear as to what you want them to achieve and how you will know that they have been successful.

Figure 13.2 Notes from an observation

Table 13.1 Example of a basic set of observation notes

Basic set of observation notes, made during the lesson	Prompt lesson start. Shared learning objectives on the board. You allowed a pupil to read this out, but think about extending this and also how you could expand the learning objectives so you clearly show what the attainment of the objective will look like.
	You reviewed prior learning and linked to the previous lesson.
	You worked hard to engage the class, which paid dividends at the end of the lesson.
	Warm up was well managed. Think about how you could use this to reinforce some aspects of the key teaching points you will use during the lesson.
	Clear questioning. You probe well, but avoid answering your own questions. You use the questions effectively to check understanding and reinforce the learning objectives.
	You need to do some work on your positioning and also the amount of time you spend giving instructions.
	There was clear evidence of progress throughout the lesson, with activities building on each other to allow the final activity to consolidate the learning.
	Plenary attempted to review progress, and is something to develop further.

Table 13.2 Example of more detailed observation notes

More detailed observation notes, developed after the lesson	**Lesson:**
	You got the lesson started promptly, but you need to think about how you manage pupils' arrival so they do not drift in.
	Warm up worked well, but consider reinforcing quality throughout so pupils are clear what it is you are looking for. Also link what they are doing in the warm up to what you want them to do during the lesson. You monitored the activity well, but use this as an opportunity to reinforce expectations, and showcase good practice. You reinforced some teaching points, but need to think about how you bring the pupils back to what you are expecting them to be able to achieve/demonstrate. There was some evidence of progression in terms of the use of the barrier, but could you have developed this further so that all pupils undertook that activity?
	Sharing of learning objectives this was done effectively but consider developing them further so that pupils are clear what achievement against these will look like. In essence, you want to be modelling a little bit more. Be clear how you want pupils to get into groups. Can you get this done before the lesson or during the warm up? You refocused the pupils back to the teaching points, but try and draw out their understanding of performing the skill a little bit more.
	Peer assessment was planned for and the resources produced supported this, but you need to make sure the pupils understand what they are meant to be doing and monitor the effectiveness of the approach.
	Activities were progressive, but think about how long you spend on each activity, and also how you can increase the opportunity for pupils to practise the skills. For example, did you give them sufficient time to decide which their preferred take off foot was? Did they need to run as far in approaching the bar?
	Plenary was evident, but think about getting pupils to reflect on what they could do to improve their performance, rather than just say what they felt they had achieved.

is a positive learning tool. A beginning teacher can observe their own practice and review, self-reflect and analyse specific parts of a lesson. Alternatively, it affords an opportunity for peer(s) to observe each other to identify areas of best practice and areas for development. Further, it enables you to identify specific visual examples to support any notes you have made on the lesson (see later).

According to van Es (2012, p.106), teachers are

> more student-centred and evidence-based in their analysis of classroom observations via video analysis; they adopt strategies in teaching to make student thinking more visible and to probe students' thinking and then use what they learn about students in these interactions to inform their teaching decisions.

van Es (2012, p.104) argued that a further benefit of videoing lessons is to allow a teacher the opportunity to develop their ability to 'notice', which she defined as 'what teachers attend to in the moment of teaching, as well as how they reason about what they observe'. In particular, she argued that it develops the ability to notice 'student thinking' and consequently pupils' progress.

Whilst the advantages of the use of video capture technology to support reflection are clear, the impact this has on the teacher and their teaching, or more importantly on pupils' progress, is less well documented. Lawrence et al. (2016) argued that when used effectively, it can produce rapid changes in teacher practices and pupil levels of activity. Now read case study 13.1.

Case study 13.1 An example of video observation to support observations

As part of the observation process, Jess, a beginning teacher, was videoed teaching a Year 8 gymnastics lesson. The mentor used an observation tool to record the lesson. An observation template was created within the tool that listed key characteristics of effective teaching. As the lesson was videoed, the mentor was able to 'tag' when specific behaviours were observed. In 'tagging' the behaviour, the tool would note when the behaviour was seen. The nature of the software was such that rather than Jess having to review the whole lesson, she could pinpoint, through the coding of the lesson, specific examples of when positive or negative behaviours relating to the focus of the observation were observed by the mentor.

Prior to her post-lesson discussion, Jess reviewed the lesson, and was able to analyse in detail the specific examples of her practice. She was able to clearly see what was happening prior to any specific behaviours, and was able to reflect on what she might do differently next time. Jess noted her thoughts and took them with her to her post-lesson discussion.

As part of the process, the mentor also reviewed the lesson based on the same criteria, thereby allowing the mentor and the beginning teacher to engage collaboratively in the post-lesson conversation.

So, having observed a beginning teacher, it is important to consider how you will use that observation to support your post-lesson activities (see Chapter 15 for further information about post-lesson discussions).

Post-lesson activities

 Post-lesson activities

It is consistently acknowledged that the process of reflecting on practice allows teachers to identify and draw out areas of good practice and areas for development. The post-lesson conversation is, therefore, an opportunity for you and a teacher to discuss the lesson you have just observed.

If you have videoed the lesson as well as made notes, you have a rich source of evidence to start your conversation. Video evidence allows focused discussion between observers around common issues as recorded on the video (Marsh and Mitchell, 2014). In this situation, judgements made become those of the beginning teacher, from their own observations. Further, van Es (2012) suggested that the opportunity provided for collaboration has the greatest impact on reflection. Therefore, it is not just about your feedback to a beginning teacher; it is about the beginning teacher watching themselves and discussing their observations with others. As with any type of feedback, the depth and specificity are more important than the breadth. However, it is important to remember that you are trying to draw out from your observations the questions you might want to ask the beginning teacher in order to develop their capacity to reflect on their own teaching and to establish targets for development. You also need to be aware of judging the beginning teacher (Hobson and Malderez (2013); see also Chapter 6 on the mentor–mentee relationship). Now complete Task 13.6.

Task 13.6   Video of a lesson

In Task 13.4, you were asked to video a lesson to identify key characteristics of teaching identified by yourself and a beginning teacher.

Record a second lesson and consider how you might use the recording to support a beginning teacher to reflect on their own teaching.

Consider carefully how you could use the record to highlight key strengths and areas for development you have identified.

Summary and key points

• Throughout this chapter, you have been asked to consider your approaches to observation and how this may influence how you undertake the observation cycle. How you engage with a beginning teacher during the observation process is important, if it is to be a productive tool to support development and progress.

• As a mentor, you are the main observer of a beginning teacher. However, it is important to acknowledge that what you see and how you might interpret that during a lesson may well differ from what others see and how they interpret it. Therefore, it is important to ensure that a beginning teacher is observed by a range of teachers as well as that they can observe themselves and others.

• When observing beginning teachers, therefore, the following key points need to be considered.

• What is the purpose and value of observing the lesson?

• How do you work through the lesson observation cycle, including pre- and post-lesson activities?

• How do you identify and share the focus of the observation?

• How are you recording lesson observations?

• How do you use any notes/recordings to support the beginning teacher?

• How do you engage a beginning teacher in observing their own practice?

Further resources

Lawrence, J. (2017) 'Reflecting on your teaching', in W. Jolliffe and D. Waugh (eds.) *NQT: The Beginning Teacher's Guide to Outstanding Practice*, London: Learning Matters, pp. 82–93.
This short chapter provides an overview of the process of reflection and how beginning teachers can be encouraged to engage in the process.

Lawrence, J., Low, K. and Phan, J (2016) 'The impact of a high intensity observation programme in Singapore', in *Proceedings of the International Conference on Education and e-Learning (EeL)*, Singapore: Global Science and Technology Forum, pp. 9–13.
This research paper provides details of a short research project based in Singapore that looked at how video observation could be used to support physical education teachers of different levels of experience to reflect upon their own and others' teaching.

Video Enhanced Observation (VEO) at www.veo-group.com
This commercially available tool allows behaviours to be tagged during the recording of lessons. Once the recording is complete, the tool will note when specific behaviours were observed (tagged), allowing the reviewer(s) to move immediately to that point within the recording to view the behaviour.

See also the companion website for this book (www.routledge.com/9781138059658).

You may also find it useful to refer to/use the text books written for student and newly qualified physical education teachers with the beginning teachers you are mentoring (see list on Page 4).

14 Supporting beginning physical education teachers to observe movement to support pupil learning

Sophy Bassett and Angela Newton

Introduction

The ability to observe and analyse movement is essential to ensure pupil progress in physical education. Indeed, 'learning is more likely to occur when you use observation to give personalised feedback to reinforce, guide and advise pupils' (Whitehead, 2016, p. 174). This chapter considers how you can support a beginning physical education teacher to develop their ability to observe and analyse movement.

Having set a task, a teacher must be able to review the success of pupils as a result of engaging in that task. Although initially a beginning teacher's response may be based around observations of safety, behaviour, organisation or clarification of the task, once they are confident with these elements, observation and analysis of the movement(s) can take place.

Observation and analysis of movement facilitates focused feedback to pupils to support their progression towards the learning objectives or intended learning outcomes (called 'intended learning outcomes' in this chapter). In order to be able to analyse movement and provide effective feedback, a beginning teacher must develop their understanding of movement in a wide variety of contexts (subject content knowledge) and their understanding of different pupils' needs (knowledge of learners and learning theory) (knowledge bases are covered in Chapter 9).

Observation and analysis of movement is a skill and, as with other teaching skills, develops over time. Your role as a mentor is to provide structured opportunities for a beginning teacher to become skilled in observation, analysis and giving supportive feedback about movement.

Objectives

At the end of this chapter, you should be able to:

- Support a beginning teacher in moving from observation for safety, behaviour, organisation or clarification of a task to observation and analysis of movement and understanding the relationship between observation, analysis and feedback;

- Support a beginning teacher in developing secure subject knowledge (both content and pedagogical) across the age phase in which they are working as a beginning teacher;
- Identify a range of strategies to support a beginning teacher to develop their ability to observe, analyse and give feedback on pupil movement.

Before reading further, we ask you to reflect on your current knowledge about observing and analysing movement (Task 14.1).

Task 14.1   Mentor reflection: Observing and analysing movement

Consider the following questions to reflect on your own ability and confidence in observing and analysing movement.

Are you confident in observing and analysing movement across all activities? With all age groups and attainment levels? If not, why not?

Can you identify how you observe and analyse movement?

Do you have a strategy for observing and analysing movement in lessons you teach? If so, can you describe this?

What methods have you used in the past to support beginning teachers to develop their skills of observation and analysis? How effective have these been?

Establishing effective positioning for movement observation

In order for a beginning teacher to observe pupil movement, you must encourage them to be positioned appropriately in relation to the class. When moving around the teaching area, they must be in a position to scan the class as a whole and/or adopt the best positions to observe the movement of pupils. As a mentor, you should be aware of a common error of many beginning teachers, whereby they focus on setting a task and then circulate around groups or individuals before standing back and scanning the whole class, or they fail to observe what the pupils are doing as they concentrate on the next aspect of the lesson. This may result in common errors being overlooked and safety and behavioural issues being neglected. Consequently, pupil engagement and learning are affected due to a lack of feed-back. In Task 14.2, you are asked to observe a beginning teacher's positioning for scanning the class and observing movement.

Task 14.2   Observation of a beginning teacher's positioning for scanning and movement observation

Identify a lesson in which the sole focus of your observation is the positioning of a beginning teacher.

- Map the positions and pathways the beginning teacher assumes throughout the lesson.

- Review the findings with the beginning teacher and challenge them to reflect on the suitability of their positioning to enable them to observe pupil movement in each phase of the lesson.
- Repeat the observation in the next lesson and plot:
  - any occasions when they stop to scan the class. Code this with X (position when scanning)
  - interventions that may arise from their observation of groups or individuals. Code this with S (safety), B (behaviour), O (organisation) and P (pupil performance)
- Challenge the beginning teacher to review the findings and evaluate their progress.

The relationship of effective observation to knowledge and understanding

The ability of a beginning teacher to observe and analyse movement depends on their knowledge and understanding of the activity they are teaching. It is useful to ask a beginning teacher to conduct an audit of their confidence across the activities you deliver in your school's curriculum. In Task 14.3, you are asked to use an audit of a beginning teacher's confidence in physical education curriculum areas to identify areas for development of subject content knowledge.

Task 14.3   Audit of confidence in physical education curriculum areas

Ask a beginning teacher to complete an audit of all the activities on the timetable for the term. An example is provided in Table 14.1 (another example of an audit is provided in Chapter 9; confidence can be added to the response for knowledge and skills).

Use the results of the audit to identify areas requiring subject content knowledge development.

Agree targets and actions for subject content knowledge development for the term.

Table 14.1 Audit tool for confidence in physical education curriculum areas

Activity	Confidence level	Level of confidence code:
Gymnastics	2	1 (Not confident to lead teach any aspect of this activity)
Orienteering	3	
Invasion games	1	2 (Confident to lead teach some aspects of this activity)
Swimming (stroke development)	2	
		3 (Fully confident to lead teach any aspect of this activity)

Note: your ongoing observations of a beginning teacher may highlight additional areas for development not identified in the audit.

The confidence of a beginning teacher will vary according to their level of development and the stage at which you are supporting them (for example, a student teacher may be less confident than a newly qualified teacher). Areas in which a beginning teacher lacks confidence (level one or, in some cases, level two from the audit of confidence) require opportunities for development, including personal research, observation of good practice/skilled practitioners, collaborative planning, team teaching leading to solo teaching, investment in governing body awards, enhancement sessions for teachers, or in-house training. The advantage of in-house training is that it can be specifically tailored towards observing movement. You may wish to reflect on the expertise you have in your school or across local schools and how this might be shared to support beginning teachers locally (see Chapter 8 for collaborative approaches to mentoring).

Where opportunities to support development are scheduled may depend on the stage of development of a beginning teacher. For a student teacher, these might be officially scheduled into their timetable, whilst for a recently qualified teacher, departmental twilight sessions might be more appropriate. Each opportunity should be considered carefully. For example, where a beginning teacher plans lessons alongside the class teacher, initially their delivery may be restricted to one or two specific lesson episodes. As confidence in the activity increases, a beginning teacher can take on increasing responsibility for planning and delivery of the lesson and ultimately, solo teaching. It is good practice to set a target for how long the process of assuming full responsibility for a lesson will take (although the time may vary from one beginning teacher to another, or even for the same beginning teacher in different activities); for example, week 1: warm up; weeks 2 and 3: warm up and selected episode(s); week 4: collaboratively planned, solo teach; week 5 and 6: solo planning and teaching.

As another example, beginning teacher observations of other practitioners should focus on how the teacher applies their subject content knowledge in learning contexts in order to enable pupils to achieve each intended learning outcome. This process also affords the opportunity to specifically identify how the teacher uses their observations of pupils to give feedback and therefore support their learning. Task 14.4 focuses on observing good practice.

Task 14.4   Observing good practice

Using the audit of confidence (Task 14.3) and findings from focused observation tasks (Task 14.2), agree three priority areas with a beginning teacher for observation of good practice. Ask them to develop a focused observation schedule that identifies points in the lesson where the experienced practitioner observes movement and gives feedback.

Review the developed schedule with the beginning teacher and challenge them to carry out observations of experienced practitioners in three different contexts. In the next mentor meeting, review the findings and identify best practice.

Observation and analysis of movement

Movement and movement patterns

All physical education teachers need an understanding of movement itself. Many beginning teachers do not come with this, so they need to develop it. They need to understand, for example, that a movement is a change of position in space and time. All activities involve movement patterns, that is, a series of movements performed in sequence, with preparation, action and recovery phases. Each movement pattern begins with the learner's preparation stage, where they assume the correct body position for transition into the second phase, the main action of the movement. The final phase, the recovery, returns the learner to an appropriate position ready for the next movement. Movement patterns can comprise a skill such as a tennis serve, or could range in complexity from a tactical move in a game context to movement in relation to others, such as group dynamics in a gymnastics sequence.

Chapter 11 looked at how to support a beginning teacher's planning, including the selection of age and attainment appropriate learning objectives and intended learning outcomes. The next section involves the concept of using intended learning outcomes to create a structured framework to support observation. This is referred to as a 'frame of reference'.

Frames of reference

In order to observe and analyse movement and provide appropriate feedback to progress learning, a beginning teacher must first establish what movements they are looking for. A frame of reference is a mental picture of the expected movement response from pupils. This expectation is set as a consequence of a carefully selected intended learning outcome, informed by secure subject content knowledge and an awareness of the ability of the pupils being taught (see example in Figure 14.1; note, further examples can be found in Figures 14.2, 14.3 and 14.4).

As an experienced practitioner, you will have refined and developed these expectations over time. A beginning teacher needs guidance to set their expectations for intended learning outcomes at an appropriate level. This involves ensuring that they pitch the quality of movement expected at the right level and give a suitable learning context; for example, a small-sided game or a contextual practice. Once the learning focus has been clearly defined, they can use the intended learning outcome to develop a mental picture of what the movement patterns of the pupils should look like. This can be structured in terms of preparation, action and recovery. A beginning teacher then needs to identify an associated list of teaching points on which they can draw in order to give appropriate, focused feedback to individuals or groups following their observations of pupil performance.

Writing a frame of reference with associated teaching points can be a useful exercise for a beginning teacher in contexts where their subject content knowledge is not yet secure. As they become more experienced observers, with expectations appropriate to the age and ability of their pupils, they automatically establish a mental picture, as you do. It is possible to create your own analysis template for a beginning teacher. Alternatively, other examples can be found in Killingbeck and Whitehead (2015). Task 14.5 looks at constructing a frame of reference.

Intended learning outcome
Pupils will be able to perform the full action serve with consistency in an isolated practice

Frame of reference
Preparation: The player stands diagonally, side on to the target, with balance and focus. Ball and racket together, pointing to target.
Action: The ball is placed high above the racket side of the body as the racket is swung in one continuous movement to meet the ball as high as possible. The ball is hit down into the service box consistently.
Recovery: Racket follows through across the body, player returns to ready position.

Teaching points for development of the skill		
Preparation	Action	Recovery
• Continental grip • Look to target (service box) • Stand behind the service line with opposite foot to racket hand forward • Weight over the front foot, feet shoulder width apart • Stand diagonally to target service box • Racket pointing towards target, ball in non-racket hand in contact with racket	• Keep throwing arm straight, swinging up to release the ball from the fingertips • Place ball higher than the height of the racket to the racket side of body • Simultaneously, swing racket down, around and behind the head • As ball drops, throw racket head up and forward at ball • Contact the ball slightly forward and with full extension of body, arm and racket • Transfer weight forward into the court	• Follow through with racket to opposite side of body • Step into court and regain balance ready for next action

Figure 14.1 An example of a frame of reference that could be used for observation and analysis of a skill in the context of a tennis episode

Task 14.5   Constructing a frame of reference from an intended learning outcome to assist observation, analysis and feedback during a lesson episode

During collaborative planning, agree an intended learning outcome for a lesson episode that you will observe and ask a beginning teacher to write a frame of reference and associated teaching points. This is used as a framework for their observation. Figures 14.1, 14.2, 14.3 and 14.4 can be used for guidance.

The beginning teacher delivers the episode, observing movement patterns against the frame of reference. They select the most appropriate teaching points to feed back to the pupils in order to help them move closer to the established frame of reference and, therefore, the intended learning outcome. Where strengths are identified, specific, positive feedback should be given.

During the lesson debrief, discuss the following:

1 The appropriateness of the written frame of reference in providing a framework for observation.
2 The effectiveness of the observation and analysis of movement in the lesson and any areas for further development.
3 Specific feedback given to selected individuals and groups. Were the identified teaching points appropriate?
4 The effectiveness of the feedback in meeting the frame of reference and supporting pupils in making progress towards the intended learning outcome.

Frames of reference can be developed initially for isolated skills with the intention to move on to more complex patterns of movement; for example, pupil response to a conditioned game, pupil creation of a group sequence in gymnastics or a motif in dance, or pupil response to a problem-solving activity in outdoor and adventurous activities. In each case, the principle is the same. A beginning teacher identifies a suitable intended learning outcome, develops a mental picture of what they want to see and writes a list of associated teaching points. Following their observation during the teaching episode, they can reflect on the effectiveness of their feedback in progressing pupil learning. Encouraging a beginning teacher to

Intended learning outcome
Pupils will be able to create space in order to attack a target as a team in a modified game
Frame of reference
Preparation: Once the team gains possession, players turn to attack their target area, scanning to show awareness of the position of the ball. They move forward confidently at pace filling channels of the court. Action: Players advance towards the target cutting into space to call for the pass if required. They hold a position/space between themselves and the target area, moving decisively when the pass is possible, showing their open side to receive the pass and challenge the target. Recovery: Once the shot has been made they position themselves for any rebound.

Teaching points to pursue the attacking team strategy		
Preparation	Action	Recovery
• Look at the ball • Maintain a balanced position, ready to move off in any direction • Look for space away from other players • Move quickly to fill channels	• Maintain a balanced position in space • Look at the ball to identify when to move • Cut decisively in to space • Show target for the pass (e.g. hands out) • Action will repeat until shot is made	• Move close to target in position for rebound

Figure 14.2 An example of a frame of reference that could be used for observation and analysis of an attacking team strategy

Intended learning outcome		
Pupils will be able to perform an imaginative sequence of six movements showing changes in level and speed with a partner		
Frame of reference		
Preparation: Pupils will assume a controlled starting position in relation to partner and space.		
Action: Pupils perform their sequence demonstrating fluency and control. They will show decisive changes in speed and movements that demonstrate low, medium and high levels and variations in relationships with their partner.		
Recovery: Finishing position held to indicate the completion of the sequence.		
Teaching points to pursue a quality sequence		
Preparation	Action	Recovery
• Hold a defined shape, showing good tension, control and stillness, • Clear relationship to partner	• All movements show good body tension • Linking movements show fluency and control • Movements incorporate changes in speed and level • Clear positioning in relationship to partner	• Hold a defined shape, showing good tension, control and stillness. • Clear relationship to partner

Figure 14.3 An example of a frame of reference that could be used for observation and analysis of a sequence in gymnastics

adopt this observation framework will support their ability to observe and analyse pupil movement responses and provide appropriate feedback. Simultaneously, their subject content knowledge will be improved, and you will start to develop a resource bank that other teachers may find useful.

Giving appropriate feedback based on teaching points

As a mentor, you should monitor whether a beginning teacher selects the most appropriate teaching points for pupils. This is more likely to be an issue in an activity in which they lack knowledge and confidence. You should also monitor the number of teaching points provided to support learning in a given episode, as they must avoid overloading pupils with too much information. You then need to consider the best time to discuss these points with a beginning teacher in a learning conversation (CUREE 2005b), for example during planning reviews/pre-lesson conversations (see Chapter 15).

The quality of the feedback a beginning teacher provides to pupils in the lesson may be an issue, even when the teaching points are used as a checklist. You may find that the feedback is presented in a negative way; for instance, saying 'your hands are too close together, move them apart' when pupils are using a push technique to shoot at goal in hockey. Encourage the idea of contextualising how the feedback will help to improve performance and progress towards the intended learning outcome; for example, 'A good attempt but you will get more control by moving your hands further apart'.

In direct contrast to specific feedback lacking in positivity, there may be occasions when praise is disingenuous or not specific to the learning intention. Even experienced practitioners occasionally offer feedback such as 'well done', 'that was good' or 'excellent'. This praise may motivate pupils but does not move learning forward. For further information on giving accurate and specific feedback, see Blair with Whitehead (2015).

If feedback is identified as an area for development, it may be beneficial to film the beginning teacher with a view to analysing movement in sections of the lesson together. Task 14.6 focuses on recording and analysing types of feedback.

Intended learning outcome
Pupils will be able to demonstrate a powerful shot put action with a selected implement.

Frame of reference
Preparation: Pupils will stand side on to the direction of the put with feet slightly offset and weight over the back foot.
Action: Pupils extend the legs, driving the hips forward and rotating the shoulders in one fluid action to push the object upwards and forwards into the throwing sector.
Recovery: The feet are adjusted to control the rotation and remain in the throwing area.

Teaching points to pursue a quality sequence

Preparation	Action	Recovery
• Object held on base of first three fingers, supported by thumb and little finger • Shot held under chin against the neck • Elbow high • Knees bent • Stand sideways, weight on back foot • Rear heel and front toe in a line • Shoulder of throwing arm facing away from the direction of the throw	• Wrist firm and elbow high throughout action • Rotation initiated by non-throwing arm • Weight transferred from rear foot to front foot • Hips drive upwards and forwards ahead of the shoulders • Throwing arm punches fast, long and high from the chin • Extend fingers	• Reverse leg position to prevent forward momentum • Lower the upper body to remain within the circle

Figure 14.4 An example of a frame of reference that could be used for observation and analysis of the shot put

Task 14.6   Recording and analysing types of feedback

Select a lesson that has been identified from the audit in Task 14.3 as an area for development for a beginning teacher.

- Film key lesson episodes, or a whole lesson where feedback is likely to be prominent, ensuring that the beginning teacher's feedback is audible and can be captured on the recording. This may require you to use a portable recording device to track the teacher.
- Following the lesson, view the recording together and analyse the quality of feedback given. Plan actions to help develop the beginning teacher's ability to give effective feedback.

A possible analysis tool, whereby you can tally the types of feedback observed, is shown in Figure 14.5.

Observation checklists

It is important to reiterate to a beginning teacher that initial scanning must take place once the task is set to ensure pupils are safe and engaged (Task 14.2 focuses on the correct positioning). Their next observation focus should be how the pupil movement response compares with the frame of reference and the associated teaching points. Stress that it is not necessary to stop the whole class unless there is a common misconception that needs to be addressed. The checklist in Figure 14.6 provides an aide memoire for a beginning teacher to guide their observation and analysis of movement.
Task 14.7 asks you to develop an observation checklist.

Task 14.7   Developing an observation checklist for observation of a beginning teacher

- Devise your own observation checklist to observe a beginning teacher's ability to observe and analyse movement
- Use the checklist to guide your observation of a beginning teacher, identifying areas of strength and areas for development
- Discuss your findings in a learning conversation as part of your post-lesson debrief
- Agree targets for further development of movement observation and analysis

Note: there are a number of observation sheets on the companion website for this book (www.routledge.com/9781138059658) designed to support observation of a range of aspects of teaching.

	Generic statement e.g. Well done	Specific e.g. Well done. You threw the ball high above your racket side	Specific corrective e.g. Well done. You placed the ball high above your racket side but keep your weight forward to hit up and over the ball
Positive			
Neutral			
Negative			

Figure 14.5 Tally chart for recording types of feedback used

1. Stand in a safe position to view the whole class
2. Scan the class
3. Intervene to resolve any issues of behaviour, safety and organisation
4. Observe movement patterns in relation to the frame of reference and teaching points
5. Identify good performance and common errors and take appropriate action (only stopping the whole group if necessary)
6. Give feedback to groups/individuals based on identified strengths and prioritised teaching points to improve performance (do not overload with too much information)
7. Observe modified movements informed by the teaching points
8. Repeat as necessary
9. Evaluation and final feedback to pupils at conclusion of episode

Figure 14.6 Observation checklist for a beginning teacher

Impact of observation and feedback on learning

A focus of any learning conversation in relation to the observation of movement must be the impact on pupils' learning. This is measured against the intended learning outcome from which the frame of reference was devised. The quality of the teaching points selected for pupils contributes to their success and may also determine whether intended learning outcomes were pitched at the correct level for all, most or some pupils. You need to prompt a beginning teacher to carefully evaluate intended learning outcomes and honestly appraise how far the feedback given to pupils supported their progression towards the learning intentions.

Finally, Task 14.8 asks you to reflect on your knowledge about observing and analysing movement after having read this chapter and undertaken the tasks therein.

Task 14.8 Mentor reflection: Observing and analysing movement

Having read this chapter and undertaken the various tasks, reflect on your confidence in observing and analysing movement across all activities. How has this developed?

Reflect on how you have developed/refined the way you undertake movement observation and analysis in your lessons.

Reflect on the changes you have made/are going to make in supporting a beginning teacher to observe and analyse movement and give effective feedback to pupils.

Summary and key points

The chapter has modelled a framework for observing and analysing movement and providing developmental feedback that can be utilised by a beginning teacher. The framework recommends that feedback in the form of teaching points should be carefully selected according to the intended learning outcomes and evaluated systematically considering its impact on pupil learning.

After working through this chapter, you should:

- Be able to support a beginning teacher to appreciate the relationship between observation, analysis and feedback in supporting effective teaching and learning
- Understand the importance of, and be able to identify, strategies for supporting a beginning teacher to develop their subject knowledge (both content and pedagogical) in the age phase in which they are working as a beginning teacher (see Chapter 9)
- Know strategies for supporting a beginning teacher to develop basic teaching skills of positioning and scanning
- Know how to support a beginning teacher's observation, analysis and developmental feedback
- Be aware of the need to support and encourage a beginning teacher's evaluation of pupil progress against intended learning outcomes in relation to the quality of feedback given.

Further resources

Maude, P. and Whitehead, M. (2008) *Observing and Analysing Learners' Movement*, CD-ROM, Worcester: Tacklesport Limited.
This resource contains over 90 video clips of children performing a variety of movement patterns shown from different angles. Different stages of development are also included. This can be used with beginning teachers to provide support for their observation of movement, particularly in less familiar curriculum activities.

Killingbeck, M. and Whitehead, M. (2016) 'Observation in PE', in S. Capel and M. Whitehead (eds.) *Learning to Teach Physical Education in the Secondary School: A Companion to School Experience*, 4th edn, London: Routledge, pp. 49–66.
This book chapter provides a good starting point for supporting a beginning teacher as they embark on the journey towards becoming effective in movement observation. It covers observation in relation to lesson organisation and management, learning and language development.

Mitchell, S.A., Oslin, J.L. and Griffin, L.L. (2013) *Teaching Sports Concepts and Skills. A Tactical Games Approach for Ages 7-18*, 3rd edn, Leeds: Human Kinetics.
This book explores a tactical approach to games teaching, including the observable components of game performance.

See also the companion website for this book (www.routledge.com/9781138059658).

You may also find it useful to refer to/use the text books written for student and newly qualified physical education teachers with a beginning teacher you are mentoring (see list on Page 4).

15 Holding pre- and post-lesson observation discussions

Julia Lawrence

Introduction

This chapter focuses on discussions you hold with a beginning teacher pre- and post-lesson observation. These are integral parts of the observation cycle (see Chapter 13), acting as bookends to the observation of teaching. O'Leary (2014, p. 3) argued that the observation of teaching 'has commonly been used as a method of assessment and is an important tool for nurturing key pedagogical skills and teacher learning'. Pre- and post-lesson discussions, therefore, provide the opportunity for reflection on what is observed in a lesson.

Although pre- and post-lesson observation discussions are designed to be beneficial to a beginning teacher, they can also be beneficial for the mentor. Belvis et al. (2013) identified benefits for a beginning teacher as improved performance, increased motivation and a feeling of support, whilst benefits for the mentor are improved performance through reflecting on their own behaviours as part of the process.

How you handle these discussions is important for allowing and encouraging reflection both by the beginning teacher and by yourself. Both parties need to adopt an open-minded approach to the process (Dewey, 1933) and establish a working relationship that encourages openness and critical thought. The mentor and the beginning teacher need to engage in a two-way discussion and reflection rather than the mentor leading and 'telling' the beginning teacher what they saw and what the teacher should do. Both the mentor and the beginning teacher need to take responsibility for active engagement as well as undertaking to engage as fully as possible with the process in order to provide opportunities for open discussion of, and reflection on, the lesson prior to and post-delivery.

Further, it is important that a range of sources are used to support discussion. The evidence to support pre- and post-lesson observation discussions with a beginning teacher is likely to come from a number of sources, including lesson plans, lesson observations and reflections by the beginning teacher. Relying on a single source reduces the opportunity for depth of reflection.

The role of the mentor is not only to support and guide a beginning teacher professionally, but also to support their emotional wellbeing. As a teacher yourself, you can appreciate how feedback from others can impact on you. Most of us thrive on positive reinforcement, but can react negatively when we feel we are receiving a negative evaluation. Therefore, you need to consider how any comments you make might impact on the beginning teacher. According to Hobson (2016, p. 87), 'judgementoring' can be 'detrimental to beginning teachers' professional learning, development and wellbeing'.

You also need to consider how you are going to engage and structure your discussions to ensure that the beginning teacher is the central focus and that they are guided through your questioning to reflect on how well they are achieving and what they need to do to make further progress.

Where any of these are missing, the value and potential outcomes of the process may be compromised.

Objectives

At the end of this chapter, you should be able to:

*   Organise pre- and post-lesson observation discussion meetings in order to make them efficient and effective;
*   Understand the role of the mentor and the beginning teacher in facilitating pre- and post-lesson observation discussions;
*   Understand how questioning for reflection can be structured to support discussion;
*   Conduct pre- and post-lesson observation discussions so that they are most productive;
*   Understand the review processes that can be undertaken during the running of a post-lesson observation discussion.

Before reading any further, complete Task 15.1 to reflect on your current practice in relation to pre- and post-lesson observation discussions.

Task 15.1   Mentor reflection: What is my current practice in relation to pre- and post-lesson observation discussions?

Using your experiences of mentoring to date, reflect on your current practice in relation to pre- and post-lesson observation discussions, making specific reference to the following:

*   Who runs the meeting?
*   What expectations do you have of a beginning teacher and yourself in preparing for a meeting?
*   How is a meeting recorded?
*   What sort of questions do you ask during a meeting?
*   Any other points in relation to your current practice?

Organising pre- and post-lesson observation discussions

Being a mentor is not likely to be the only role you undertake in school. Although you are busy, it is important to prioritise pre- and post-lesson observation discussions so that they happen in a timely manner. Allowing time after a pre-lesson observation discussion for a beginning teacher to make any changes to a lesson plan can enhance a lesson, as well as their learning and development. Allowing a short period of time after a lesson before holding a post-lesson observation discussion enables some reflection on/evaluation of the lesson prior to the meeting, but ensures the lesson is still fresh in both your and the beginning teacher's mind. However, it is very important that a beginning teacher knows when these meetings are going to take place.

Time in schools is precious. The organisation and management of any meeting with a beginning teacher are important if it is to be efficient and effective in its use of time. Ensuring that pre- and post-lesson observation discussions have a clear and concise structure focuses attention on what is expected from the meeting. Franko et al. (2016) highlighted the need to establish a clear structure to meetings to ensure that both parties understand the purpose of, and what is to be addressed during, the meeting, as well as establishing specific roles and responsibilities for each party. Thus, it is important to establish ground rules for both the mentor and the beginning teacher. Ground rules could include the following:

- What needs to be done prior to the meeting?
    - Does any documentation need to be circulated before the meeting and by when?
        - Lesson plans?
        - Notes from the previous meeting?
    - Who will confirm when and where the meeting will take place?
- How will the meeting be conducted?
    - Who will lead the meeting?
    - What will be the focus of the meeting?
    - How will the meeting be recorded?
- How will the meeting be followed up?
    - Who will circulate meeting notes and by when?

Maintaining a consistency in ground rules for both pre- and post-lesson observation discussions provides less opportunity for both the beginning teacher and the mentor to become confused. I am sure we've all heard 'Well I didn't think I needed to do this for this meeting.' If it helps, produce a checklist for both you and the beginning teacher for each meeting (see examples in Tables 15.1 and 15.2).

It is important that a beginning teacher shares the lesson plan with you in advance of the meeting. This allows you to read and annotate the plan (adding comments to the text is a good way of doing this). It can then be returned to the beginning teacher prior to the meeting so they have some time to think about how they might respond to the queries you have raised. If time allows, the beginning teacher should make modifications based on the feedback provided and bring a revised plan to the pre-lesson observation discussion. However, this is not always the case, so modifications may well be undertaken after the pre-lesson observation discussion and before they teach the lesson (unless this meeting is being held immediately before the lesson itself).

Table 15.1 Example of roles and responsibilities for a pre-lesson observation discussion

Beginning teacher	Mentor
Confirms where and when the meeting is taking place	Ensures they prioritise meeting to meet in a timely manner
Sends lesson plan prior to meeting	Reads lesson plan and makes notes for discussion
Identifies key areas they wish to discuss	Asks questions of the beginning teacher to draw out their understanding of how the lesson will be delivered and any issues that may arise
Makes notes of the meeting and distributes them following the meeting	Signs the meeting notes to confirm that they reflect the discussions
Makes any changes to lesson plan prior to delivery	

Table 15.2 Example of roles and responsibilities for a post-lesson observation discussion

Beginning teacher	Mentor
Confirms where and when the meeting is taking place	Ensures they prioritise meeting to meet in a timely manner
Provides an evaluation of the lesson based on their own initial reflections	Provides written feedback on the lesson observed
Highlights key areas they wish to discuss	Asks questions of the beginning teacher to draw out their understanding of how the lesson was delivered and any issues that may have arisen
Provides clear evidence of how the pupils have met the learning objectives	Focuses the discussion on strengths and areas for development
Works with mentor to develop targets for the next lesson	
Makes notes of the meeting and distributes them following the meeting	Signs the meeting notes to confirm they reflect the discussions
Incorporates any agreed targets into next lesson plans	

Most beginning teachers want feedback as soon as possible after a lesson; however, it can be beneficial to delay the meeting until the beginning teacher has had some time to reflect upon their teaching. If this is the case, a small amount of feedback may be appropriate to reassure them and to offer some areas on which they might reflect prior to the meeting. If the lesson has been videoed (see Chapter 13), it is good practice to give a copy to the beginning teacher to look at and review prior to meeting. This allows them to spend some time analysing their own teaching. We now look in more detail at what the meetings themselves might look like in practice.

Engaging in pre- and post-lesson observation discussions

Facilitating a pre-lesson observation discussion

A beginning teacher has crafted a lesson plan based on their knowledge and understanding of the class and their current level of progress. A pre-lesson observation discussion is an opportunity for a beginning teacher and a mentor to reflect on a lesson prior to it being taught.

It provides space for the beginning teacher to think about what they want their pupils to learn, what this will look like and how they have planned to achieve this. For the mentor, it provides an opportunity to develop an understanding of what the beginning teacher is thinking and what it is they want to achieve in the lesson. Therefore, as the facilitator, you should aim to draw out the rationale for the plan and to understand the beginning teacher's thoughts. For example, it is important to establish what the end of the lesson will look like. What is it specifically that the beginning teacher wants the pupils to have achieved by the end of the lesson, and what evidence will they have that allows them to say they have achieved it and at what level? Immediately, the beginning teacher is challenged to think about the purpose of the lesson, to draw out success criteria and therefore focus on pupil outcomes and behaviours, rather than their own teaching.

It also allows any issues that may occur during the teaching of the lesson to be identified, discussed and addressed prior to the lesson being taught. It allows questioning for clarification and, if necessary, allows modification to be made to the plan.

In summary, by setting time aside prior to the lesson being taught, both the beginning teacher and the mentor/observer can understand what is going to be taught and how pupil progress will be demonstrated. It also allows changes to be made to the plan, as well as providing an opportunity for a beginning teacher to reflect on their planning and ideas. As a result, a beginning teacher should enter the lesson more confidently, which should, in turn, be reflected in their teaching.

Structuring a pre- and post-lesson observation discussion

One key component of a successful pre- or post-lesson observation discussion is structuring the discussion in order to create an environment in which both you and the beginning teacher feel comfortable to discuss in depth the lesson you are going to observe/have observed. This includes structuring questions to allow a beginning teacher to share their thoughts effectively.

Understanding questioning to support a positive and productive pre- and post-lesson observation discussion

It is important to be clear what it is you want to focus on prior to a meeting. Questioning could be based around a specific aspect of the lesson that might have been identified as a result of a previous lesson. For example, a beginning teacher may spend too much time talking to the class, so questioning might focus on how much information the pupils need to be able to undertake the activity, with a view to reducing beginning teacher talk.

The ability to reflect evolves over time, based on experiences and understanding of the reflective process. Thus, when engaging in a pre- and post-lesson observation discussion, the approach adopted should evolve alongside the development of the beginning teacher's capacity for reflection. For a meaningful and productive discussion to take place, there should be a change from mentor- to beginning teacher-led discussions, and questions should move from descriptive to reflective. However, there is no fixed model or timeframe for this to occur; it should evolve as appropriate.

Reflection can occur at three levels, related to the depth of reflection and the focus of the reflection. For example, at level 1 in simple reflection, the focus is predominantly on describing organisational and technical aspects of lessons. As reflection becomes deeper at level 2, theory is used to underpin and, in some cases, justify the approaches adopted within the lesson. At the deepest level of reflection (level 3), the focus is on skills, knowledge and understanding, but also the impact of teaching on the wider social and emotional learning of the pupils taught. This is important because, as the mentor, you need to consider what you can expect from a beginning teacher at each stage of their development; it is important not to expect a beginning teacher to engage in in-depth reflection early on. See Chapter 10 on supporting the development of a beginning teacher's reflection. Task 15.2 asks you to look at how and why meetings change over time.

Task 15.2   Changes to pre- and post-lesson observation discussions over time

Consider a recent mentoring experience you have engaged in:

* Did the pre- and post-lesson observation discussion meetings change over time? If so, how and why?
* How did you conduct meetings at the start of the mentoring experience?
* How did you encourage the beginning teacher to take increasing responsibility for the meetings?
* How did you encourage reflection by the beginning teacher?
* How did you conduct the meetings later on in the mentoring experience?
* What caused any changes?

Early in a beginning teacher's development (normally early in the initial teacher education (ITE) phase), discussions are likely to focus on organisational and technical aspects of teaching such as planning, time management or the activities delivered. For example, a beginning teacher might describe why they have chosen the activities they have, or not be aware of the amount of time they are spending talking to pupils, which is limiting the amount of time pupils have to practice.

Over time, the focus moves towards contextual aspects of teaching; for example, how pupil characteristics are taken into account, the skill level of individual pupils in the class, the purpose of each activity, and how resources are used to support learning. For example, a beginning teacher may discuss how activities link together, how activities have been differentiated and why. They will include a range of resources to support learning and assessment.

At a later stage of ITE and into the newly qualified and early career experiences, discussion is more reflective, with a greater emphasis on aspects such as specific needs of pupils, the affective domain and the lesson climate. There will be clear evidence of links to theory and connections made to specific pupils and approaches adopted; for example, how activities are differentiated to meet pupils' needs, how pupils are grouped, and the roles they undertake in the lesson to ensure that all pupils have opportunities to assess and review their own learning. Further, a beginning teacher may have been exploring more innovative teaching approaches.

Structuring questions

Questions related to the what, why, when, how, where and who are asked to encourage a beginning teacher to reflect on a lesson and the impact their teaching has had on pupils' progress. To elicit depth to the responses, key words such as 'tell me, explain, describe, precisely, in detail, exactly' (also known as TED PIE (Metropolitan Police Service, 2003)) can be asked. Questions should be structured but open-ended to request specific information about what has happened. For example, if you want to find out why a beginning teacher delivered an activity in a certain way, you can ask: *Why did you deliver your warm up in that way?* or *Describe in detail how you delivered the warm up, and explain why you adopted this approach.* The subtle change in the question focuses the beginning teacher much more on providing detail of what is needed, and encourages the use of evidence to support what they are saying. Task 15.3 focuses on asking the right questions.

Task 15.3   Asking the right questions

Record one each of your pre- and post-lesson observation discussions. Listen back to them and write down the questions you ask.

1.   How do your questions encourage reflection from the beginning teacher?
2.   What aspects of the lesson do you focus on?
3.   Do the questions differ between the pre- and post-lesson observation discussion?
4.   Do you ask common questions in both meetings?
5.   Do the questions you ask elicit the information you are seeking? If not, why not?
6.   What do you need to do to enhance your questioning technique?

Questions you may ask in a pre-lesson observation discussion

Table 15.3 provides examples of questions you might ask in a pre-lesson observation discussion to facilitate reflective thinking.

As a result of the pre-lesson observation discussion, both you and the beginning teacher should have a clear understanding of how the lesson will progress, and what the focus on the observation will be. Now complete Task 15.4.

Task 15.4   Questions for a pre-lesson observation discussion

1.   Having completed Task 15.3 and looked at Table 15.3, consider what questions you might ask at the next pre-lesson observation discussion you hold with a beginning teacher.

Table 15.3 Questions you might ask in a pre-lesson observation discussion

Key question	Purpose
What are your learning objectives and how will you know that the pupils have achieved these?	To establish what the pupils are expected to have achieved by the end of the lesson, with evidence of what this will look like. This will also support the beginning teacher to reflect on whether the learning objectives are achievable, and what the success criteria are.
How will you assess progress during the lesson?	To allow the beginning teacher to reflect on their assessment strategies and how they will track progress during the lesson, and also to consider when mini plenaries are appropriate and questions they might ask pupils to monitor their understanding.
Talk me through the lesson.	The beginning teacher provides a verbal overview of the lesson. In doing so, issues they might not have considered might arise; for example, whether the activities flow, or the organisation of groups and equipment.
Are there any particular parts of the lesson you are most concerned about?	This allows the beginning teacher to consider where any problem might arise and what alternative strategies they might have to adopt.
What specifically would you like me to focus on during the observation?	The focus of the observation is handed to the beginning teacher. They will have their own targets for development, and this is their opportunity to identify those on which they want focused feedback.

Questions you may ask in a post-lesson observation discussion

As with a pre-lesson observation discussion, the management of time is important. Asking questions targeted on achievement of the learning objectives, including when discussing a video of the lesson, as well as on the agreed focus of the observation draws a beginning teacher's attention to key aspects of the lesson and their teaching, rather than requiring them to provide an analysis of each part of the lesson. For example, questions might include:

1. Based on your learning objectives, what specific evidence do you have that the pupils achieved these and made progress?
2. Today the lesson observation focused on the quality of pupils' work and clarity of instruction.
   a. Based on your lesson, how would you describe the quality of the pupils' work, and what might you do to enhance it further?
   b. How would you evidence that you presented your instructions in a meaningful, clear and concise manner?
3. From your lesson, describe in detail two of the things you were most pleased with.
4. From your lesson, describe in detail one thing you would like to improve.
5. Based on your evaluation, what are you intending to teach in your next lesson?
6. Based on your evaluation. what would you like the focus of the next observation to be?

As with a pre-lesson observation discussion, the questions asked in a post-lesson observation discussion are, in many ways, guided by the beginning teacher's current level of reflection. You should encourage a beginning teacher to draw on specific evidence from their observations to provide informed comment about, and reflection on, pupils' learning and their teaching. The use of specific examples allows consideration of whether informed decisions have been made in the delivery of the lesson, and also the extent to which reflection is taking place within the lesson to support modifications to the teaching, and therefore learning, that is taking place (see Chapter 10 on reflection). For example, if behaviour management was a focus of the observation, you might draw the beginning teacher's attention to specific incidents within the lesson to discuss, for example:

1.   When you were organising the groups after the warm up, pupils became more disruptive. How did you feel at this time?
2.   Why did you allow the pupils to choose their own groups?
3.   How might you change the way you group pupils in the next lesson?

Such questioning requires the beginning teacher to identify specific examples. These may be drawn from, for example, observations made, including video evidence if the lesson has been recorded, or evaluation by the beginning teacher. Now complete Task 15.5.

Task 15.5   Questions for a post-lesson observation discussion

During your next lesson observation, jot down key questions that emerge during the lesson and review these with the beginning teacher during the post-lesson observation discussion.

The review process

One way of approaching the post-lesson observation discussion is by using the review process (Lawrence and Mellor, 2011) (see Table 15.4). The review process provides a clear structure to support reflection. It follows six key steps, starting with reassurance and moving to a conclusion of setting new targets for development.

Each of these steps is now considered in turn.

During the reassure phase, the focus is on settling the beginning teacher and focusing the discussion. If there has been a period of time between the lesson and the meeting, both the beginning teacher and the mentor should bring with them notes about the lesson and any specific issues they would like to discuss. This is an opportunity for the mentor to start to draw out some key positive points from the observation. For example:

> I really liked the way you managed the class today, you clearly thought about the transitions between each activity, especially between the warm up and the first activity, and as a result the disruptive behaviour we saw last week has been reduced. Well done.

The establish phase provides an opportunity to focus on what the beginning teacher planned for the pupils to achieve by the end of the lesson. This builds on the pre-lesson observation

Table 15.4 The review process

Stage	Focus	Characteristics/key questions
Reassure	The beginning teacher about the lesson	Mentor provides reassurance about the lesson, which may include specific examples of what went well.
Establish	What the beginning teacher wanted pupils to have achieved during the lesson	Mentor asks questions of the beginning teacher about the objectives for the lesson. The beginning teacher explains the extent to which they felt these had been achieved by pupils.
Review	Pupil progress, beginning teacher progress against targets and against specific teaching standards	The mentor poses specific questions that encourage the beginning teacher to reflect on specific aspects of the lesson, paying particular attention to examples of both pupils' and their own progress. The beginning teacher is encouraged to provide specific examples from the lesson to expand the depth of their answers.
Input	Your observations	The mentor provides specific feedback based on their observations, bringing in aspects that have not previously been covered. Emphasis is placed on the provision of specific examples from the lesson (this might include the use of video evidence).
Emphasise	Provide a summary of the discussion	The beginning teacher provides a summary of the discussion to draw key aspects out. This is later written up by the beginning teacher and shared with the mentor.
Way forward	Identify targets for the next observation and focus for development	The beginning teacher and the mentor identify strengths from the lesson and targets for development based on discussion.

discussion in establishing what the learning objectives were for the lesson and the evidence available to support the achievement of these. Key questions might therefore be, for example:

> Looking at your learning objectives, describe specifically what evidence you have that you achieved these.

Or

> In your learning objectives you identified (give specific example) was the key success criteria. What specifically were you looking for from the pupils to achieve this?

The review phase focuses on the beginning teacher evidencing the progress made by pupils in the lesson. This should predominantly refer to what they have observed during the lesson in relation to progress against the learning objectives. The beginning teacher should be encouraged to consider what they feel are the key aspects of pupil progress they might need to focus on moving forward. Throughout, reference to the focus of the observation should be made, and consequently, the evidence to support this phase should be provided predominantly by the beginning teacher.

It is also important that the beginning teacher is provided with an opportunity to identify areas of strength and potential areas for development. This can be a challenging section of the discussion, as the tendency, from experience, is for a beginning teacher to focus on the negative aspects of the lesson. In physical education lessons, we seek to encourage pupils to reflect upon their own performance and identify areas for development; all we are doing within the post-lesson observation discussion is encouraging a beginning teacher to do the same. Key questions may therefore be, for example:

> One of your targets for development was around giving instructions. How would you evidence that you presented your instructions in a meaningful, clear and concise manner?
> From your lesson, describe in detail two of the things you were most pleased with.
> From your lesson, describe in detail one thing you would like to improve next time.

The input phase is the opportunity for you to make your contribution based on your observation of the lesson. It is possible that if questions have been appropriately structured, the beginning teacher has already identified some of the issues you have observed. You need to consider how your input/feedback is framed, as many beginning teachers are seeking reassurance and approval/guidance from you. It should be constructive and identify potential improvements. For example:

> I thought you questioned the group well. You had clearly thought about the appropriateness of the questions for different pupils and really got them to expand their answers to show their depth of understanding.

Or

> I was concerned about how you moved from one activity to another. There was not always a clear transition and you may wish to think about how you summarise the learning after each activity using a mini plenary.

In the emphasis phase, the discussion is summarised. The beginning teacher should have been making notes throughout the discussion, which they can use for the summary as well as to refer to later. A beginning teacher may ask to audio record meetings, but that should be at your discretion.

The final phase is that of target setting or ways forward. New target(s) are set. The focus of the next observation can be established, and also possible activities that will provide evidence to support achievement of the target(s) through the observation focus. Task 15.6 asks you to look at your approach in a post-lesson discussion and how you might modify it. In Task 15.7, you are asked to reflect on your practice in relation to holding pre- and post-lesson observation discussions.

Task 15.6   The approach I adopt in my post-lesson observation discussions and how I might modify it

1. Reflect on your last post-lesson discussion with a beginning teacher.

    a.   Who controlled the discussion?

   b. What percentage of time were you speaking, and how much input did the beginning teacher have?

   c. How effectively did you draw out observations and reflection from the beginning teacher?

   d. How satisfied were you with the way you handled the discussion? Do you know how the beginning teacher felt?

   e. Having reviewed the section on post-lesson discussions, how might you modify your approach in your next post-lesson observation discussions?

An example of the review process in practice is provided in case study 15.1. The discussion focuses on pupils' achievement of the learning objectives.

Case study 15.1 The review process in practice

Context: Sam is a beginning teacher who has been observed teaching a Year 8 rounders lesson. Sam's learning objectives were to engage pupils in throwing and catching practices, building up to a full game where pupils would be able to demonstrate these skills in a competitive situation.

Pre-lesson observation discussion: Through the pre-lesson discussion, Sam demonstrated a clear understanding of what he wanted pupils to learn during the lesson and how this would be demonstrated.

During the lesson, it became clear that Sam had not fully considered that the pupils had significant prior knowledge of throwing and catching, as they had completed a unit of work on cricket in Year 7.

(Part of) Post-lesson observation discussion:

Mentor: Thank you Sam, I enjoyed watching your lesson, and it is clear that you have a sound understanding of the skills and knowledge required for rounders (*reassure*). Can you remind me what your learning objectives were and how you feel you achieved these (*establish*)?

Sam: My learning objective focused on developing pupils' throwing and catching skills, and then for them to apply these in a games situation. I started by reviewing different ways of throwing, but it was clear I had not thought enough about what they might already know and be able to do, as many were achieving above what I had planned for them to learn. Therefore, on reflection I think the objectives were too simplistic and the lesson lacked the required level of challenge.

Mentor: So, you have identified that there was a lack of challenge for some pupils. What evidence do you have that this was causing a problem (*review*)?

Sam: It was clear that when I introduced the activities, the majority of pupils could already do the activity. Some of them started to talk and mess around. When they went away to practice, this continued. I thought they were just being disruptive, but when one of them told me that they had done this before, it made me think that perhaps their behaviour reflected a level of boredom. This was also evident when I called them in to move the activity on.

Mentor: Sam, I would agree that the lack of challenge did impact on pupils' behaviour. It was clear that you had underestimated their ability (*input*). You must consider what other activities the pupils have engaged in and how the skills you are looking to develop might already have been developed. One way to do this is to get the pupils to reflect on what they already know and how they can use existing skills across areas of activity (*emphasis*). So, Sam, what would you do differently next time (*ways forward*)?

Sam: I think for next time, I'll look to start with some small-sided games where the emphasis is on throwing and catching. This will allow me to identify more clearly the skill level of different pupils. I'll also take a look at the grades they have for other activities they have been taught that might include throwing and catching and then identify how I might group them on ability. In terms of developing their skills further, I'll develop more differentiated activities, which will allow them to challenge themselves further. In terms of transitions, I think I'll try the approach I've used in some of my other lessons, whereby I work with a specific group to develop the next activity and then get the rest of the class to come and watch them, or just move each group on as and when I think it is appropriate.

Task 15.7   Mentor reflection: Reviewing pre- and post-lesson observation discussions

Having read the chapter:

* How will you make sure that a beginning teacher understands what is expected of them during pre- and post-lesson observation discussions?
* What are the key questions you should ask during a pre-lesson observation discussion?
* What are the key questions you will ask during each phase of the review process in a post-lesson observation discussion?
* What changes can/would you make to how you facilitate pre- and post-lesson observation discussions?

Summary and key points

This chapter has highlighted some of the key characteristics that can make successful pre- and post-lesson observation discussions. Specifically,

* Effective pre- and post-lesson discussions allow you and a beginning teacher to develop a clear understanding of what they are hoping to achieve in a lesson, how this will be

achieved and what it will look like, and then the opportunity to review the lesson based on the jointly agreed focus of the observation.

- Ensuring that discussions are well planned, structured and managed will allow the beginning teacher to reflect in depth about their strengths and areas for development.
- In focusing on aspects of questioning, we have encouraged you to think about how your questions can facilitate reflective thought and use evidence to support discussions.
- Central to the success of the discussions is the opportunity for a beginning teacher, supported by your questioning, to lead the sessions, thereby taking greater responsibility for their own development over time.

Further resources

O'Leary, M. (2014) *Classroom Observation: A Guide to the Effective Observation of Teaching and Learning*, Abingdon: Routledge.
This easy-to-read text provides clear guidance regarding the observation of teaching and learning. Whilst the main focus is on observation, chapter 7 focuses on how observations can be used to support critical reflection.

Lawrence, J. (2017) 'Reflecting on your teaching', in W. Jolliffe and D. Waugh (eds.) *NQT: The Beginning Teacher's Guide to Outstanding Practice*, London: Learning Matters.
This short chapter provides an overview of the process of reflection and how beginning teachers can be encouraged to engage in the process.

See also the companion website for this book (www.routledge.com/9781138059658).

You may also find it useful to refer to/use the text books written for student and newly qualified physical education teachers with a beginning teacher you are mentoring (see list on Page 4).

16 Holding weekly briefings

*Gill Golder, Jackie Arthur, Alison Keyworth
and Julie Stevens*

Introduction

Hobson et al. (2016) suggested that international research evidence supports the claim that there are substantial benefits to providing mentors to support the professional learning and development of teachers. A beginning teacher is involved in a range of informal and formal mentoring experiences. A weekly meeting between you as mentor and a beginning physical education teacher is a requirement on many initial teacher education (ITE) courses. It is a formal experience that is a crucial component of mentoring.

A weekly meeting provides a 'safe space' within which a beginning teacher should feel able to speak openly and honestly to you about their perceived weaknesses and learning and development needs, as well as celebrate strengths or areas of significant progress. Their progress against previous targets is monitored and evaluated, and targeted goals and objectives are developed, aligned with the beginning teacher's needs (Ragins, 2016).

The most successful weekly meetings act as a tool for teacher empowerment and professional enhancement for the beginning physical education teacher. They enable you, as mentor, to reflect on your own practice, learn from the beginning teacher and develop key attributes needed to be an effective mentor. Ragins (2016, p. 231) described this as relational mentoring, which 'acknowledges that mentors can also learn and grow from the relationship'.

The expertise of you both is brought together to generate a critical evidence base to support a practically grounded reflection on what a beginning teacher has achieved as well as informed action for further development. Thus, the best weekly meetings are collaborative in nature. McCaughtry et al. (2005) suggested that this collaborative professional learning contains a number of key characteristics, including semi-structured design that responds to emerging needs; contextualisation of learning specific to the school and the classes the beginning teacher is working with; relevance to the beginning teacher in terms of their stage of development (see Katz, 1995, chapter 1); practical and ready-to-incorporate ideas in terms of subject content and pedagogical knowledge; and reflection centred on active learning.

For a mentor, a subtle mixture of rich and sophisticated content, curricular and pedagogical knowledge (Stroot et al. 1998), as well as strong listening and communication skills that can support, motivate and emotionally engage a beginning teacher, are important for holding effective weekly meetings. Another skill is being able to select the most effective way to conduct a weekly meeting to ensure that it meets its intended outcomes. The manner in which you conduct meetings is affected by both external drivers, such as policy directions, frameworks for working or professional requirements, and internal drivers, such as how your school structures learning, other professional responsibilities, or ITE partnership arrangements. It is also affected by both your own and the beginning teacher's personality and their current stage of development.

Objectives

At the end of this chapter, you should be able to:

- Understand the importance of a regular and structured weekly meeting with a beginning teacher;
- Be aware of the external and internal drivers that might impact on how you organise and conduct a weekly meeting;
- Understand the shifting relationship in the weekly meeting as a beginning teacher develops over time;
- Draw upon the evidence base to structure a weekly meeting, setting an appropriate focus based on individual beginning teacher need;
- Negotiate appropriate targets to move a beginning teacher's practice forward;
- Reflect on your own ability in holding weekly meetings and what you might need to develop in this area.

Before proceeding, complete Task 16.1.

Task 16.1   Mentor reflection: Ability to run a weekly meeting

Use the following questions to reflect on the current effectiveness of weekly meetings you are holding with a beginning teacher.

- What aspects of the weekly meeting do you find most rewarding? Why?
- What aspects of the weekly meeting do you find most challenging? Why?
- How has the weekly meeting supported the beginning teacher to progress?
- How has the weekly meeting supported your development?
- To be a more effective mentor, what aspects of the weekly meetings would you like to develop?

The weekly meeting

A weekly meeting is significant in supporting a beginning teacher to make sense of the range of learning experiences to which they have been exposed over the period of a week. In this way, it is distinct from a lesson debrief, which places a magnifying glass on why a beginning teacher chose specific objectives/pedagogies/strategies with a specific group of pupils (see Chapter 15). A weekly meeting draws together learning from all a beginning teacher's formal and informal experiences and provides an opportunity for them and for you to reflect and look at the bigger picture of their progress over time, rather than the minutiae of an individual teaching episode. Whilst it is a formal undertaking with a scheduled and regular meeting time, the manner in which you conduct a weekly meeting needs to be dynamic in nature, since the context in which a beginning teacher is working (time, schools, mentors) is in constant flux.

Task 16.2 focuses on recognising differences between a weekly meeting and a lesson debrief.

Task 16.2   Recognising different learning outcomes of a weekly meeting versus a lesson debrief

Using ideas presented in Chapter 15, identify a unique core purpose of both a weekly meeting and a lesson debrief. Consider how they are different. Consider both yourself as a mentor and a beginning physical education teacher.

What can a mentor learn from facilitating a weekly meeting?	What can a beginning teacher learn from engaging in a weekly meeting?
What can a mentor learn from carrying out a lesson debrief?	What can a beginning teacher learn from a lesson debrief?

External drivers/frameworks and internal drivers

External drivers/frameworks

Chapter 1 explored some external drivers that impact on all aspects of your mentoring. These provide a useful framework to help you structure and plan a weekly meeting. These external drivers in relation to England, and how you might use these in a weekly meeting, are considered in this section. If you are mentoring a beginning teacher in another country, refer to the specific external drivers for your country (see Chapter 1 for some examples from other countries).

The feedback a beginning physical education teacher receives on their lessons and their own self-evaluation of their teaching enable you to identify areas of strength and areas for development on which to focus discussions. An external driver such as the 'Teachers' Standards' (Department for Education (DfE), 2011a) can be used to explore specific elements of a beginning teacher's teaching to support pupils' learning. They can be used in your weekly meeting to determine where a beginning teacher is already demonstrating excellent practice in relation to that standard or area(s)/standard(s) where additional development might be needed.

Another external driver might be a core curriculum for ITE (for example DfE, 2016a). You can use the content of the core curriculum as a checklist to ensure that a beginning teacher receives a good grounding in elements of good classroom practice in teaching physical education and to design specific development activities to help them move their practice forward.

It can be useful to refer to mentoring standards (for example DfE, 2016b) to reflect on your own skills as a mentor, establish a different way of working if there appears to be a breakdown in communication, or help a beginning teacher overcome barriers to development they may be experiencing. Using these to look at aspects of a weekly meeting when challenges occur, or a beginning teacher does not seem to be progressing or is plateauing, can enable you to explore elements of the standards and reflect on the characteristics of effective mentoring that impact on a beginning teacher's overall experience. In England (DfE 2016b), there are four standards, and targeting one of these, for example teaching or professionalism, may enable a beginning teacher to develop a more personalised development plan.

A national mentoring framework (e.g. CUREE, 2015b) can provide a really useful tool as you design the weekly meeting structure, in order to consider how you have embedded the different principles that underpin the framework; for example, in relation to self-evaluation of practice and helping you identify areas for further improvement in your mentoring practices. As a beginning teacher progresses, they can start to take ownership for their own development, adopting the principles themselves in their work or making suggestions of what they would like to cover; for example, how to apply their experiences of being mentored to working with pupils in their care.

It is possible to discuss standards for teachers' professional development (e.g. DfE, 2016c) with a beginning teacher and plan accordingly to address the areas that focus on professional development. The professional code of conduct, for example developing trust, ethics and treating pupils with dignity, can sometimes be difficult to set targets for, and hence should be a particular focus in relation to both a beginning teacher and your own development as a mentor (e.g. establish trusting relationships, empathise with the challenges a beginning teacher faces and model high standards of practice). If you are working with a beginning teacher as they complete their ITE, it is good to use the professional development standards to structure discussion and set targets for the newly qualified teacher year.

Task 16.3 focuses on frameworks that influence your setting.

Task 16.3   Frameworks that influence your setting

Read through, and become familiar with, the core content of the various frameworks that influence your setting (as a starter, you may want to refer to the list in Chapter 1). For each, write one sentence:

'I can use this in my weekly meeting to.......'

List those for which you have difficulty in identifying how you can use them in your weekly meeting, and discuss with another mentor how they do this.

Internal drivers

Internal drivers impact on the way in which you conduct a weekly meeting. One of the biggest internal factors is the other roles and responsibilities you have. This can affect how a beginning teacher sees you. If you are in a position of leadership, they may see you in a different way than if you have recently qualified yourself. It is important to ensure that how you establish the relationship and conduct a weekly meeting acknowledges the 'other hats' you might wear, but that this does not distract from, or overtake, the meeting. In addition, the structure of your school day influences when, where and for how long you can meet. Some schools ensure a free period each week to enable a meeting to take place, but this can be anything from 30 minutes to 100 minutes long, depending on the structure of your school day. Other schools expect a weekly meeting to take place after the teaching day has finished. However, in physical education, fitting this in with meetings or extra-curricular activities can sometimes be challenging.

An additional internal driver may relate to an aspect of practice or learning on which the school is focusing; for example, a whole-school focus on reading might be in place. You may want to discuss this specifically in a weekly meeting. Your own school policies are also an internal driver. There might, for example, be a specific approach to marking which all staff, including a student teacher, are required to follow. However, whilst they need to adopt the school policy, it is important that they also reflect on other approaches, as this will prepare them better for employment in other schools. Chapter 2 looked at the physical education-specific context. This is also important in relation to your weekly meeting.

Task 16.4 asks you to consider internal drivers that affect weekly meetings.

Task 16.4   Common internal drivers to consider when establishing the format and purpose of your weekly meeting

Discuss with mentors of beginning teachers, experienced staff, or staff new to the school, internal drivers in your school setting that affect their weekly meetings. Find out:

- Do they have a set agenda they must follow (linked to department structures or school policy)?
- Who decides how they run their meetings?
- What are the challenges they face in making time for planning and holding their meeting?
- How do they overcome the challenges?
- What can you learn from the experiences of others?

Planning a weekly meeting to meet a beginning teacher's individual needs: Changing needs and roles

A weekly meeting changes and evolves over time as a beginning teacher becomes more independent and autonomous. In order for you to be able to best support a beginning teacher as they develop over time, it is vital that you are aware of how your role within the mentor-mentee relationship needs to be both flexible and adaptable.

In Chapter 1, three models of mentoring were presented: Daloz (2012), Katz (1995) and Clutterbuck (2004). In each model, there was a suggestion that a mentee's needs change over time, and as a result, the way you plan, conduct and evaluate your weekly meeting needs to reflect this.

Your ability to identify and assess the developmental stage of a beginning teacher at any given time is a significant aspect of your being effective in structuring a weekly meeting to ensure growth takes place. Of equal importance, however, is your skill in adapting your own approach to fit the developmental needs of the beginning teacher. It is worth remembering that none of the models are linear in structure, and, therefore, it is likely that a beginning teacher will move 'to and fro' between the stages/zones.

Task 16.5 looks at models of mentoring and stages of development.

Task 16.5   Stages of development

Consider the Katz (1995) stages of development model outlined in Chapter 1. Explore which model you might adopt in order to support a beginning teacher at each of the four developmental stages.

Stage of development (Katz, 1995)	What models of mentoring might you refer to? Why?	What questions might you ask during a weekly meeting that will support a beginning teacher at this particular stage?	How might you appropriately challenge a beginning teacher during the weekly meeting?	What support mechanisms might you put in place to enable a beginning teacher to learn effectively and make good or better progress?
Survival				
Consolidation				
Renewal				
Maturity				

Purpose and structure of a weekly meeting

Some of a beginning teacher's initial concerns in the early phases of development are logistical ones, and you need to set out clearly how you will work, answering questions such

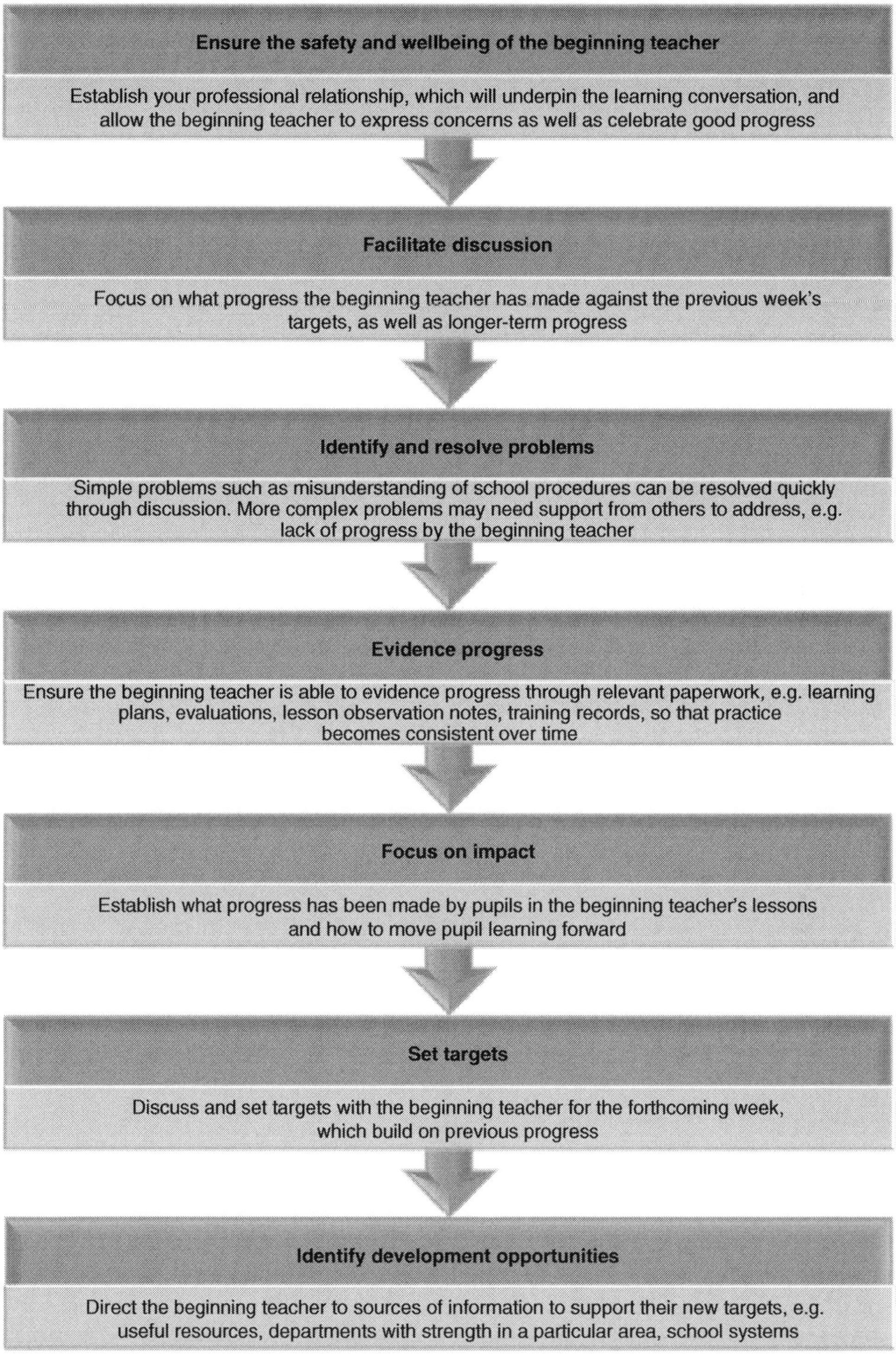

Ensure the safety and wellbeing of the beginning teacher

Establish your professional relationship, which will underpin the learning conversation, and allow the beginning teacher to express concerns as well as celebrate good progress

Facilitate discussion

Focus on what progress the beginning teacher has made against the previous week's targets, as well as longer-term progress

Identify and resolve problems

Simple problems such as misunderstanding of school procedures can be resolved quickly through discussion. More complex problems may need support from others to address, e.g. lack of progress by the beginning teacher

Evidence progress

Ensure the beginning teacher is able to evidence progress through relevant paperwork, e.g. learning plans, evaluations, lesson observation notes, training records, so that practice becomes consistent over time

Focus on impact

Establish what progress has been made by pupils in the beginning teacher's lessons and how to move pupil learning forward

Set targets

Discuss and set targets with the beginning teacher for the forthcoming week, which build on previous progress

Identify development opportunities

Direct the beginning teacher to sources of information to support their new targets, e.g. useful resources, departments with strength in a particular area, school systems

Figure 16.1 The general principles around the purpose of the weekly meeting

as: How often do we meet? Who takes responsibility for setting up the meeting? Where will we meet? How long do we meet for? Once the logistics are set, you can turn your attention to the purpose and structure of the meeting. Do not underestimate the value a beginning teacher places on the weekly meeting; they see it as essential to their progress and praise a mentor who prioritises this regular slot on the timetable. This is reinforced by the DfE (2016b, p.11), who explicitly identified as one of the mentor standards for ITE in England that mentors should 'make time for the trainee and prioritise meetings and discussions with them'.

The purposes of a weekly meeting are multi-faceted, and both external drivers, such as a new framework for managing behaviour in schools, and internal drivers, such as a particular focus in the school on developing literacy levels, as well as the developmental stage of a beginning teacher, influence the agenda. Figure 16.1 outlines the general principles around the purposes of the weekly meeting.

The meeting should be held in a room where discussion can flow and you will not be interrupted or overheard; there may be instances when a beginning teacher may feel overwhelmed or upset, and this safe space allows them to take stock and reflect. The professional relationship you establish makes or breaks the success of the meeting (Roberts, 2000; Hargreaves and Fullan, 2000; Daloz, 2012) (the mentor–mentee relationship is addressed in Chapter 7). Both you as mentor and the beginning teacher should ensure that you are able to meet each week for an appropriate length of time; you should both have completed the necessary preparation to ensure that the meeting is effective and outcomes are met (Wang and Odell, 2002). Task 16.6 asks you to consider preparing for the meeting. In completing the task, consider the following considerations for a well-designed meeting.

In a well-designed meeting, you and the beginning teacher:

- Identify positive experiences from the work in which the beginning teacher has engaged in the school, in lessons and with pupils and staff
- Identify how these activities have enabled the beginning teacher to establish themselves as part of the learning community
- Collate evidence against targets set in the previous meeting to help the beginning teacher see clearly where they are in their development and provide evidence of progress
- Recognise the degree of consistency across the range of evidence supporting progress over time; for example, consider whether the lesson observation of a beginning teacher's teaching agrees with their own evaluation, pupil assessment and initial planning
- Appreciate the relationship between the types of evidence, enabling the evidence collated to help focus progress required against targets set and specific requirements, for example the Teachers' Standards
- Recognise that the beginning teacher has played a significant part in designing the most appropriate development pathway.

Task 16.6   Preparing for the meeting

Devise a checklist of documents required at the meeting, from both your perspective and the beginning teacher's. Consider the range of sources of evidence; for example, beginning teacher practice, pupil practice, school practice, resources and training materials.

What do I need to bring to the meeting?	What does the beginning teacher need to bring to the meeting?

Common practices for structuring meetings with a beginning teacher include:

- Have a set way in which to record the meeting, including a pre-meeting reflection opportunity;
- Ensure that all paperwork is available for both you and the beginning teacher, either in hard copy or electronically, and that both are familiar with it;
- Open the meeting with a question the beginning teacher can respond to positively (see Table 16.1 for starter questions);
- Review the previous week's targets systematically, discussing key evidence in learning plans, evaluations, observations, assessments, resources and so on;
- Discuss opportunities for the beginning teacher to be engaged in development activities that might not be directly linked to their specific targets;
- Discuss what further progress is required in the beginning teacher's practice to become consistent and effective. Some practice will take longer to develop, for example 'Adapting teaching to respond to strengths and needs of all pupils' (DfE, 2011);
- Provide an opportunity for the beginning teacher to express concerns and feelings, emotions, anxieties or frustrations as well as their professional development;
- Discuss and set appropriate targets for the following week to ensure progress over time;
- Ensure that the beginning teacher leaves the meeting feeling able to make progress against agreed targets, knowing what action to take and recognising where they are in their development, that is, from survival stage to maturity (Katz, 1995).

The documentation from the weekly meeting is in itself a source of evidence for development (e.g. against the Teachers' Standards (DfE, 2011a) or other targets you might be setting). The meeting should clearly document any wider professional development and experience the beginning teacher has undertaken, for example parents' evening, professional studies sessions, staff meetings, after-school clubs and fixtures, school trips and visits, and so on, which may not be documented in any other form. This avoids time-consuming activities such as signed letters indicating that the beginning teacher has attended an activity. Figure 16.2 illustrates the type of record the beginning teacher might keep of their meeting with you. It is useful for the beginning teacher to have noted aspects in each section that they would like to discuss with you before the meeting, so that the meeting time can be spent discussing rather than note taking. The example in Figure 16.2 makes suggestions of the sort of thing a beginning teacher might make notes on in each section; however, it is important to note that the content will change as a beginning teacher becomes more autonomous and develops confidence and competence.

Weekly meeting No. 5/30	Date:	Days absent: *Keep a record of this as this may be a cause of lack of progress*
Development opportunities taken this week	• To be completed by the beginning teacher in advance of the meeting • List the different development activities they have been engaged in e.g. Whole-school meeting, lesson observations of beginning teacher teaching, observation of experience teacher, support with planning etc.	
LOOKING BACK:		Reference to Professional Standards you are working towards
1. Progress made on previous targets since last week's meeting: • To be completed by the beginning teacher in advance of the meeting • In this section, the beginning teacher reviews progress against previous targets. They should include where to find evidence for the statement they have made e.g. Year 8 gymnastics group demonstrated more precision in the performance of routines because my focus on subject content knowledge development resulted in more focused ability to identify and remedy common faults in static and dynamic balance (evidence in lesson plan, lesson evaluation, video of pupil work) • This should identify the impact of actions taken on pupils' learning, progress and attainment as well as their own development.		In this section provide an overview of targets set against each section of the professional standards
2. Areas for further development of previous targets since last week's meeting (aspects to carry over to this week): • To be completed by the beginning teacher in advance of the meeting • This section should recognise where more consolidation is required of the targets set		
REFLECTING ON THIS WEEK		
In this section, break down the different sections of the Professional Standards the beginning teacher is working towards to ensure targeted and specific rather than general reflection.	• In this section note down discussion around experiences that have led to progress since the previous meeting. Where appropriate, progress against standard(s) should be highlighted. • In addition, where gaps in knowledge/understanding have been highlighted because of activities the beginning teacher has been engaged in, these could be notes to feed into future targets, e.g. not being certain how to support an English as an Additional Language (EAL) learner in a football lesson so wanting help creating resources to support spoken instruction. • The beginning teacher could jot down aspects they want to discuss in advance and show this to you to aid your planning for the meeting and help you decide in advance which 'helping to learn' approach might be best.	

Figure 16.2 An example of a weekly meeting record document

There also needs to be a section on target setting, which is discussed under the outcomes of the meeting section.

Outcomes and targets of the weekly meeting

As Katz (1995) suggested, in the early stage of their development, a beginning teacher is in survival mode, often displaying low confidence and self-esteem, doubting their competence to make the desired progress. They need to be able to evidence and explain their development in confidence arising from progress against agreed targets. Therefore, a clear action relating to a target is needed, so that the beginning teacher knows what you expect to see as a learning outcome. As the beginning teacher matures within the learning environment, they are able to recognise the impact their progress is having on pupil progress over time.

The discussions that take place in a weekly meeting, and specific learning conversations that evolve from them, are integral to negotiating the next steps in the beginning teacher's development and, hence, the targets you agree at the end of the meeting. However, asking the right questions that enable the appropriate blend of support and challenge (see Daloz's (2012) model) can be difficult, and it becomes all too easy for a mentor to end up dominating the conversation or answering the questions you want the beginning teacher to discover for themselves. Table 16.1 provides an illustration of questions for different foci of the meeting that might help lead you and the beginning teacher to set new targets. You may need to ask different styles of question for different development areas or outcomes: for example, a focus on subject content knowledge, pedagogy or the beginning teacher's wider role as a teacher, or a question by which you want to draw out understanding of policies, develop critical evaluation of approaches to teaching, or justify the strategies the beginning teacher adopted. Sometimes, however, it is more important to talk about how the beginning teacher is feeling and explore issues related to their wellbeing. This makes a nice opening or closing question, as it may dictate how the rest of the meeting goes or the nature of targets you set.

By the time the meeting is over, there should be a very clear joint understanding between you and the beginning teacher about the next steps they will take, including agreed targets.

Figure 16.3 is an example of the final phase of the meeting: the agreement of targets, actions and success criteria.

Clarifying what you expect a beginning teacher to do between this meeting and the next is important. Therefore, there need to be effective actions resulting from the meeting:

- You and the beginning teacher should be able to visualise how these new targets will materialise.
- You need to end the meeting with clearly established learning opportunities/activities the beginning teacher can access, either across the whole school or within the physical education department (or in another school), that will help provide scaffolding for successful progress to be made.
- The beginning teacher needs to know they are in the driving seat and be proactive, networking across the learning community to maximise opportunities initiated.

Table 16.1 Examples of questions for different foci

Opening Questions
- We planned to meet at this time; is it still a good time to carry out the meeting?
- How do you feel about yourself as a teacher this week?
- What has been the most enjoyable experience you have been involved with this week?
- Has there been anything that has made you anxious or uncertain this week?

Whole-School Outcomes
- Were there any whole-school events this week with which you were involved?
- Which groups of staff have you met this week and what did you learn from them?
- As the staff bulletin was encouraging a focus on oracy, how did you see this develop across your tutor group/physical education classes?
- The staff briefing on Monday identified issues of bullying across the school; what have you seen to suggest the community is aware of, and working to address, bullying?

Physical Education Subject Content Knowledge-Specific Outcomes
- In what ways were you able to able to develop pupils' technique and improve their performance this week?
- How successful was your work with Year 9 on developing strategies to overcome opponents? What can they do now that they could not do last week?
- As netball is your strongest area of subject content knowledge, how did it feel to deliver it at Key Stage (KS) 3 and then again at KS 4?
- Since aquatics is your least strong area of activity, what successes have you had over the week?

Physical Education Pedagogy-specific outcomes
- How did your most successful class make you feel this week?
- Did you have sufficient assessment data and information to design appropriate learning objectives?
- How effective were your learning objectives in terms of the progress pupils made in lessons which you have been given sole responsibility to plan and deliver this week?
- How effectively was time on task managed?
- In a lesson you felt was less successful, what impact did your learning objectives have on pupil behaviour or engagement?
- What are you able to tell me about the best progress made by any pupil in your classes this week?
- What action have you taken to ensure progress next week?

Probing Questions
- Your target was ....; what would you suggest is the most robust evidence you have to indicate pupil progress as a result of your development?
- In your plan you have specified the need to differentiate for the high-achieving pupils; where can you show me the impact this had on the outcome of their learning?

Improving Questions
- Recognising the need for consistently positive learning experiences, where can you reflect on reliable pupil progress over time through your evidence?
- If you are satisfied with the level of progress being made by your Year 9 class, how will you establish further challenge to ensure they are stretched and challenged?

End of Meeting
- What do you think have been the most critical incidents this week in your development (see Chapter X for critical incidents)?
- How will the/these critical incident(s) make a difference to how you work next week?
- Are there any changes to the way we arrange our meetings you would like to make for next week?

LOOKING FORWARD: The beginning teacher writes these from discussion, and in agreement, with the mentor.

Agreed targets set at the conclusion of the meeting for the forthcoming week from reflection sections above and success criteria	Action required to address these targets	Related Teachers' Standards
• Targets should be specific and the impact measurable	Identify any actions to be taken or support needed to enable the target to be met and evidenced by the next meeting	
• Set a maximum of three targets for the week, based on all discussions		
• Link these to Standards (and sections of Standards)		
• What will it look like when the beginning teacher has met the target?		
• What evidence do you want to see to show this?		
• How will this result in an impact on pupil learning?		
Issues which give **cause for concern**. If a beginning teacher is not making expected progress, is not responding to advice, appears to be struggling with mental health or health issues, or has missed a significant amount of time in school through, for example, illness, an intervention, or a specific action plan to support them, may be needed.		

Figure 16.3 An example of the final phase of the meeting

- Targets set with the beginning teacher need to be made transparent for staff/coaches working with them to help support progress.
- You need to engage with the school's continuing professional development lead or other key staff to create learning opportunities, for example:
  - Focused observation
  - Scaffolded teaching experience
  - Personal, Social and Health Education (PSHE) engagement
  - Whole-school issues or priorities
- Attention to key indicators for pupil progress, with particular attention to different groups of learners, need to feature as measureable impacts on pupil progress.

Task 16.7 focuses on using evidence to set targets.

Task 16.7   Using evidence to set targets

- A beginning physical education teacher spent a long time planning for an activity area they see as a weakness. They bring a lesson plan, lesson evaluation and resource card to a weekly meeting. They were trying to develop pupils' ability to use more advanced techniques to improve their performances, but were frustrated that the pupils did not grasp the concept.
- How would you support/challenge them to help close the subject content knowledge gap or perceived limited confidence?
  - What targets would you set?

- What actions/development activities/tasks would you plan?
- What success criteria would you suggest?

Reflection on your ability to hold weekly meetings

Löfström and Eisenschmidt (2009) argued that 'It is vital that mentors analyse their own work, question their practices and develop themselves professionally' (p. 688). One way to do this is to make judgements about your professional development needs to successfully support a beginning teacher through the weekly meeting process. It is possible to explore these from different perspectives:

- You can consider it from the perspective of organisation and management; that is, are you providing adequate time to plan, conduct and evaluate the meeting?
- Alternatively, you can reflect upon the outcome of the meeting for the beginning teacher. Have they made the expected progress in their practice as a result of your involvement at the weekly meeting?
- A third perspective would be the impact of the beginning teacher on the pupils they are working with. Are the pupils showing expected progress because of the way the beginning teacher is working with them?
- A more introspective approach would be to look at the benefits you are gaining from the experience of being a mentor. Is your position in the school feeling more worthwhile because of the work you are doing as a mentor?
- You can also explore how your professional development has progressed through the meetings. What characteristics of an effective mentor have I exhibited this week?
- Finally, you can reflect on the skills you have developed or need to develop to be more effective in carrying out the weekly meeting.

Task 16.8 focuses on improving your ability to run a weekly meeting.

Task 16.8   Mentor reflection: Ability to run a weekly meeting

Return to Task 16.1 and answer the questions in light of your reading of this chapter. Identify aspects of your weekly meetings which have developed as a result of reading the chapter and areas in which you need to undertake further work.

Summary and key points

This chapter has highlighted the importance of the weekly meeting. The weekly meeting encapsulates self-evaluation and reflection, resulting in areas for further development, for mentors in a formal process.

- The weekly meeting is a fundamental tool available to you as a mentor to enable *self-reflection* to happen.
- A beginning physical education teacher places a great deal of *importance* on this meeting in enabling them to make good progress against *personal* and *professional targets*.
- The weekly meeting establishes *effective learning conversations* that monitor, review and sustain a beginning teacher's progress over time.
- At the heart of this, *building rapport* by maintaining a transparent process is a crucial starting point.
- The effectiveness of the weekly meeting is underpinned by *active listening* and *questioning*.
- Reflecting back is often the most useful and powerful thing a mentor can do. *Act as a mirror* that allows the beginning teacher to see and hear themselves as others see and hear them. Then summarise to *check for mutual understanding*, to *agree on a way forward* and agree a plan of action.
- It is crucial that the beginning teacher feels they are *moving forward* in their ability to become *less dependent* on you as a mentor. Ragins (2016, p. 242) found that today's mentees are tomorrow's mentors: 'people who have been mentee in the past are more likely to become a mentor in the future than those who have never been in a mentoring relationship'.

Further resources

Clutterbuck, D. (2004) *Everyone Needs a Mentor: Fostering Talent in Your Organisation*, 4th edn, London: Chartered Institute of Personnel and Development (CIPD).
This text provides a useful overview of a variety of 'help to learn' strategies that can be used in planning, facilitating and evaluating weekly meetings.

Ragins, B. (2016) 'From the ordinary to the extraordinary: High quality mentoring relationships at work', *Organizational Dynamics* 45, 228-244.
This text explores relational mentoring, which illuminates the path for creating high-quality mentoring relationships at work. In particular, it focuses on developing a professional relationship in which both mentor and mentee actively learn and grow with each other.

Montgomery, B.L. (2017) 'Mapping a mentoring roadmap and developing a supportive network for strategic career advancement', *SAGE Open* April–June, 1-13.
Montgomery outlines a mentoring roadmap concept that comprises four steps: (a) self-reflection, (b) establishment of mentor–mentee relationship(s), (c) maintenance of mentoring relationships and (d) advancing in mentoring relationship(s), all of which have relevance for the effective facilitation of weekly meetings.

See also the companion website for this book (www.routledge.com/9781138059658).

You may also find it useful to refer to/use the text books written for student and newly qualified physical education teachers with a beginning teacher you are mentoring (see list on Page 4).

17 Challenging beginning physical education teachers beyond mastery of the basics

Kerry Whitehouse

Introduction

Capel (2010, p. 286) reminded us that teacher professional development 'begins whilst you are a student teacher, extends into your first/induction year of teaching as a Newly Qualified Teacher (NQT) and continues throughout your teaching career'.

After concerns about themselves surviving in the classroom, the early focus in learning to teach for most beginning teachers is what they are teaching. As they gain experience in a school setting, read literature and engage in dialogue with fellow professionals, their knowledge of teaching increases and they reach the point where they have well-planned and organised lessons and positive relationships with pupils, who are busy and active within lessons. Further, their knowledge and understanding of pupil learning increases as the principles of assessment, monitoring progress, and providing pupils with relevant feedback become embedded classroom practice. At this point, a beginning teacher is likely to have met requirements for their early development; they are able to teach many aspects of the curriculum effectively and have the confidence to adapt to meet the needs of the pupils they teach with a positive impact on progress and outcomes. Essentially, the focus has moved from 'What am I doing in my teaching?' to 'What are pupils learning and what progress are they making?'

Once they have mastered the basics, have met the requirements for their development, and feel competent and confident, there is a danger that a beginning teacher may feel they have completed their learning journey. As a result, they continue with comfortable, tried and tested practices, and reach a plateau. After all, if practices are working and pupils are progressing and achieving, why make changes? This plateau can be exacerbated if the mentor does not encourage further learning and development. Thus, it is important to remember that when a beginning teacher has mastered the basics, their professional learning should not stop, and, in your role, you can support, nurture and encourage them to develop new knowledge, understanding and skills to move their practice forward by continually reflecting on practice, challenging routines and questioning what they do in the classroom and beyond.

As a mentor, you should ask yourself 'How can I support a beginning teacher who has mastered the basics? How can I challenge them to move their practice forward to enhance pupil learning? How can I continue to develop myself professionally?' This is not always an easy task, and you may find that your own knowledge, understanding, skills and confidence are challenged along the way. It is, therefore, important to remember that learning and development is a continual process, and that you can develop your knowledge, understanding and skills alongside a beginning teacher.

This chapter aims to help you move a beginning teacher on once they have mastered the basics so as to continually enhance their teaching practices, ensure pupil learning and sustain professional aspirations. It considers how to support a beginning teacher in today's increasingly changing world, where they need to continually reflect and adapt to meet the demands of physical education teaching. It explores practical strategies to help you, as a mentor, to understand ways in which you can support and challenge a beginning teacher to reflect on the many aspects of effective teaching and learning and to move out of their comfort zone to enhance pupil learning within lessons.

Objectives

At the end of this chapter you should be able to:

- identify a starting point for supporting the development of a beginning teacher's practice beyond mastery of the basics;
- understand how you can support a beginning teacher to reflect on and challenge their practice;
- consider practical strategies you can use to support a beginning teacher to develop their practice beyond mastery of the basics;
- reflect on the views and experiences of a beginning teacher to support you in developing your mentoring skills further;
- identify potential barriers and ways to overcome them.

Before reading further, complete Task 17.1.

Task 17.1 Mentor reflection: Challenging a beginning teacher to move beyond mastery of the basics

In relation to any beginning teachers you have mentored, reflect on how you have challenged them once they have mastered the basics and met the relevant standards for their stage of development.

Have you enabled them to continue with comfortable, tried and tested practices or have you challenged them to continue to develop their knowledge, understanding and practice? How have you done this?

Identifying a starting point for future development

You may know the beginning teacher you are working with well, or you may have only just met. Either way, it is important to identify a starting point for development, including their current level of knowledge, understanding and skill, the amount of practical experience they have and their confidence to try new things. In doing this, it is prudent to remember that we are all different and make progress at different rates. You can identify a starting point from existing information you may have, information-gathering tools and professional dialogue.

When you first meet a beginning teacher, it is likely you will have a copy of their curriculum vitae (CV) and information from their application to either an initial teacher education course or a teaching post. This information gives you initial insights into their experience and qualifications. You may also have information from a previous placement/work in schools through, for example, a placement report, accompanied by a personal reflection on progress. This can be an insightful document, as it provides a dual viewpoint, that of a previous mentor alongside views of the beginning teacher. In order to identify an accurate starting point, you should ensure that information is current and considers both factual experience and qualifications alongside the beginning teacher's own feelings and reflections. One way of gathering this information is through audits (see Chapter 9 and the companion website for this book (www.routledge.com/9781138059658), which gives examples of formats for three audits: a subject content knowledge audit (Figure 17.4); a Teachers' Standards audit (for England) (Figure 17.5) and a pedagogic knowledge audit (Figure 17.6)). An audit enables a beginning teacher to track their progress by identifying and reflecting on evidence. It is usual for a beginning teacher to engage in reflective dialogue with their mentor to consider the evidence (see Chapters 15 and 16).

Task 17.2 asks you to work through a subject content knowledge audit with a beginning teacher.

Task 17.2   Work through the subject content knowledge audit with a beginning teacher

During a meeting, support a beginning teacher to work through a subject content knowledge audit (see the companion website for this book (www.routledge.com/9781138059658) for Figure 17.4 or refer to Chapter 9) to find out their levels of knowledge and experience. This is important underpinning for a beginning teacher's development as a teacher. You may wish to use this opportunity to point out the priorities for the curriculum in your school or to see where a beginning teacher could provide pupils with new experiences. Identify, with the beginning teacher, ways for them to develop the knowledge gaps they may have.

Since the work of Muska Mosston (1966) on teaching styles in physical education, there have been a number of developments in pedagogy. These range from Teaching Games for Understanding (Bunker and Thorpe, 1982) to Sport Education (Siedentop, 1994) to Cooperative Learning (Metzler, 2005), to name a few.

A pedagogic knowledge audit could be the focus of discussion for one of your first meetings with a beginning teacher you are mentoring. This should provide a holistic picture as a starting point. A beginning teacher may not be aware of some of those pedagogies listed in the audit (Figure 17.6), so an audit of pedagogic experience may prove challenging. In this case, further time or exploration of these by reading, discussion and sharing your own knowledge may be necessary. Likewise, it may take time for a beginning teacher to remember occasions when they have used such pedagogies. The audit can then be a focus in a meeting periodically to enable a beginning teacher to reflect on the use of different pedagogies and their impact on pupils' learning, as well as to identify further practical experiences needed for further development.

Likewise, as a mentor, it is important that you are knowledgeable about a range of pedagogies and, if necessary, develop your knowledge through, for example, attending conferences, dialogue with fellow professionals, use of social media such as Twitter, and reading up-to-date practitioner- or research-related literature (see examples in 'Further resources' at the end of the chapter).

Task 17.3 focuses on a beginning teacher's pedagogic knowledge audit.

Task 17.3   Auditing and developing pedagogy

Step 1: Plan a meeting with a beginning teacher to focus on a pedagogic knowledge audit.

Step 2: Consider briefly each of the pedagogies in Figure 17.6 in turn, to gain a baseline of a beginning teacher's prior knowledge of each. Add any other pedagogies you and/or the beginning teacher are aware of.

Step 3: Ask the beginning teacher to record their 'Practical Experience Gained' in up to three examples of pedagogy.

Step 4: Discus the audit with the beginning teacher and either

Step 4a: If a beginning teacher has a number of examples of pedagogies they have practised, ask them to add all information in preparation for a second meeting

or

Step 4b: If a beginning teacher has only a few examples, arrange a second meeting.

Once steps 3 and 4 are complete, you will have a better understanding of a beginning teacher's experience and can adapt your approach to the second meeting you arrange to focus on development of pedagogy.

Step 5: During your second meeting, focus on development of pedagogy:

Step 5a: Identify any pedagogies a beginning teacher has a good knowledge of, but has not applied in practice.

Step 5b: Identify one pedagogy a beginning teacher is not familiar with and ask them to research information on this before your next meeting. If necessary, you may need to find out more information on the pedagogy so that you can fully support the beginning teacher.

For both 5a and 5b, decide together which group or lesson this pedagogy can be used in. You may need to support the beginning teacher during both planning and teaching. When this has been taught, you can add reflections and evaluations to the audit.

This process can be repeated for all pedagogies stated and others you may be aware of.

Lesson observations

You have gained an insight into the qualifications and experiences of a beginning teacher through information available at interview and also audits. To add to your growing knowledge of a beginning teacher, you gain knowledge from regular and focused lesson observations (see Chapter 13), alongside regular and open professional dialogue. Continuing these in a focused and critically reflective way provides ongoing opportunities for beginning teacher reflection and development beyond mastery of the basics (see Figure 17.1).

Other examples of questions are found on the companion website for this book (www.routledge.com/9781138059658) (Figure 17.7).

Once you have a clear picture of a beginning teacher's starting point, you are able to support them by planning professional learning to move them beyond mastery of the basics that is relevant to their individual needs.

Supporting a beginning teacher to reflect on and challenge their practice: Developing a mindset for challenge and positive risk-taking

Positive risk-taking

The notion of risk in physical education is often considered in relation to risk management and the balance between involvement in risk-associated activities and avoiding the potential for injury (Coelho, 2001). This chapter invites you to consider an alternative viewpoint, that of positive risk-taking for professional development. This type of risk is defined as an action or activity undertaken by choice to achieve a learning benefit. It requires a beginning teacher to reflect on an element of professional practice they wish to develop and to challenge their practices and routines by moving out of their comfort zone (Whitehouse, 2015, unpublished). For Dreger (2011), risk-taking in teaching involves employing teaching strategies that teachers are not familiar with or employing behaviours that break down traditional practices and structures so as to promote better pupil learning. Moving a beginning teacher on beyond established and comfortable practices necessitates engagement with ideas and practices that are new to them, and maybe new to you. Positive risk-taking is, therefore, trying something new, working outside the comfort zones, and balancing the probability of a successful

---

1. How well does the planning and structure of the lesson:
   • promote learning?
   • secure an engaging learning environment?
   • promote positive and effective behaviour for learning?
2. How well are the needs of individual pupils being met?
   • How are those pupils who are having difficulty learning being supported?
   • How are those who find learning easier being challenged?
3. How does feedback secure pupil progress?
   • What types of feedback are evident within the lesson?
4. How well has an effective environment been created to promote positive behaviour and engagement in the lesson?

Figure 17.1 Questions which a mentor can use to help focus observation and professional dialogue with a beginning teacher to move their practice on

outcome in terms of benefits to pupil learning and/or personal professional development versus a non-successful outcome. It is, therefore, important that, before embarking on a risk or challenge, the potential gains this may have are identified. Seale (2012) reinforced this point when she argued that the conceptualisation and implementation of positive risk-taking involve negotiating and making decisions that weigh risks against benefits.

Davies (1999) considered taking risks when teaching to be a means of creativity, arguing that, despite the limited freedom schools are given to augment creative work, taking risks in teaching can have positive impacts. Whitehouse (2015, unpublished) asked beginning teachers who had taken risks in their practice during their initial teacher education year, and mentors who had supported them, what they thought the potential gains were of challenging their practice and taking risks. Their responses were as follows:

- Pupils were more engaged in their learning
- Pupils were excited and looked forward to lessons because they were different and more fun
- Working independently and being able to direct their own learning led to better pupil understanding
- Pupil behaviour in the lesson improved because everyone had a responsibility.

Taking risks requires you, as a mentor, to encourage and support a beginning teacher to try practices that are new to them so that they continue to learn in situations with an element of uncertainty. In order to support a beginning teacher in positive risk-taking, it is helpful to reflect on your own attitude towards risk-taking and question whether you willingly engage in new practices that may challenge you. If you engage with risk-taking yourself, you can model practice to help a beginning teacher develop further. However, if you are risk-averse in your practice, you need to keep an open mind towards risk-taking by a beginning teacher.

Moving a beginning teacher from their comfort zone to a courage/challenge zone

In Warrell's (2013) model, taken from business (see Figure 17.2), risk involves moving beyond one's comfort zone into a courage/challenge zone where growth and opportunity prevail.

When they begin teaching, a beginning teacher does not start in the comfort zone. As they master the basics, become more confident and competent with their teaching and pupil learning, and become more comfortable in their practice, they move into their comfort zone. At this point, it is important to encourage them to move beyond the comfort zone and to work in their courage/challenge zone. However, it is important that a beginning teacher is not pushed too quickly and challenged beyond their capabilities, as this may lead to a lack of confidence and fear of engaging with new practices.

It is in the courage/challenge zone that, Warrell (2013) argued, the best rewards are gained. The first steps are to help a beginning teacher to reflect on their practice and accept a need for change. Suggestions of new ideas, alternative pedagogies and creative practices can be discussed and collaboratively planned and employed with the aim of developing practice further.

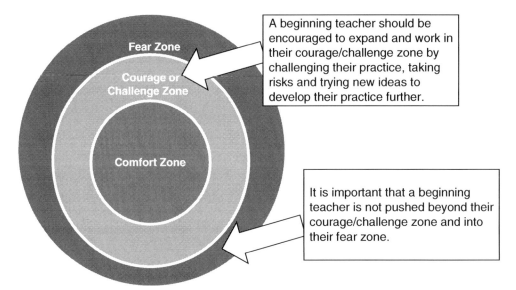

Figure 17.2 Comfort Zone to Courage/Challenge Zone
(Source: adapted from Warrell, 2013)

As a mentor, it is important to remember that your role is one of support and acceptance for a beginning teacher who is taking risks. A beginning teacher should consider taking risks as an opportunity to explore new practices, without worrying about making mistakes or not getting it right first time. Hence, supporting a beginning teacher to take risks should be separate from any required assessment of a beginning teacher.

Clarke et al. (2012) asked experienced mentors and beginning teachers who had supported and taken risks what they considered to be risky or challenging practices for a beginning teacher. Some responses included:

- Going beyond a personal comfort zone
- Trying something new that you are not sure will work. These may be ideas from colleagues or those you have read
- Managing and using new learning technologies
- Dealing with difficult pupil–teacher relationships, especially emotional or behavioural relationships, or tackling difficult issues
- Stepping up for extra professional duties
- Being prepared to have less control of the lesson or the class
- Allowing independent learning and handing over the responsibility to pupils
- Teacher taking a step back to consider pupil learning within the lesson

These suggestions may give you and a beginning teacher some ideas as a starting point to challenge practice through positive risk-taking. Now complete Task 17.4.

Task 17.4   Reflection and action to challenge practice

After considering a beginning teacher's audits and observing them teach, you will have built up a good picture of their abilities and strengths.

Identify aspects of practice the beginning teacher is comfortable with (inner circle in Figure 17.2). Discuss with the beginning teacher how they can enhance their practice in those areas by adopting new approaches that challenge them (they may need some ideas from you) (the second circle in Figure 17.2).

Support the beginning teacher in trying out these approaches in their lessons and evaluating their success and further areas for development.

You can help a beginning teacher to consider how to action their new ideas by encouraging them to:

*   be open to self-awareness and self-reflection
*   consider the time or resources that may need to be invested into the new idea
*   consider any external opportunities or barriers related to their ideas
*   consider what benefits the new idea may bring to pupils and themselves.

If a beginning teacher is able to plan for their ideas independently, you may just need to be on hand if they have a question. For a less confident beginning teacher, you may wish to plan and/or teach collaboratively with them the first time to try their ideas.

The importance of critical reflection in supporting positive risk-taking

Critical reflection is a challenging process in itself, particularly for a beginning teacher new to the environment or learning new skills and particularly for many of those who have generally experienced successes in teaching, coaching or the sport they play. Dewey (1933) saw reflection as a continual process of evaluation, whereby a subject, behaviour or practice is considered over and over in a critical way so as to find new conclusions or situations. A reflective practitioner asks searching questions about their practice; they consider their own and the wider context of education and its settings. Furthermore, reflective practitioners 'demonstrate a commitment to continuous learning by seeking new ideas, evaluating and reflecting on their impact and trying out new practices and ways of working to improve their own effectiveness in the teaching environment' (Zwozdiak-Myers, 2015a, p. 233). Reflection is an internal process that explores personal assumptions, emotions, actions and beliefs (King and Kitchener, 1994). As a mentor, you cannot make a beginning teacher reflect; however, you can encourage critical reflection for change, raise awareness through careful questioning, and develop an open, supportive relationship with a beginning teacher. The following examples can help a beginning teacher engage with reflective practice:

*   Questioning their own practice critically and reflectively
*   Continually considering the learning pupils are achieving

- Observing other teachers
- Their teaching being observed
- Undertaking Action Research

Examples of ways of supporting the development of reflection by a beginning teacher are addressed in Chapter 10. In the following section, a risk-taking learning cycle is considered that supports a beginning teacher to plan, action and evaluate risks taken.

Risk-taking learning cycle

One way to help a beginning teacher reflect and engage in practice that challenges them and for them to expand or move outside of their comfort zone is to consider a risk-taking learning cycle in relation to either a problem they may have or an area they wish to develop further to enhance pupils' learning or develop their professional practice. The risk-taking learning cycle in Figure 17.3 is adapted from the work of Schön (1983) and his concept of reflection-on-action and reflection-in-action. Here, the action would be considered the risk that a beginning teacher is taking and would be in their challenge zone (see Figure 17.2). Reflection-on-action involves thinking over a situation either before it is actioned or after it has happened. This may occur when planning for, or following, a lesson when you sit with a beginning teacher to engage in dialogue regarding the lesson. Reflection-in-action

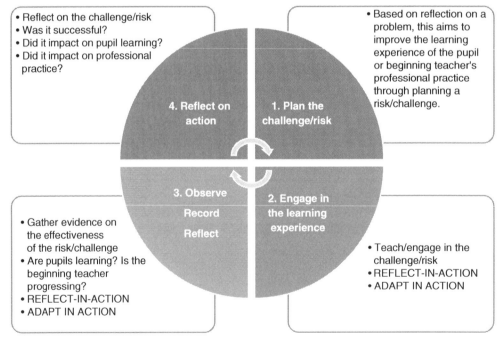

Figure 17.3 Risk-taking Learning Cycle
(Source: adapted from Lawson and Whitehouse, 2017 based on the work of Schön, 1983)

involves taking action during a lesson or whilst teaching. It involves continual adaptation to the circumstances and situations in which the teacher finds themselves whilst teaching. This may lead to adaptations being made during the lesson. This takes time and experience to develop.

You can use the risk-taking learning cycle with a beginning teacher as follows:

Stage 1: Plan the challenge/risk: Allow a beginning teacher time to think and plan 'the risk/challenge'. It is useful for you to consider how a beginning teacher has planned and, if necessary, ask them questions on how they visualise the outcomes of the risk/challenge if it is successful.

Stage 2: Engage in the learning experience: Encourage a beginning teacher to reflect on the challenge whilst it is underway. They may adapt the risk/challenge 'in action', and the success of this can be considered following the lesson. You can also encourage a beginning teacher to gather evidence during the challenge. This could be in the form of personal reflections on engagement or behaviour, formative checks on learning or, peer/group reflections and task outcomes.

Stage 3: Observe, record, reflect: You may have the opportunity to observe the 'risk/challenge' a beginning teacher undertakes, thus enabling you to gather evidence and provide feedback first-hand from your observations.

Stage 4: Reflect-on-action: Take time after the challenge to sit down and talk through the risk/challenge with a beginning teacher, considering first what was successful and then how things could be developed further. Challenging one's own practice can also be a very emotional time, so be mindful to consider how a beginning teacher may have felt during and after the challenge. These reflections can then be used to inform future lessons and planning.

In Task 17.5, you are asked to engage with the risk-taking learning cycle.

Task 17.5   Engaging with the risk-taking learning cycle

Based upon all of the information you have collaboratively gathered during engagement with the tasks in this chapter, now consider with a beginning teacher an aspect of practice they would like to develop. This will inform stage 1 (**Plan the challenge/risk**) of the risk-taking learning cycle (Figure 17.3). The aspect of practice may relate to, for example, pupil progress, learning or behaviour, or may originate from an idea they have seen or information they have read. You need to be sure the beginning teacher is not playing it safe and trying something they can already do. Then, support the beginning teacher as they work through the stages of the risk-taking cycle. In engaging with this process with the beginning teacher, you may undertake a challenge or risk during the same week as a beginning teacher to develop your own practice.

Case studies 17.1 and 17.2 consider the experiences of two beginning teachers who followed the risk-taking learning cycle to challenge their practice. After reading the case studies, complete Task 17.6.

Case study 17.1 Jennifer's story

Jennifer was over half way into her initial teacher education year and had settled into her second placement school. She had been teaching GCSE physical education theory lessons to a lower-ability boys' group, whom she found to be disaffected within the classroom environment. Jennifer knew the boys really enjoyed practical 'hands on' activities and wanted them to enjoy and engage in classroom lessons in the same way. She considered carefully what she could do to engage these pupils in learning and conversed with her school mentor to stimulate ideas. Jennifer's idea was for the group to engage in an activity whereby the pupils dissected hearts to learn about the cardio-vascular system and heart function. Jennifer's mentor supported her with this idea, helped her to plan what she needed to do, and put her in contact with colleagues in the school who could offer support and guidance. Jennifer sought the assistance of the school's science department to develop her own knowledge of this procedure. Science colleagues were more than willing to help and taught Jennifer the correct technique for dissecting a heart and also the health and safety considerations for this activity. For Jennifer, this was an area in which she had very little knowledge; it was new to her and a perceived risk in relation to her own skills and the engagement of pupils. Jennifer planned the lesson thoroughly, and her mentor gave her encouragement, was present within the lesson and provided feedback at the end. Jennifer taught an extremely successful and effective lesson in which pupils showed a significant increase in enthusiasm and engagement. When she later tested the knowledge of the class, she found that effective learning had taken place. This lesson also impacted on the pupils, who went on to attend future lessons motivated, engaged and willing to learn. Jennifer continued to plan practical 'hands on' lessons for this group, which were successful. She was, however, careful that pupils also understood there were times when they needed to apply and use their knowledge in a written sense, particularly in preparation for their GCSE examination.

Case study 17.2 Megan's story

Megan was an NQT who had been teaching in her first school for six months. She had developed positive relationships with the pupils and knew many of the girls in her Year 9 basketball group very well, as they were in the school netball team she coached. With the help of her mentor's questioning, Megan reflected on the high ability of her all-girls' basketball group and felt she needed to challenge them in order to ensure higher levels of learning, which went beyond the skills of the activity. Megan and her mentor took time during a scheduled meeting to consider pedagogic strategies they were aware of from either her initial teacher education reading or past experience. Megan decided that within the unit of work she would make links to the GCSE theory syllabus and also encourage the group to take greater responsibility for their learning by planning the lessons through a sport education model (Siedentop, 1994). This approach had been explained during her initial teacher education and Megan had tried out some of its ideas within the 'safety net' of her placement school but never as a full unit of work. Megan planned the Sport Education module into this unit of work and asked her mentor to look at the planning with a critical eye so as to provide support and confidence in the delivery. She planned the unit to gradually give pupils more responsibility and lead lessons. Pupils were given different roles (team players, coaches, referees, medics) and the opportunity to learn independently about the expectations of each role. Furthermore, pupils were expected to share their own learning, through their role, with others.

This was a challenge for Megan, as it involved pupils working independently for the first time and taking the lead in every element of the lesson. Being an NQT, she also felt nervous because she was teaching alone. It was also a new pedagogy to her and one in which she did not as yet feel confident. This encouraged Megan to take a step back during lessons, allowing learning to evolve, and gave her the opportunity to 'reflect-in-action.' Megan had regular supportive conversations with her mentor, which gave her the confidence to apply the Sport Education model to her lessons. Megan commented:'These lessons worked really well. It was great to be able to watch the girls adapt to different roles and show a willingness to learn independently. It also allowed me to take a step back to get a clear picture of learning as pupils didn't rely on me to give them instructions. They were essentially in charge of the lesson. At the end, we used the data medics had collected to analyse heart rate during exercise and linked this to theory. The pupils were really engaged and worked well together! It also gave me the confidence to try new ideas in the future.'

Task 17.6 Learning from the case studies

Having read the preceding case studies, identify:

1. What aspect of practice the beginning teacher wished to challenge themselves with.
2. Where the beginning teacher found information and support to help them plan their challenge/risk.
4. The positive outcomes for pupils and the beginning teacher.

Overcoming potential barriers

Having looked at the experiences of Jennifer and Megan, you have seen the benefits of encouraging a beginning teacher to challenge themselves and try new ideas. As may be expected, both a beginning teacher and a mentor may meet with barriers to taking risks and moving practice forward. These may take the form of, for example, time, curriculum constraints, facilities, space or resources. It is important to factor these into the planning phase. When faced with such potential barriers, you, as the mentor, have the knowledge and experience of school procedures and can help a beginning teacher to approach relevant colleagues, source new equipment or additional space that may be needed, or possibly consider alternative times to take the risk.

Further barriers may include resistance from other staff. The attitudes of both yourself and colleagues to a beginning teacher taking risks will impact on their confidence to move their practice forward and try new things. It is, therefore, important that you are aware of how your own and others' attitudes impact on and influence a beginning teacher's practices and confidence to try new things. Creating, and encouraging others to create, an environment where open dialogue and discussion of hopes and fears can occur provides a positive environment, which is conducive to challenging current practices and risk-taking and gives you an ongoing picture of the progress and thoughts of a beginning teacher.

You also need to be mindful that moving out of their comfort zone is an emotional experience for a beginning teacher. A beginning teacher may be afraid that they may make mistakes and things may not go to plan. Reid (2010) highlighted the emotional experience of risk-taking behaviour, as it lies within uncertainty, whilst Dreger (2011) argued that it is through overcoming these uncomfortable and uncertain practices that real learning takes place. As a mentor, it is important that you support a beginning teacher to develop their confidence to engage with and overcome the emotion of moving out of their comfort zone by encouraging an environment where making mistakes is accepted as a time when learning and professional development occur and new practices (including those which a beginning teacher was once afraid to try out or were not aware of) become embedded into normal practice. This also inspires a beginning teacher to welcome future engagement with challenge and trying new practices.

How can you support a beginning teacher to move their practice on?

- It is important to create a supportive and non-judgemental environment, where a beginning teacher feels secure that it is all right to try new things and make mistakes. In keeping an open mind to learning from mistakes, new ideas are cultivated, practice develops and further learning takes place. It is easy to continue with tried and tested practices that lead to a desired outcome; however, trying new things often leads to an even better way.
- Empower a beginning teacher with knowledge by planning new pedagogic models or ideas collaboratively. Agree to read about the same pedagogic model or idea and then discuss your learning before planning collaboratively to move a beginning teacher's practice forward.
- Find time to model new ideas and share good practice with a beginning teacher. Ask for feedback on your own lessons where you are working out of your comfort zone. This further builds confidence, allows dialogue over shared experience and shows some of the benefits that can be achieved. Modelling may also be set up with other members of the department or school colleagues, which encourages a beginning teacher to try out new ideas, especially any successful ones they have seen.
- Create opportunities to celebrate beginning teacher successes, engage in shared dialogue and reflect on successful classroom practice. This provides new ideas to all, develops a positive self-esteem and empowers a beginning teacher as they share their successes.

- Although it is sometimes difficult, it is important that a beginning teacher feels that you trust their ideas and judgements. Allowing a beginning teacher to act on their own initiative and work independently develops their confidence to take risks and try new ideas.

Summary and key points

This chapter has looked at ideas and strategies that may be useful in supporting a beginning teacher to move on beyond mastery of the basics of teaching. Specifically, it has identified the following points:

- Auditing tools and observation can be used as means of finding a starting point to ascertain a beginning teacher's current level of knowledge and understanding.
- Once a starting point is clear, encouraging open and supportive dialogue and reflection by a beginning teacher to develop practice further (to move from comfort zone to courage/challenge zone) is advocated.
- Using a reflective risk-taking cycle encourages challenging practice and reflecting 'on action' and 'in action' for a beginning teacher to move on, beyond mastery of the basics.
- The benefits of reflecting on, challenging and taking positive risks in practice builds confidence and empowers a beginning teacher to continually develop their practice.
- Creating a non-judgemental environment, modelling ideas yourself, and engaging with theory and pedagogic research are ways in which you can support a beginning teacher to move on when they have mastered the basics.
- The experiences of mentors and beginning teachers who have successfully collaborated to move beyond mastery of the basics offer examples and practical suggestions that may help both you and a beginning teacher you support to develop as critical and reflective practitioners who are willing to challenge themselves so as to continually enhance practice and become lifelong learners.

Further resources

Lawson, S. and Whitehouse, K. (2017) 'Challenging the competent trainee – taking risks in the classroom', in T. Wright (Ed.) *How to Be a Brilliant Mentor*, London: Routledge, pp. 92–107.
This chapter considers practical ways in which a mentor can challenge competent student teachers to take risks in the classroom. It explores what risk or challenge may look like and draws on cross-subject examples and case studies. Barriers and benefits to risk-taking are considered and conclusions drawn, advocating that mistakes are where the greatest learning can be achieved.

Wright, T. (2008) 'Reflection and evaluation', in T. Wright (Ed.) *How to Be a Brilliant Trainee Teacher*, London: Routledge, pp. 115–126.
This chapter approaches reflection and evaluation from the perspective of a student teacher. It draws on real-life experience, offering practical suggestions on how to move from a good to a brilliant student teacher. The reader is challenged to question their understanding and practice, and reflection and evaluation are advocated as continuing tasks to improve practice.

Zwozdiak-Myers, P. (2012) *The Teacher's Reflective Practice Handbook: Becoming an Extended Professional through Capturing Evidence-Informed Practice*, London: Routledge. This book explores in detail what it means to be a reflective practitioner and offers good advice, underpinned by theoretical concepts and research, to help a beginning teacher reflect to enhance classroom practice and hence pupil learning, as well as for professional development. It includes reflective tasks, links to online resources and ideas for further reading to enhance reflective practice.

Zwozdiak-Myers, P. (2015) Chapter 15. 'Teacher as a Researcher/Reflective Practitioner', In S. Capel and M. Whitehead (eds.) *Learning to Teach Physical Education in the Secondary School: A Companion to School Experience,* 4th edn, London: Routledge, pp. 235–255.
This chapter introduces the reader to the concepts of teacher as researcher and reflective practitioner. It considers strategies to support research and reflection, including teacher observation of self and others, self-reflection and Action Research as a means of thinking critically and investigating practice.

Practitioner magazines/journals
Physical Education Matters, published by the Association for Physical Education (AfPE)

Practitioner webpages
Association for Physical Education (AfPE), www.afpe.org.uk
1st4sport.com: sports coaching, training and physical education books and resources

Twitter resources
Association for PE (@afPE_PE) on Twitter
PE4Learning.com (@PE4Learning) on Twitter
PE Geeks (@PEgeeks) on Twitter
PE Scholar (@PEScholar) on Twitter
PE Tip of the Day (@PE_TotD) on Twitter
@TeacherToolkit (@TeacherToolkit) on Twitter

See also the companion website for this book (www.routledge.com/9781138059658).

You may also find it useful to refer to/use the text books written for student and newly qualified physical education teachers with a beginning teacher you are mentoring (see list on Page 4).

18 And finally ...

Susan Capel

Teaching is a challenging profession, regardless of level of experience. Mentoring supports a teacher to face these challenges. It supports them to develop and deepen understanding of their practice, teaching and learning, and the curriculum; introduce and experiment with alternative teaching and learning strategies, with the focus on the impact on pupil learning outcomes, both physical education specific and broader outcomes; and review and renew established practice. Simply having many years of teaching experience is not enough to be an effective mentor; you need to understand and demonstrate best practices in physical education as well as be able to support a beginning teacher to understand and develop best practice. Thus, you need to want to be a mentor, because you see the role as important, not because you are a body to fill the role.

This book has looked at mentoring of beginning teachers (defined as student, newly qualified and early career teachers). It is important that all those involved with mentoring beginning teachers are explicit about initial teacher education (ITE) being initial and begin-ning being beginning – so that beginning teachers fully understand they are not the 'finished product' and need to develop further throughout their career.

Hence, mentoring does not finish after ITE, or, indeed, after the first few years in teaching. Mentoring is valuable throughout a teacher's career, particularly at career transitions; for example, when preparing for, or undertaking, a new role, such as a middle or senior leader. Mentoring supports a teacher to meet new challenges, to understand and respond to the demands of the new role, and to understand the responsibilities of the role. Further, it supports the development, across a department or a school, of a culture of openness; for example, mutual support for and critique of professional practice.

The knowledge, skills and understanding covered in this book are all relevant in these new contexts and with a range of people (teachers, as well as others who you may be involved in mentoring in school, e.g. adults other than teachers, coaches). However, specific requirements may change (e.g. a weekly meeting is frequently a requirement on an ITE course, but not after ITE or for others working in schools). Likewise, in ITE a range of activities are planned to gradually introduce a student teacher to teaching (e.g. co-planning and teaching, observing other teachers teaching, shadowing a pupil), which may not be appropriate, or possible, with others you are mentoring. Thus, it is important to consider which activities are appropriate and possible in which context.

It is also important to consider where a teacher you are mentoring is in their development. A newly qualified teacher might need to focus initially on further developing the 'basics' of teaching (perhaps in a new setting), but, once they have mastered the basics, it is important that they continue to develop; something they need to do throughout their career. They might need advice on, for example, where to find sources of information relating to the range of professional developmental activities available; different developmental pathways, courses and qualifications available, including the transition from teacher to teacher educator; how to undertake classroom-based (action or practitioner) research; or current research into, and practice of, mentoring. They also need to be able to access a range of learning opportunities, including, for example, groups undertaking classroom-based research and whole-school professional development.

As a mentor, you need good subject content, pedagogical and curriculum knowledge. You are expected to demonstrate best practice in teaching physical education. You are a role model. A beginning teacher tends to follow your example in both teaching and professional behaviour. You, therefore, need to consider how you are developing your own subject knowledge. For example, are you a member of a subject association and/or subject mentor network – both of which give access to resources and online support? However, you also need a broader range of professional knowledge. No one person can be an expert in everything; hence, it is also important that you continue to learn and develop. An important aspect of your development is taking time to reflect on your own practice and on your development as a mentor. You also need to be able to deconstruct your practice and explain it to someone else. Keeping an evidence folder or personal diary/journal allows you to chart activities that support your ability to reflect on your learning and development of your mentoring practice.

Further, it is important that you reflect on your impact as a mentor on both the teacher you are mentoring and the wider school. How effective is your mentoring for the person you are mentoring? How does your role as a mentor benefit the subject department and/or school? Have you supported the development of a culture of openness (e.g. mutual support for and critique of professional practice) in the department or across the school?

Although, as a mentor, you work with a beginning (or experienced) teacher (or anyone else working in the school), they also need support from others, both in the school and outside (e.g. in a neighbouring school, a sports context) to effectively support the transition from a student teacher to a newly qualified teacher or to undertake a new role. A range of support means that a teacher is more likely to thrive (rather than just survive), have higher job satisfaction and remain in the teaching profession.

However, different arrangements may be appropriate, for example co-mentoring or peer mentoring. It is important that, whomever you are mentoring, you consider the requirements of mentoring in the specific context and the specific needs of that person and then select the most appropriate models and approaches to mentoring.

Thus, as a mentor, you work as part of a team. You can learn a lot from others with whom you work as a mentor. However, broader collaboration amongst teachers and mentors is important, as is encouraging teachers to share practice through participation in national and international teaching networks/forums/associations. You should, therefore, encourage teachers whom you mentor to collaborate. This can be done by, for example, establishing communities of learning within the school or engaging in lesson study activities. As a mentor, you should be encouraging a learning school, that is, a whole-school culture of continuous development.

Remember, today's mentee might want to become tomorrow's mentor.

REFERENCES

Aderibigbe, S.A. (2013) 'Opportunities of the collaborative mentoring relationships between teachers and student teachers in the classroom: The views of teachers, student teachers and university tutors', *Management in Education* 27(2), 70-74.

Aderibigbe, S., Colucci-Gray, L. and Gray, D.S. (2016) 'Conceptions and expectations of mentoring relationships in a teacher education reform context', *Mentoring & Tutoring: Partnership in Learning* 24(1), 8-29.

AITSL (Australian Institute for Teaching and School Leadership) (2011) *The Australian Professional Standards for Teachers,* Melbourne: AITSL, viewed 25 January 2018, from www.aitsl.edu.au/teach/standards

Arshavskaya, E. (2016) 'Complexity in mentoring in a pre-service teacher practicum: A case study approach', *International Journal of Mentoring and Coaching in Education* 5(1), 2-19. doi: http://dx.doi.org/10.1108/IJMCE-07-2015-0021

Arthur, J. and Capel, S. (2015) 'How planning and evaluation support effective learning and teaching', in S. Capel and M. Whitehead (2015) *Learning to Teach Physical Education in the Secondary School: A Companion to School Experience*, 4th edn, Abingdon: Routledge, pp. 31-48.

Aspfors, J.F.G. (2015) 'Research on mentor education for mentors of newly qualified teachers: A qualitative meta-synthesis', *Teaching and Teacher Education* 48, 75-86.

Banville, D. (2015) 'Novice physical education teachers learning to teach', *Journal of Teaching in Physical Education* 34(2), 259-277.

Belvis, E., Pineda, P., Armengol, C. and Moreno, V. (2013) 'Evaluation of reflective practice in teacher education', *European Journal of Teacher Education* 36(3), 279-292.

Black, P.E. and Plowright, D. (2010) 'A multi-dimensional model of reflective learning for professional development', *Reflective Practice* 11(2), 245-259.

Blair, R. with Whitehead, M. (2015) 'Designing teaching approaches to achieve intended learning outcomes' in S. Capel and M. Whitehead (eds.) *Learning to Teach Physical Education in the Secondary School: A Companion to School Experience*, 4th edn, Abingdon: Routledge, pp. 204-218.

Bolton, G. (2014) *Reflective Practice: Writing and Professional Development*, 4th edn, London: Sage.

Bonanno, H., Jones, J. and English, L. (1998) 'Improving group satisfaction: Making groups work in a first-year undergraduate course', *Teaching in Higher Education* 3(3), 365-382.

Borton, T. (1970) *Read, Touch and Teach: Student Concerns and Process Education*, New York: McGraw Hill.

Boultona, H. and Hramiak, A. (2012) 'E-flection: The development of reflective communities of learning for trainee teachers through the use of shared online web logs', *Reflective Practice* 13(4), 503-515.

Bowler, M., Bassett, S. and Newton, A. (2014) 'Assessing pupils' learning' in S. Capel and P. Breckon (eds.) *A Practical Guide to Teaching Physical Education in the Secondary School*, 2nd edn, Abingdon: Routledge, pp. 197–210.

Brisk, M.E. (2008) *Language, Culture and Community in Teacher Education*, New York: Lawrence Erlbaum.

Brooks, C.M. and Ammons, J.L. (2003) 'Free-riding in group projects and the effects of timing, frequency and specificity of criteria in peer assessments', *Journal of Education for Business* 78(5), 268–272.

Brophy, J. (ed.) (2004) *Using Video in Teacher Education*, Amsterdam: Elsevier.

Brown, T.D. (2011) 'More than glimpses in the mirror: An argument for self-study in the professional learning of physical education teachers', *Asia-Pacific Journal of Health, Sport and Physical Education* 2(1), 19–32.

Buchanan, M.T. and Stern, J. (2012) 'Pre-service teachers' perceptions of the benefits of peer review', *Journal of Education for Teaching: International Research and Pedagogy* 38(1), 37–49.

Bunker, D. and Thorpe, R. (1982) 'A model for the teaching of games in the secondary school', *Bulletin of Physical Education* 10, 9–16.

Caddick, P. (2017) *Building Effective Mentoring Relationships*, viewed 25 January 2018, from http://pcaddick.com/page5.html

Cajkler, W. and Wood, P. (2016) 'Lesson study and pedagogic literacy in initial teacher education: Challenging reductive models', *British Journal of Educational Studies* 64(4), 503–521.

Capel, S. (2010) 'Continuing professional development in PE', in S. Capel and M. Whitehead (eds.) *Learning to Teach Physical Education in the Secondary School*, 3rd edn, Abingdon: Routledge, pp. 286–304.

Capel, S. (2015) 'Starting out as a PE teacher' in S. Capel and M. Whitehead (eds.) *Learning to Teach Physical Education in the Secondary School: A Companion to School Experience*, 4th edn, Abingdon: Routledge, pp. 6–17.

Capel, S. and Katene, W.H. (2000) 'Secondary PGCE PE students' perceptions of their subject knowledge', *European Physical Education Review* 6(1), 46–70.

Capel, S. and Whitehead, M. (2015) *Learning to Teach in the Secondary School: A Companion to School Experience*, 4th edn, Abingdon: Routledge.

Carter, M. and Francis, R. (2001) 'Mentoring and beginning teachers' workplace learning', *Asia-Pacific Journal of Teacher Education* 29(3), 249–262.

Chalies, S., Bertone, S., Flavier, E. and Durand, M. (2008) 'Effects of collaborative mentoring on the articulation of training and classroom situations: A case study in the French school system', *Teaching and Teacher Education* 3(24), 550–563.

Chambers, F (2015) *Mentoring in Physical Education and Sports Coaching*, Abingdon: Routledge.

Chappell, A. (2015) 'Teaching safely and safety in PE', in S. Capel and M. Whitehead (eds.) *Learning to Teach Physical Education in the Secondary School: A Companion to School Experience*, 4th edn, Abingdon: Routledge, pp. 184–203.

Child, A. and Merrill, S. (2005) *Developing as a Secondary School Mentor: A Case Study Approach for Trainee Mentors and their Tutors*, Exeter: Learning Matters.

Cho, C., Ramanan, R. and Feldman, M. (2011) 'Defining the ideal qualities of mentorship: A qualitative analysis of the characteristics of outstanding mentors', *The American Journal of Medicine* 124(5), 453–458.

CIPD (Chartered Institute of Personnel and Development) (2012) *Coaching and Mentoring Fact Sheet*, viewed 25 January 2018, from www.cipd.ae/knowledge/factsheets/coaching-mentoring

CIPD (2017) *Search*: @cipd, viewed 21 February 2017, from www.cipd.co.uk/search

Clarke, P., Howarth, S., Whitehouse, K. and Wood Griffiths S. (2012) 'Perspectives on teacher education: Risk-taking in the workplace; challenging trainee teachers to develop their practice', *Worcester Journal of Learning and Teaching* 7, July, pp. 18-23, viewed 3 June 2018, from https://rteworcester.files.wordpress.com/2017/05/wyatt_howarth_whitehouse_woodgriffiths_perspectives_on_teacher_education_risk-taking.pdf.

Clutterbuck, D. (2004) *Everyone Needs a Mentor: Fostering Talent in Your Organisation*, 4th edn, London: Chartered Institute of Personnel and Development (CIPD).

Clutterbuck, D. (2014) *Everyone Needs a Mentor*, 5th edn, London: Chartered Institute of Personnel and Development.

Coe, R., Aloisi, C., Higgins, S. and Major, L.E. (2014) *What Makes Great Teaching? Review of the Underpinning Research*, London: Sutton Trust.

Coelho, J.D. (2001) 'Risk management in quality physical education programs', *Strategies: A Journal for Physical and Sport Educators* 14(6), 32-35.

Collins-Brown, E. (2015) *Writing Observable and Measurable Learning Objectives*, ScholarWorks at Western Michigan University, viewed 12 December 2017, from https://scholarworks.wmich.edu/cgi/viewcontent.cgi?referer=https://www.google.co.uk/&httpsredir=1&article=1038&context=assessment_day

Cordingley, P., Bell, M., Rundell, B. and Evans, D. (2003) 'The impact of collaborative continuing professional development on classroom teaching and learning', in *Research Evidence in Education Library*, London: EPPI-Centre, Social Science Research Unit, Institute of Education, University of London.

Cordingley, P., Higgins, S., Greany, T., Buckler, N., Coles-Jordan, D., Crisp, B., Saunders, L. and Coe, R. (2015) *Developing Great Teaching: Lessons from the International Reviews into Effective Professional Development*, London: Teacher Development Trust, viewed 25 January 2018, from http://tdtrust.org/wp-content/uploads/2015/10/DGT-Summary.pdf

Crème, P. (2005) 'Should student learning journals be assessed?', *Assessment and Evaluation in Higher Education* 30(3), 287-296.

Cummins, J.P., Brown, K. and Sayers, D. (2007) *Literacy, Technology and Diversity: Teaching for Success in Changing Times*, Washington: Pearson.

CUREE (Centre for the Use of Research and Evidence in Education) (2005a) *National Framework for Mentoring and Coaching*, viewed 25 January 2018, from www.curee.co.uk/files/publication/1219313968/mentoring_and_coaching_national_framework.pdf

CUREE (2005b) *Mentoring and Coaching CPD Capacity Building Project 2004-2005; National Framework for Mentoring and Coaching*, Warwick: CUREE/DfES.

Curtner-Smith, M. (1999) 'The more things change the more they stay the same: Factors influencing teachers' interpretations and delivery of National Curriculum Physical Education', *Sport, Education and Society* 4(1), 75-97.

Daloz, L.A. (2012) *Mentor: Guiding the Journey of Adult Learners*, Wiley: New York.

d'Arripe-Longueville, F., Gernigon, C., Huet, M-L., Cadopi, M. and Winnykamen, F. (2002) 'Peer tutoring in a physical education setting: Influence of tutor skill level on novice learners' motivation and performance', *Journal of Teaching in Physical Education* 22, 105-123.

Danielowich, R.M. and McCarthy, M.J. (2013) 'Teacher educators as learners: How supervisors shape their pedagogies by creating and using classroom videos with their student teachers', *Action in Teacher Education* 35(3), 147-164.

Danielson, C. (2011) 'Evaluations that help teachers learn', *Educational Leadership* 68(4), 35-39.

Davies, T. (1999) 'Taking risks as a feature of creativity in the teaching and learning of design and technology', *The Journal of Design and Technology Education* 4(2), 101-108.

Day, C. (1993) 'Reflection: A necessary but not sufficient condition for professional development', *British Educational Research Journal* 19(1), 83-93.

Dewey, J. (1933) *How We Think: A Restatement of the Relation of Reflective Thinking to the Educative Process*, New York: D.C. Heath and Company.

DfE (Department for Education) (2011a) *The Teachers' Standards*, London: DfE, viewed 25 January 2018, from www.gov.uk/government/publications/teachers-standards

DfE (2011b) *Teachers' Standards: Guidance for School Leaders, School Staff and Governing Bodies*, London: viewed 25 January 2018, from www.gov.uk/government/uploads/system/uploads/attachment_data/file/665520/Teachers__Standards.pdf.

DfE (2016a) *A Framework of Core Content for Initial Teacher Training (ITT)*, London: Crown, viewed 25 January 2018, from www.gov.uk/government/uploads/system/uploads/attachment_data/file/536890/Framework_Report_11_July_2016_Final.pdf

DfE (2016b) *National Standards for School-based Initial Teacher Training (ITT) Mentors*, London: Crown, viewed 25 January 2018, from www.gov.uk/government/uploads/system/uploads/attachment_data/file/536891/Mentor_standards_report_Final.pdf

DfE (2016c) *Standards for Teachers' Professional Development*, London: Crown, viewed 25 January 2018, from www.gov.uk/government/uploads/system/uploads/attachment_data/file/537031/160712_-_PD_Expert_Group_Guidance.pdf

DfE (2016d) *Initial Teacher Training: Government Response to Carter Review*, viewed 25 January 2018, from www.gov.uk/government/uploads/system/uploads/attachment_data/file/536916/Govt_response_-_ITT.pdf

DfE (2016e) *Initial Teacher Training Criteria and Support Advice: Information for Accredited Initial Teacher Training Providers*. London: DfE.

Dreger, A. (2011) *Taking Risks in the Classroom*, viewed 25 January 2018, from www.msu.edu/~taprog/thoughts/tt2.doc

Driscoll, L.G., Parkes, K.A., Tilley-Lubbs, G.A., Brill, J.M. and Pitts Bannister, V.R. (2009) 'Navigating the lonely sea: Peer mentoring and collaboration among aspiring women scholars', *Mentoring and Tutoring: Partnership in Learning* 17, 5–21.

Eliahoo, R. (2016) 'An analysis of beginning mentors' critical incidents in English post-compulsory education. Navigating stormy waters', *International Journal of Mentoring and Coaching in Education* 5(4), 304–317.

Eraut, M., Alderton, J., Cole, G. and Senker, P. (1998) 'Development of knowledge and skills in employment; Research Report No5, Brighton: University of Sussex'; cited in M. Griffiths (2011) 'Mentoring as a professional learning strategy', in K. Armour (ed.) *Sport Pedagogy: An Introduction for Teaching and Coaching*, Essex: Pearson, p. 300.

Everley, S. (2011) 'Evaluation of the adventure experience: the inside view, how do we make sense of evidence?' in M. Berry and C. Hodgson (eds.) *Adventure Education: An Introduction to Effective Facilitation*, Abingdon: Routledge.

Everley, S. and Flemons, M. (2015) 'Teacher beliefs', in S. Capel and M. Whitehead (eds.) *Learning to Teach Physical Education in Secondary School: A Companion to School Experience*, 4th edn, London: Routledge, pp. 256–270.

Farrell, T.S.C. (2004) *Reflective Practice in Action*, Thousand Oaks, CA: Corwin Press.

Feiman-Nemser, S. (2012) 'Beyond solo teaching', *Educational Leadership* 69(8), 10–16.

Feiman-Nemser, S. and Parker, M. (1993) 'Mentoring in context: A comparison of two U.S. programs for beginning teachers', *International Journal of Educational Research* 19(8), 699–718.

Fletcher, S. (2000) *Mentoring in Schools: A Handbook of Good Practice*, London: Kogan Page.

Franko, D.L., Rinehart, J., Kenney, K., Loeffelholz, M., Guthrie, B. and Claigiuri, P. (2016) 'Supporting faculty mentoring through the use of creative technologies: There's an app for that', *International Journal of Mentoring and Coaching in Education* 5(1), 54–64.

Furlong, J. (2015) 'Teaching tomorrow's teachers. Options for the future of initial teacher education in Wales', viewed 25 January 2018, from http://gov.wales/docs/dcells/publications/150309-teaching-tomorrows-teachers-final.pdf

Gallwey, T. (2015) *The Inner Game of Tennis*, Oxford: Pan Brooks.

Gibbs, G. (1988) *Learning by Doing: A Guide to Teaching and Learning Methods*, Oxford: Oxford Further Education Unit.

Giddens, A., Duneier, M., Appelbaum, R.P. and Carr, D. (2014) *Introduction to Sociology*, 9th edn, London: W.W. Norton.

Goleman, D. (1998) *Emotional Intelligence*, New York: Bantam.

Greenwalt, K.A. (2008) 'Through the camera's eye: A phenomenological analysis of teacher subjectivity', *Teaching and Teacher Education* 24, 387-399.

Grout, H. and Long, G. (2009) *Improving Teaching and Learning in Physical Education*, Maidenhead: Open University Press.

Haggard, D.L., Dougherty, T.W., Turban, D.B. and Wilbanks, J.E. (2011) 'Who is a mentor? A review of evolving definitions and implications for research', *Journal of Management* 37, 280-304. doi:10.1177/0149206310386227

Hagger, H. and McIntyre, D. (2006) *Learning Teaching from Teachers: Realising the Potential of School-based Teacher Education*, Maidenhead: Open University Press.

Harford, J., MacRuairc, G. and McCartan, D. (2010) 'Lights, camera, reflection: Using peer video to promote reflective dialogue among student teachers', *Teacher Development: An International Journal of Teachers' Professional Development* 14(1), 57-68.

Hargreaves, A. and Dawe, R. (1990) 'Paths of professional development: Contrived collegiality, collaborative culture and the case of peer coaching', *Teaching and Teacher Education* 6(3), 227-241.

Hargreaves, A. and Fullan, M. (2000) 'Mentoring in the new millennium', *Theory into Practice* 39(1), 49-56.

Hattie, J.A. (2009) *Visible Learning: A Synthesis of over 800 Meta-analyses Relating to Achievement*, Abingdon: Routledge.

Hay McBer Associates (2000) *Research into Teacher Effectiveness: A Model of Teacher Effectiveness* (Research Report RR216), London: DfEE.

Haydn-Davies, D. (2011) 'Learning and teaching approaches', in M. Whitehead (ed.) *Physical Literacy throughout the Lifecourse*, Abingdon: Routledge, pp. 164-174.

Herbert, C.P. (2005) 'Changing the culture: Interprofessional education for collaborative patient-centred practice in Canada', *Journal of Interprofessional Care* 19(1), 1-4.

Higgins, M.C. and Thomas, D.A. (2001) 'Constellations and careers: Toward understanding the effects of multiple developmental relationships', *Journal of Organizational Behavior* 22, 223-247.

Hobbs, V. (2007) 'Faking it or hating it: Can reflective practice be forced?', *Reflective Practice* 8(3), 405-417.

Hobson, A. (2002) 'Student teachers' perceptions of school-based mentoring in initial teacher training (ITT)', *Mentoring and Tutoring: Partnership in Learning* 10(1), 5-20.

Hobson, A.J. (2016) 'Judgementoring and how to avert it: Introducing ONSIDE mentoring for beginning teachers', *International Journal of Mentoring and Coaching in Education* 5(2), 87-110.

Hobson, A.J. and Malderez, A. (2013) 'Judgementoring and other threats to realizing potential of school-based mentoring in teacher education', *International Journal of Mentoring and Coaching in Education* 2(2), 89-108.

Hobson, A.J., Ashby, P., Malderez, A. and Tomlinson, P.D. (2009) 'Mentoring beginning teachers: What we know and what we don't', *Teacher and Teacher Education* 25(1), 207-216.

Hobson, A.J., Astanheira, P., Doyle, K., Csigás, Z. and Clutterbuck, D. (2016) *The Mentoring Across Professions (Map) Project: What Can Teacher Mentoring Learn from International Good Practice in Employee Mentoring and Coaching?* London: The Gatsby Charitable Foundation.

Hudson, P. (2016) 'Forming the mentor–mentee relationship', *Mentoring and Tutoring: Partnership in Learning* 24(1), 30-43.

Hudson, P. and Hudson, S. (2016) 'Mentoring beginning teachers and goal setting', *Australian Journal of Teacher Education* 41(10), 48-64.

Illeris, K. (2007) *How We Learn: Learning and Non-learning in School and Beyond*, Abingdon: Routledge.

Ingersoll, R. and Smith, T.M. (2004) 'Do teacher induction and mentoring matter?' *NAASP Bulletin* 88(638), 28-40.

Jay, J.K. and Johnson, K.L. (2002) 'Capturing complexity: a typology of reflective practice for teacher education', *Teacher and Teacher Education* 18, 73–85.

Jenkins, J.M. (2002) 'Peer coaching for preservice teachers in a field setting', *Journal of Sport Pedagogy* 8, 20–37.

Jenkins, J.M., Hamrick, C. and Todorovich, J. (2002) 'Peer coaching: Implementation and data collection tools', *Journal of Physical Education, Recreation and Dance* 73, 47–53.

Johnson, B.J. and Ridley, C.R. (2004) *The Elements of Mentoring*, New York: Palgrave Macmillan.

Jones, E. and Simmons, G. (2010) *The National Coaching Foundation. Recruit into Coaching: Mentoring Guide*, Leeds: Sports Coach UK: Coachwise.

Jones, M. (2009) 'Supporting the supporters of novice teachers: An analysis of mentors' needs from twelve European countries presented from an English perspective', *Research in Comparative and International Education* 4(1), 4–21.

Jones, M. and Straker, K. (2006) 'What informs mentors' practice when working with trainees and newly qualified teachers? An investigation into mentors' professional knowledge base', *Journal of Education for Teaching* 32(2), 165–184.

Katene, W., Lawrence, A., Coombes, A., Bluett, S. and Eveleigh, J. (2017) 'The impact of collaborative learning on student learning gain in a second year undergraduate module: The shape of things to come?' Paper presented at the Annual Education Conference, University of Exeter, 5 May, 2017.

Katz, L.G. (1995) *Talks with Teachers: A Collection*, Norwood, NJ: Ablex.

Kay, W. (2004) 'Are mentors and students talking the same language?' *British Journal of Teaching Physical Education* Autumn, 19–22.

Keay, J. (2006) 'Collaborative learning in physical education teachers' early-career professional development', *Physical Education and Sport Pedagogy* 11(3), 285–305.

Keel, M.I. (2009) *Mentoring: Program Development, Relationships and Outcomes. Education in a Competitive and Globalizing World Series*, New York: Nova Science.

Kell, S. and Forsberg, N. (2014) 'The role of mentoring in physical education teacher education: A theoretical and practical perspective', *Physical and Health Education Journal* 80(2), 6–11.

Kell, S. and Forsberg, N. (2016) 'The role of mentoring in physical education teacher education: Mentoring in practice', *Physical and Health Education Journal* 81(3), 1–16.

Kemmis, S., Heikkinen, H.L.T., Fransson, G., Aspfors, J. and Edwards-Groves, C. (2014) 'Mentoring of new teachers as a contested practice: Supervision, support and collaborative self-development', *Teaching and Teacher Education* 43, 154–164.

Kennett, P. and Lomas, T. (2015) 'Making meaning through mentoring: Mentors finding fulfilment at work through self-determination and self-reflection', *International Journal of Evidence Based Coaching and Mentoring* 13(2), 29–44.

Kerry, T. and Shelton-Mayes, A. (eds.) (1995) *Issues in Mentoring*, London: Routledge.

Killingbeck, M. and Whitehead, M. (2015) 'Observation in PE', in S. Capel and M. Whitehead (eds.) *Learning to Teach Physical Education in the Secondary School: A Companion to School Experience*, 4th edn, Abingdon: Routledge, pp. 49–66.

King, P.M. and Kitchener, K.S. (1994) *Developing Reflective Judgment: Understanding and Promoting Intellectual Growth and Critical Thinking in Adolescents and Adults*, San Francisco: Jossey-Bass.

Kleinknecht, M.G.A. (2016) 'Fostering preservice teachers' noticing with structured video feedback: Results of an online- and video-based intervention study', *Teaching and Teacher Education* 59, 45–56.

Kolb, D. (1984) *Experiential Learning: Experience as the Source of Learning and Development*, Englewood Cliffs, NJ: Prentice Hall.

Kooloos, J.G.M., Klaassen, T., Vereijken, M., van Kuppeveld, S., Bolhuis, S. and Vorstenbosch, M. (2011) 'Collaborative group work: Effects of group size and assignment structure on learning gain, student satisfaction and perceived participation', *Medical Teacher* 33, 983–988.

Korthagen, F., Loughran, J. and Russell, T. (2006) 'Developing fundamental principles for teacher education programs and practices', *Teaching and Teacher Education* 22(8), 1020–1041.

Kroll, J. (2016) 'What is meant by the term group mentoring?' *Mentoring and Tutoring: Partnership in Learning* 24, 44–58.

Kyriacou, C. (2014) *Essential Teaching Skills*, 4th edn, Cheltenham: Stanley Thornes.

Lane, G. and Clutterbuck, D. (2004) *The Situational Mentor: An International Review of Competences and Capabilities in Mentoring*, London: Routledge.

Langdon, F. (2011) 'Shifting perception and practice: New Zealand beginning teacher induction and mentoring as a pathway to expertise', *Professional Development in Education* 37(2), 241–258.

Lawrence, J. (2014) 'Creating an effective learning environment', in S. Capel and P. Breckon (eds.) *A Practical Guide to Teaching Physical Education in the Secondary School*, 2nd edn, Abingdon: Routledge, pp. 145–157.

Lawrence, J. and Mellor, P. (2011) *The Review Process*, unpublished manuscript, Leeds Metropolitan University.

Lawrence, J. and Whitehead, M. (2015) 'Lesson organisation and management', in S. Capel and M. Whitehead (eds.) *Learning to Teach Physical Education in the Secondary School: A Companion to School Experience*, 4th edn, Abingdon: Routledge, pp. 87–106.

Lawrence, J., Low, K. and Phan, J. (2016) 'The impact of a high intensity observation programme in Singapore', *International Conference on Education and e-Learning (EeL) Proceedings; Singapore:* 9–13, Singapore: Global Science and Technology Forum.

Leask, M. and Moorehouse, C. (2005) 'The student teacher's role and responsibilities', in S. Capel., M. Leask and T. Turner (eds.) *Learning to Teach in the Secondary School: A Companion to School Experience*, 4th edn, Abingdon: Routledge, pp. 18–31.

Le Cornu, R. (2005) 'Peer mentoring: Engaging pre-service teachers in mentoring one another', *Mentoring and Tutoring: Partnership in Learning* 13(3), 355–366.

Löfström, E. and Eisenschmidt, E. (2009) 'Novice teachers' perspective on mentoring: The case of Estonian induction year', *Teaching and Teacher Education* 25, 681–689.

Lord, P., Atkinson, M. and Mitchell, H. (2008) *Mentoring and Coaching for Professionals: A Study of the Research Evidence*, Slough: NFER, viewed 29 January 2018, from www.nfer.ac.uk/publications/MCM01/MCM01.pdf

Lowe, M. and Redfern, C. (2016) 'Taking responsibility for the whole lesson', in S. Capel, M. Leask and S. Younie (eds.) *Learning to Teach in the Secondary School: A Companion to School Experience*, 7th edn, Abingdon: Routledge, pp. 122–137.

Manross, D. and Templeton, C. (1997) 'Expertise in teaching physical education', *Recreation and Dance* 68, 29–35.

Marsh, B. and Mitchell, N. (2014) 'The role of video in teacher professional development', *Teacher Development* 18(3), 403–417.

Mason, K.O. and Klein, S.R. (2013) 'Land, sea and sky: Mapmaking as reflection in pre-service teacher education', *Reflective Practice* 14(2), 209–225.

Maynard, T. (2000) 'Learning to teach or learning to manage mentors? Experiences of school-based teacher training', *Mentoring and Tutoring: Partnership in Learning* 8(1), 17–30.

Maynard, T. and Furlong, J. (1995) 'Learning to teach and models of mentoring', in T. Kerry and A. Shelton-Mayes (eds.) *Issues in Mentoring*, London: Routledge, pp. 10–14.

McAteer, M., Hallett, F. and Murtagh, L. (2010) *Achieving Your Masters in Teaching and Learning*, Exeter: Learning Matters.

McCaughtry, N., Cothran, D., Hodges Kulinna, P., Martin, J. and Faust, R. (2005) 'Chapter 3: Teachers mentoring teachers: A view over time', *Journal of Teaching in Physical Education* 24, 326–343.

McGrath, C.H., Guerin, B., Harte, E., Frearson, M. and Manville, C. (2015) *Learning Gain in Higher Education*, London: HEFCE.

Meirink, J.A., Meijer, P.C. and Verloop, N. (2007) 'A closer look at teachers' individual learning in collaborative settings', *Teachers and Teaching: Theory and Practice* 13(2), 145–164.

Mena, J., Hennissen, P. and Loughran, J. (2017) 'Developing pre-service teachers' professional knowledge of teaching: The influence of mentoring', *Teaching and Teacher Education* 66, 47–59.

Metropolitan Police Service (2003) *The Problem Solver's Guide*, London: Territorial Police Headquarters.

Metzler, M.W. (2005) *Instructional Models for Physical Education*, Scottsdale, AZ: Holcomb Hathaway.

Metzler, M.W. (2011) *Instructional Models for Physical Education*, Scottsdale, AZ: Holcomb Hathaway.

Ministry of Education / Physical Education Sport Teacher Academy (2013) *Physical Education Lesson Observation Tool*, Singapore: Ministry of Education.

Ministry of Education and Research (2010) *Differentiated Primary and Lower Secondary Teacher Education Programmes for Years 1–7 and Years 5–10*, Oslo: Ministry of Education and Research.

Moon, J. (1999) *Reflection in Learning and Professional Development: Theory and Practice*, London: Routledge-Falmer.

Montgomery, B.L. (2017) 'Mapping a mentoring roadmap and developing a supportive network for strategic career advancement', *SAGE Open* April–June, 1–13.

Mosston, M. (1966) *Teaching Physical Education*, Columbus, OH: Merill.

Mosston, M. and Ashworth, S. (2008) *Teaching Physical Education*, 1st online edn, viewed 5 February 2018, from www.spectrumofteachingstyles.org/e-book-download.php

Murata, A. (2011) 'Introduction: Conceptual overview of lesson study', cited in L.C. Hart, A.S. Alston and A. Murata (2011) *Lesson Study Research and Practice in Mathematics Education*, New York: Springer.

National Board for Professional Teaching Standards (2016) *Physical Education Standards; for Teachers of Students ages 3–18+*, 2nd edn, USA: NBPTS.

National College for Teaching and Leadership (2017) *NCSL Modular Curriculum*, viewed 25 January 2018, from www.nationalcollege.org.uk/transfer/open/mentoring-and-coaching-core-skills/mccore-s02/mccore-s02-t03.html

Nevid, J. (2013) 'Using action verbs as learning outcomes: Applying Bloom's Taxonomy in measuring instructional objectives in introductory psychology', *Journal of Education and Training Studies* 1(2), 19–32.

New Teacher Center (2011) *NTC Continuum of Mentoring Practice*, Santa Cruz: New Teacher Center.

Newton, A. and Bowler, M. (2015) 'Assessment for and of learning in PE', in S. Capel and M. Whitehead (eds.) *Learning to Teach Physical Education in the Secondary School: A Companion to School Experience*, 4th edn, Abingdon: Routledge, pp. 140–155.

Nordberg, D. (2008) 'Group projects: More learning? Less fair? A conundrum in assessing postgraduate business education', *Assessment and Evaluation in Higher Education* 33(5), 481–492.

Normore, A.L.K. (2006) 'Avoiding the pitfalls of the rookie year: How a mentor can help', *Kappa Delta Pi Record* 43(1), 25–29.

O'Leary, M. (2014) *Classroom Observation: A Guide to the Effective Observation of Teaching and Learning*, Abingdon: Routledge.

Ofsted (Office for Standards in Education) (2012) *Initial Teacher Education Inspection Handbook*, London: Ofsted.

Ohio Department for Education (2015) *Ohio Standards for Professional Development*, Ohio: Department for Education, viewed 25 January 2018 at http://education.ohio.gov/Topics/Teaching/Professional-Development/Organizing-for-High-Quality-Professional-Development

Online Etymology Dictionary (2017) Available at: www.etymonline.com/

Ovens, A. and Fletcher, T. (2014) *Self-Study in Physical Education Teacher Education: Exploring the Interplay of Practice and Scholarship*, New York, NY: Springer.

Palmer, P.J. (1998) *The Courage to Teach: Exploring the Inner Landscape of a Teacher's Life*, San Francisco: Jossey-Bass.

Pavlovich, K. (2007) 'The development of reflective practice through student journals', *Higher Education Research and Development* 26(3), 281-295.

Perry, R.R. and Lewis, C.C. (2009) 'What is successful adaptation of lesson study in the US?' *Journal of Educational Change* 10(4), 365-391.

Placek, J.H. (1983) 'Conceptions of success in teaching: Busy, happy and good', in T.J. Templin and J.K. Olson (eds.) *Teaching in Physical Education*, Champaign, IL: Human Kinetics, pp. 46-56.

Pollard, A. (2014) *Reflective Teaching in Schools*, 4th edn, London: Bloomsbury.

Portner, H. (2003) *Mentoring New Teachers*, London: Sage.

Ragins, B. (2016) 'From the ordinary to the extraordinary: High quality mentoring relationships at work', *Organizational Dynamics* 45, 228-244.

Reid, S. (2010) *Teaching Risk Taking in the College Classroom*, viewed 10 March 2014, from www.facultyfocus.com/articles/teaching-and-learning/teaching-risk-taking-in-the-college-classroom/

Richter, D., Kunter, M., Lüdtke, O., Klusmann, U., Anders, Y and Baumert, J. (2013) 'How different mentoring approaches affect beginning teachers' development in the first years of practice', *Teachers and Teacher Education* 36, 166-177.

Roberts, A. (2000) 'Mentoring revisited: A phenomenological reading of the literature', *Mentoring and Tutoring: Partnership in Learning* 8(2), 145-170.

Rovegno, I. and Bandhauer, D. (2013) *Elementary Physical Education: Curriculum and Instruction*, Burlington, MA: Jones and Bartlett Learning.

Salovey, P. and Mayer, J.D. (1990) 'Emotional intelligence', *Imagination, Cognition and Personality* 9, 185-211.

Saric, M. and Steh, B. (2017) 'Critical reflection in the professional development of teachers: Challenges and possibilities', *Center for Educational Policy Studies (CEPS) Journal* 7(3), 67-85.

Schatz-Oppenheimer, O. (2017) 'Being a mentor: Novice teachers' mentors' conceptions of mentoring prior to training', *Professional Development in Education* 43(2), 274-292.

Schön, D.A. (1983) *The Reflective Practitioner. How Professionals Think in Action*, New York: Basic Books.

Schön, D.A. (1987) *Educating the Reflective Practitioner: Towards a New Design for Teaching and Learning in the Professions*, San Francisco, CA: Jossey-Bass.

Seale, J. (2012) *Transforming the Discourse of Positive Risk Taking in Special and Inclusive Education*, from https://ore.exeter.ac.uk/repository/bitstream/handle/10871/9945/Transforming%20the%20discourse%20of%20positive%20risk.pdf?sequence=2

Sherin, M. and Han, S. (2004) 'Teacher learning in the context of a video club', *Teaching and Teacher Education* 20(2), 163-183.

Shulman, L.S. (1986) 'Those who understand: Knowledge growth in teaching', *Educational Researcher* 15(2), 4-14.

Shulman, L.S. (1987) 'Knowledge and teaching: Foundations of the new reform', *Harvard Educational Review* 57(1), 1-22.

Siedentop, D. (1994) *Sport Education: Quality PE through Positive Sport Experiences*, Champaign, IL: Human Kinetics.

Sørenson, P. (2014) 'Collaboration, dialogue and expansive learning: The use of paired and multiple placements in the school practicum', *Teaching and Teacher Education* 44, 128-137.

Spackman, L. (2002) 'Assessment for learning: The lessons for physical education', *The Bulletin of Physical Education* 38(3), 179-195.

Springer, L., Stanne, M.E. and Donovan, S.S. (1999) 'Effects of small-group learning on undergraduates in science, mathematics, engineering and technology', *Review of Educational Research* 69(1), 21-51.

Standal, O.F. and Moe, V.F. (2013) 'Reflective practice in physical education and physical education teacher education: A review of the literature since 1995', *Quest* 65, 220-240.

Stanulis, R.N. and Ames, K.T. (2009) 'Learning to mentor: Evidence and observation as tools in learning to teach', *The Professional Educator* 33(1), 28-38.

Stidder, G. and Hayes, S. (2016) 'Learning and teaching in physical education', in S. Hayes and G. Stidder (eds.) *The Really Useful Physical Education Book*, 2nd edn, Abingdon: Routledge, pp. 18-36.

Stiles, V.H. and Katene, W.H. (2013) 'Improving physical education student teachers' knowledge and understanding of applied biomechanical principles through peer collaboration', *Physical Education and Sport Pedagogy* 18(3), 235-255.

Stronge, J.H. (2007) *Qualities of Effective Teachers*, 2nd edn, Alexandria, VA: ASCD.

Stroot, S., Keil, V., Stedman, P., Lohr, L., Faust, R. and Schincariol-Randall, L. (1998) *Peer Assistance and Review Guidebook*, Columbus, OH: Ohio Department of Education.

Tabachnik, R. and Zeichner, K. (2002) 'Reflections on reflective teaching', in A. Pollard (ed.) *Readings for Reflective Teaching*, London: Continuum, pp. 13-16.

Taggart, G.L. and Wilson, A.P. (2005) *Promoting Reflective Thinking in Teachers: 50 Action Strategies*, 2nd edn, Thousand Oaks, CA: Corwin.

TDA (Training and Development Agency for Schools) (2009) *Including Pupils with SEN and/ or Disabilities in Primary Physical Education*, Manchester: TDA.

Teaching Schools Council (2016) *National Standards for School-based Initial Teacher Training (ITT) Mentors*, London: Crown.

The State Education Department/The University of The State of New York (2011) *The New York State Mentoring Standards*, Albany, NY: The State Education Department/The University of The State of New York, viewed 25 January 2018, from http://usny.nysed.gov/rttt/docs/MentoringStandards.pdf

Thornton, K. (2014) 'Mentors as educational leaders and change agents', *International Journal of Mentoring and Coaching in Education* 3(1), 18-31.

Tinker-Sachs, G., Fisher, T. and Cannon, J. (2011) 'Collaboration, mentoring and co-teaching in teacher education', *Journal of Teacher Education for Sustainability* 13(2), 70-86.

Towers, J. (2007) 'Using video in teacher education', *Canadian Journal of Learning and Technology* 33(2), viewed 21 January 2018, from www.cjlt.ca/index.php/cjlt/article/view/26451/19633

Tschannen-Moran, M. and Carter, C.B. (2016) 'Cultivating the emotional intelligences of instructional coaches', *International Journal of Mentoring and Coaching in Education* 5(4), 287-303.

Tuckman, B. (1965) 'Developmental sequence in small groups', *Psychological Bulletin* 63(6), 384-399.

Turner-Bisset, R. (1999) 'The knowledge bases of the expert teacher', *British Educational Research Journal* 25(1), 39-55.

Valli, L. (1997) 'Listening to other voices: A description of teacher reflection in the United States', *Peabody Journal of Education* 72(1), 67-88.

van Es, E.A. (2012) 'Examining the development of a teacher learning community: The case of a video club', *Teaching and Teacher Education* 28, 182-192.

van Es, E.A. and Sherin, M.G. (2002) 'Learning to notice: Scaffolding new teachers' interpretations of classroom interactions', *Journal of Technology and Teacher Education* 10, 571-596.

van Ginkel, G., Oolbekkink, H., Meijer, P.C. and Verloop, N. (2016) 'Adapting mentoring to individual differences in novice teacher learning: The mentor's viewpoint', *Teachers and Teaching* 22(2), 198–218.

Van Manen, M. (1977) 'Linking ways of knowing with ways of being practical', *Curriculum Inquiry* 6(3), 205–228.

Van Zundert, M., Sluijsmans, D. and Van Merrinboer, J. (2010) 'Effective peer assessment processes: Research findings and future directions', *Learning and Instruction* 20, 270–279.

Varner, D. and Peck, S.R. (2003) 'Learning from learning journals: The benefits and challenges of using learning journal assignments', *Journal of Management Education* 27(1), 52–77.

Vygotsky, L. (1978) *Mind in Society: The Development of Higher Psychological Processes*, Cambridge, MA: Harvard University Press.

Walsh, B. (2008) 'Being a mentor is like what?' *Innovations in Practice*, LJMU Open Journals Service 1(1), 44–50.

Walsh, B., Nixon, S., Walker, C. and Doyle, N. (2015) 'Using a clean feedback model to facilitate the learning process', *Journal of Creative Education* 6(10), 953–960.

Wang, J. and Odell, S.J. (2002) 'Mentored learning to teach according to standards-based reform: A critical review', *Review of Educational Research* 72(3), 481–546.

Warrell, M. (2013) 'Why getting comfortable with discomfort is crucial to success', viewed 25 January 2018, from www.forbes.com/sites/margiewarrell/2013/04/22/is-comfort-holding-you-back/#3e2d49274d47

Welsch, R.G. and Devlin, P.A. (2012) 'Developing preservice teachers' reflection: Examining the use of video', *Action Teacher Education* 28(4), 53–61.

Whitehead, M. (2016) 'Learner-centred teaching – a physical literacy perspective', in S. Capel and M. Whitehead (eds.) *Learning to Teach Physical Education in the Secondary School: A Companion to School Experience*, 4th edn, Abingdon: Routledge, pp. 171–183.

Whitehouse, K. (2015) 'Risk-taking in the workplace; Challenging PE trainee teachers to develop their practice', Unpublished.

Whitehouse, K., Barber, L. and Jones, V. (2015) 'Developing and maintaining an effective learning environment', in S. Capel and M. Whitehead (eds.) *Learning to Teach Physical Education in the Secondary School: A Companion to School Experience*, 4th edn, Abingdon: Routledge, pp. 121–139.

Williams, A. (1996) *Teaching Physical Education: A Guide for Mentors and Students*, London: David Fulton.

Williams, J.B. (2010) 'The nature of the mentor/trainee relationship in PE initial teacher training', Unpublished PhD Thesis, University of Brighton.

Winson, A. and Wood-Griffiths, S. (2010) 'Reflective practice: The mentoring conversation', in T. Wright (ed.) *How to Be a Brilliant Mentor: Developing Outstanding Teachers*, Abingdon: Routledge, pp. 47–63.

Wright, T. (2010) (ed.) *How to Be a Brilliant Mentor: Developing Outstanding Teachers*, Abingdon: Routledge.

Yiend, J., Weller, S. and Kinchin, I. (2012) 'Peer observation of teaching: The interaction between peer review and developmental models of practice', *Journal of Further and Higher Education* 38(4), 465–484.

Zachary, L. (2012) *The Mentor's Guide*, London: Wiley and Sons, viewed 25 January 2018, from www.dawsonera.com/readonline/9781118103326

Zwozdiak-Myers, P.N. (2015a) 'Teacher as a researcher/reflective practitioner', in S. Capel and M. Whitehead (eds.) *Learning to Teach Physical Education in Secondary School*, 4th edn, Abingdon: Routledge, pp. 235–255.

Zwozdiak-Myers, P.N. (2015b) 'Communication in PE', in S. Capel and M. Whitehead (eds.) *Learning to Teach Physical Education in the Secondary School: A Companion to School Experience*, 4th edn, Abingdon: Routledge, pp. 67–86.

AUTHOR INDEX

GENERAL INDEX

Printed in Great Britain
by Amazon

84716097R10167